W9-AEC-041

A SHEARWATER BOOK

The Most Important

Fish in the Sea

The Most

Important

Fish

in the Sea

Menhaden and America

H. Bruce Franklin

Island Press / SHEARWATER BOOKS

Washington · Covelo · London

A Shearwater Book
Published by Island Press

Copyright © 2007 H. Bruce Franklin

First Island Press cloth edition, April 2007
First Island Press paperback edition, October 2008

All rights reserved under International and Pan-American
Copyright Conventions. No part of this book may be reproduced
in any form or by any means without permission in writing from
the publisher: Island Press, 1718 Connecticut Ave. NW, Suite 300,
Washington, DC 20009.

SHEARWATER BOOKS is a trademark of
The Center for Resource Economics.

The Library of Congress has cataloged the hardcover edition as follows:
Franklin, H. Bruce (Howard Bruce), 1934–
The most important fish in the sea : menhaden and America /
H. Bruce Franklin.
p. cm.
Includes bibliographical references and index.
ISBN-13: 978-1-59726-124-1 (alk. paper)
ISBN-10: 1-59726-124-6 (alk. paper)
1. Menhaden — United States — History.
2. Menhaden fisheries — United States — History. I. Title.
QL638.C64F73 2007
597'.45 — dc22   2006035635

ISBN 13: 978-1-59726-507-2
ISBN 10: 1-59726-507-1

British Cataloguing-in-Publication data available.

Printed on recycled, acid-free paper ♻

Design by David Bullen Design

Manufactured in the United States of America

10 9 8 7 6 5 4 3 2

For Jane

Contents

The Most Important
Fish in the Sea

Now You See Them, Now You Don't

First you see the birds—gulls and terns wheeling over-head, then swooping down to a wide expanse of water dimpled as though by large raindrops and glittering with silver streaks. The sea erupts with frothy splashes, some from the diving birds, others from foot-long fish with deeply forked tails frantically hurling themselves out of the water, only to fall back into their tightly packed school. More and more birds materialize as if from nowhere, and the air rings with their shrill screams. Boats too begin to converge on the scene: the boiling cloud of birds has told anglers everywhere within view that a school of menhaden, perhaps numbering in the tens of thousands, is being ravaged by a school of bluefish.

Attacking from below and behind to slash the menhaden bodies with their powerful jaws, the razor-toothed blues are in a killing frenzy, gorging themselves with the severed backs and bellies of their prey, some killing even when they are too full to eat, some vomiting half-digested pieces so they can kill and eat again. Terns skim gracefully over the surface with their pointed bills down, dipping to pluck bits of flesh and entrails from the bloody swirls. Gulls plummet and flop heavily into the water, where a few splash about and squabble noisily over larger morsels. As some lift with their prizes, the squabbles turn aerial and a piece occasionally falls back into the water, starting a new round of shrieking skirmishes. Hovering high above the other birds, a male osprey scans for targets beneath the surface, then suddenly folds its gull-shaped wings and power-dives through the aerial tumult, extends its legs and raises its wings high over its head an instant before knifing into the water in a plume of spray, emerges in another plume, and laboriously flaps its four-foot wingspan as it slowly climbs and soars away with a writhing menhaden held headfirst in its talons. Beneath the blues, iridescent weakfish begin to circle, snapping at small lumps sinking from the carnage. Farther below, giant but tooth-less striped bass gobble tumbling heads and other chunks too big for the mouths of the weakfish. From time to time, bass muscle their way up through the blues, swallow whole menhaden alive, and propel themselves back down with their broom-like tails, leaving telltale swirls on the surface. On the mud below, crabs scuttle to scavenge on leftovers.

The panicked school of menhaden desperately races like a single creature, erratically zigging and zagging, diving and surfacing, pursued relentlessly by fish and birds. Small boats follow the chase, with excited anglers shouting and casting lures that mimic the darting menhaden. Fishing rods are bent double as some of the marauding bluefish and striped bass strike the lures. Bluefish battle until they are finally hooked with gaffs and brought aboard boats, where their blood splatters decks and jubilant anglers.

Then, as suddenly as it began, the wild scene dissipates. The water becomes surprisingly tranquil, disturbed only by wind and wave and the wakes of departing boats. Except for a few gulls lazily circling down and settling on the surface, the birds have disappeared.

The menhaden school survives and swims on, its losses dwarfed by plentitude. But a greater danger than predatory fish lurks nearby.

The birds have attracted a spotter-plane pilot who works for Omega Protein, a Houston-based corporation that does nothing but catch vast numbers of menhaden and turn their flesh into manufactured products. As the pilot approaches, he sees the school as a neatly defined purplish mass the size of a football field. He radios to a nearby ship, whose 170-foot hull can hold more than a million menhaden. The ship maneuvers close enough to launch two forty-foot-long aluminum boats. The boats share a single purse seine—a net almost a third of a mile long threaded with lines to close it up like a purse. The pilot directs the boats as they swing in a wide arc away from each other to deploy the purse seine, surrounding and trapping the entire school. Hydraulic power equipment begins to tighten the seine. As the fish strike the net, they thrash frantically, churning up a wall of white froth that marks the net's inexorably shrinking circumference. The net may now contain tens of thousands of menhaden. The factory ship pulls alongside, inserts a giant vacuum tube into the midst of the trapped fish, sucks and pumps the menhaden into its refrigerated hold, and soon heads off to unload them at the Omega port and factory complex in Reedville, Virginia. There the fish will become part of the hundreds of millions of pounds of menhaden annually processed in this tiny town on Cockrell's Creek, thus making it in tonnage the second-largest fishing port in the United States.

Not one of these fish is destined for a supermarket, a canning factory, or a restaurant. Menhaden are oily, foul smelling, and packed with tiny bones. No one eats them—not directly, anyhow. Hardly anyone has even heard of them except for those who fish or study our eastern and southern salt waters. Yet menhaden are the principal fish caught along the Atlantic and Gulf coasts, exceeding the tonnage of all other species combined.

Almost all of these fish are caught by Omega Protein, which has a nearly total monopoly on what is known as the menhaden reduction industry. Omega's fleet of sixty-one ships and thirty-two spotter planes annually captures billions of menhaden. At the company's five production facilities in Virginia, Louisiana, and Mississippi, these hundreds of thousands of tons of fish are converted into industrial commodities — hence the term "reduction." The menhaden are "reduced" into oil, solids, and meal. The oil from their bodies is pressed out for use in cosmetics, linoleum, health food supplements, lubricants, margarine, soap, insecticide, and paints. Their dried-out carcasses are then pulverized, scooped into huge piles, containerized, and shipped out as feed for domestic cats and dogs, farmed fish, and, most of all, poultry and pigs.

Menhaden have always been an integral, if unheralded, part of America's history. This was the fish that Native Americans taught the Pilgrims to plant with their corn. This was the fish that made larger-scale agriculture viable in the eighteenth and early nineteenth centuries for those farming the rocky soils of New England and Long Island. As the industrial revolution transformed the nation, this was the fish whose oil literally greased the wheels of manufacture, supplanting whale oil as a principal industrial lubricant and additive by the 1870s. Hundreds of ships hunted schools, schools sometimes forty miles long, up and down the coast from Maine to Florida. Strewn along the entire eastern seaboard, dozens of factories processed the fish into oil and fertilizer, making the menhaden fishery itself one of nineteenth-century America's largest industries. During the First World War, the U.S. Navy helped guide the menhaden fleets to their prey. In the middle of the twentieth century, *National Geographic* and *LIFE* magazines were headlining menhaden as "Uncle Sam's Top Commercial Fish" and "Biggest Ocean Harvest." In the twenty-first century, Omega Protein's annual catch still exceeds that of those hundreds of nineteenth-century vessels, though most of the menhaden now come from the Gulf of Mexico, not the Atlantic. Overall, from the 1860s to the present, catching menhaden has been far and away the nation's largest fishery. In fact, during many of these decades and years, the annual haul of menhaden weighed more than the combined commercial catch of all other finned fish put together, including Atlantic and Pacific cod, tuna, salmon, halibut, pollock, herring, swordfish, haddock, ocean perch, flounder, scup, striped bass, whiting, croaker, snapper, sardines, anchovies, dogfish, and mackerel.[1]

ALL THESE roles menhaden have played in America's national history are just minor parts of a much larger story of menhaden in America's natural history. For menhaden play dual roles in marine ecology perhaps unmatched anywhere on the planet. And this is why the story of menhaden is the tale of the most important fish in North America.

Although hardly any of those hundreds of billions of captured menhaden have ever been caught to eat, we do eat them. No, you won't see menhaden in the fish market or supermarket seafood section, but they are present in the flesh of many other fish lying there on the ice. Menhaden are crucial to the diet of Atlantic tuna, cod, haddock, halibut, mackerel, bluefish, weakfish, striped bass, swordfish, king mackerel, summer flounder, drum, and other predatory fish. The great nineteenth-century ichthyologist G. Brown Goode exaggerated only slightly when he declared that people who dine on Atlantic saltwater fish are eating "nothing but menhaden."

Menhaden are also a major component of the diet of many marine birds and mammals, including porpoises and toothed whales. In his monumental volume *A History of the Menhaden*, published in 1880, Goode expressed his wonderment at menhaden's role in the natural world: "It is not hard to surmise the menhaden's place in nature; swarming our waters in countless myriads, swimming in closely-packed, unwieldy masses, helpless as flocks of sheep, close to the surface and at the mercy of any enemy, destitute of means of defense or offense, their mission is unmistakably to be eaten."[2]

But Goode was only half right. What he did not fathom was menhaden's other—equally stupendous mission—in marine ecology.

Where did this enormous biomass of menhaden, so crucial to the food chain above it, come from? Just as all those saltwater fish are composed mainly of menhaden, all those billions of tons of menhaden are composed almost entirely of billions of tons of the tiny particles of vegetable matter known as phytoplankton. For menhaden, eating is just as crucial an ecological mission as being eaten.

Eons before humans arrived in North America, menhaden evolved along the low-lying Atlantic and Gulf coasts, where nutrients flood into estuaries, bays, and wetlands, stimulating potentially overwhelming growth of phytoplankton. From this superabundance of phytoplankton emerged the superabundance of these fish—and the fish that eat these fish. Although menhaden are the major herbivorous fish of these coasts, they don't chomp on the plants they consume. They are filter feeders that live primarily on tiny or even microscopic plants and other suspended matter, much of it indigestible or toxic to most other aquatic animals. Dense schools of menhaden, sometimes numbering in the hundreds of thousands, pour through these waters, toothless mouths agape, slurping up plankton, cellulose, and just plain detritus like a colossal submarine vacuum cleaner as wide as a city block and as deep as a train tunnel. Each adult fish filters about four gallons of water a minute.[3] Purging suspended particles that cause turbidity, this filter feeding clarifies the water, allowing sunlight to penetrate. This in turn encourages the growth of aquatic plants that release dissolved oxygen while also harboring a host of fish and shellfish.

Even more important, the menhaden's filter feeding prevents or limits devastating algal blooms. Most of the phytoplankton consumed by menhaden consists of algae. Excess nitrogen can make algae grow out of control, and that's what happens when overwhelming quantities of nitrogen flood into our inshore waters from runoff fed by paved surfaces, roofs, detergent-laden wastewater, over-fertilized golf courses and suburban lawns, and industrial poultry and pig farms. This can generate deadly blooms of algae, such as red tide and brown tide, which cause massive fish kills, then sink in thick carpets to the bottom, where they smother plants and shellfish, suck dissolved oxygen from the water, and leave dead zones that expand year by year.

In the natural ecosystem, the bonanza of phytoplankton stimulated a tremendous profusion of another filter-feeding consumer of algae: oysters. These two wonderful filter feeders kept inshore waters clear, clean, balanced, and healthy: oysters clinging to the bottom and menhaden cruising through all the upper layers. But oysters have been driven to near extinction in many bays and estuaries by overfishing and pollution. Clams and mussels also filter-feed on the algae, but neither has the enormous mass of the bygone oyster reefs or the gargantuan menhaden schools. The only remaining significant checks on the phytoplankton that cause algal blooms and dead zones are those menhaden schools, and they are now threatened by the ravages of unrestrained industrial fishing. By the end of the twentieth century, the population and range of Atlantic menhaden had virtually collapsed. The estimated number of sexually mature adult fish had crashed to less than 13 percent of what it had been four decades earlier.[4] Although northern New England had once been the scene of the largest menhaden fishery, adult fish had not been sighted north of Cape Cod since 1993.[5]

Marine biologist Sara Gottlieb, author of a groundbreaking study on menhaden's filtering capability, compares their role with the human liver's: "Just as your body needs its liver to filter out toxins, ecosystems also need those natural filters." Overfishing menhaden, she says, "is just like removing your liver."[6]

If a healthy person needs a fully functioning liver, consider someone whose body is subjected to unusual amounts of toxins—just like our Atlantic and Gulf coasts. If menhaden are the liver of these waters, should we continue to allow huge chunks to be cut out each year, cooked into industrial oils, and ground up to be fed to chickens, pigs, and pets? Menhaden have managed to survive centuries of relentless natural and human predation. But now there are ominous signs that we may have pushed our most important fish to the brink of an ecological catastrophe.

The New World of Fish

chapter 2

The Fish They Came For

When Giovanni Cabotto, better known as John Cabot, "discovered" North America for England's King Henry VII in 1497, what he actually found was a rather desolate island he called "New Found Land" adjacent to seas teeming with fish. Excited stories about these fish spread like feverish rumors of gold in a Europe bursting out of feudalism and prowling with mercantile capitalists craving new sources of wealth. The Duke of Milan received this report from his ambassador to England about that epic voyage of "Zoane Caboto":

> This Messer Zoane, as a foreigner and a poor man, would not have obtained credence, had it not been that his companions, who are practically all English and from Bristol, testified that he spoke the truth. . . . They assert that the sea there is swarming with fish, which can be taken

not only with the net, but in baskets let down with a stone, so that it sinks in the water. I have heard this Messer Zoane state so much. These same English, his companions, say that they could bring so many fish that this kingdom would have no further need of Iceland, from which place there comes a great quantity of fish called stockfish.[1]

As eager as sharks, Breton, Norman, Basque, Spanish, Portuguese, and English fishermen began ravenously hunting these North American fish. Within a decade of Cabot's voyage, a seasonal fleet of fishing vessels was streaming each year into these rich waters, and soon regular fishing colonies were sprouting. By 1517, there were reports of a hundred and fifty European fishing vessels based in Newfoundland.[2] From the southern shores of Newfoundland they steadily expanded, first hugging the coasts west into the Gulf of Saint Lawrence and then south into the Gulf of Maine, later venturing offshore first to the Grand Bank southeast of Newfoundland, then working their way around the continental shelf to the phenomenal Georges Bank off New England.[3] The Basques even pushed north to hunt fish and whales from the frigid harbors of Labrador. Throughout the sixteenth century the incredible fish tales of "Zoane Caboto" proved true, as a torrent of wealth poured from American waters to Europe. And those American fish kept luring more and more fishermen, explorers, and colonists.

In 1614, seven years after his fateful arrival in Jamestown, Captain John Smith set sail on another historic voyage to survey the land he named, upon arrival, "New England." His explorations ranged south from the Maine coast to a peninsula jutting out into waters so thick with fish that a previous British voyager in 1602 had already named it Cape Cod. Smith was mainly seeking gold and whales, but he found no gold and his crew was unable to kill any whales. What he found instead as a source of potential riches was "an incredible abundance of most sorts of fish."[4] So Smith devoted many pages in his 1616 volume *A Description of New England* to arguing for fishing as a lucrative way to colonize the lands he had mapped from Cape Cod to Penobscot Bay.

Fish are so bountiful in "the harbors we frequented," he wrote, that "with a casting-net" his crew caught "thousands when wee pleased," and "a little boye" fishing from the ship's stern could catch more "than sixe or tenne can eate in a daie." There is "no River where there is not plenty of Sturgion, or Salmon, or both," and almost anyplace "a man may take with a hooke or line what he will" of "Cod, Cuske, Holybut, Mackerell, Scate." Since someone would have to be "a very bad fisher" who "cannot kill in one day with his hooke and line, one, two, three hundred Cods," "may not the servant, the master, and the merchant, be well content with this gaine?"[5]

Even children and old women could participate in the effortless fishery he observed among the Indians: "Now, young boyes and girles Salvages, or any other, be they never such idlers, may turne, carry, and return fish, without either shame, or any great paine: he is very idle that is past twelve yeares of age and cannot do so much; and she is very olde, that cannot spin a thred to make engines to catch them." In the margin beside this sentence, Smith wrote "Imployment for poore people and fatherlesse children," conjuring up a fish-based social utopia. Life among this plethora of fish would be not just profitable but wonderfully pleasurable, Smith argued, a kind of carefree fishy Eden. "You shall scarce find any Baye or shallow shore, or Cove of sand, where you may not take many Clampes [clams], or Lobsters, or both, at your pleasure." Future colonists will be able "to recreate themselves before their owne doores, in their owne boats upon the Sea, where man woman and childe, with a small hooke and line, by angling, may take diverse sorts of excellent fish, at their pleasures. . . . Now that Carpenter, Mason, Gardiner, Taylor, Smith, Sailer, Forgers, or what other, may they not make this a pretty recreation though they fish but an houre in a day, to take more then they eate in a weeke. . . . And what sporte doth yeeld a more pleasing content, and lesse hurt or charge then angling with a hooke, and crossing the sweet ayre from Ile to Ile, over the silent streames of a calme Sea?"[6]

Smith's book, designed largely to stimulate colonization of "New England," was published just as the Puritans who had fled to Holland were looking for a new place to settle. So then it's no wonder that, motivated "chiefly for the hope of present profit to be made by fishing in that country," as William Bradford wrote in *Of Plymouth Plantation*, they decided to establish a fishing colony in New England.[7] When these Pilgrims requested permission from King James to charter this colony, he asked how they would gain "profits." Their representative replied, "Fishing." To which the king responded, "'tis an honest Trade, 'twas the Apostles owne calling."[8]

But when their *Mayflower* landed at Cape Cod and they established their nearby Plymouth Plantation in 1620, the Pilgrims had neither the fishing experience nor the fishing tackle to take advantage of nature's vast marine bounty. Though surrounded by freshwater and saltwater fish and shellfish, half the colonists died, mainly from malnutrition, during the first winter. The stranding of a single small fish was a bonanza, as indicated by their recording of this major occurrence: "Fryday the fifth of *Ianuary*, one of the Saylers found aliue vpon the shore an Hering, which the Master had to his supper, which put vs in hope of fish, but as yet we had got but one Cod; we wanted small hookes."[9]

Living among the neighboring Wampanoag Indians and observing all this incompetence was Tisquantum, or "Squanto," an ex-captive Indian brought back from England by John Smith only to find his own people entirely wiped out by a disease carried by Europeans. The Wampanoag decided to use Tisquantum to form a tactical alliance with the English. When Tisquantum showed up in March, one of his first missions was to teach the Pilgrims how easy it was to catch fish: "*Squanto* went at noone to fish for Eeles, at night he came home with as many as he could well lift in one hand, which our people were glad of, they were fat & sweet, he trod them out with his feete, and so caught them with his hands without any other Instrument."[10] By the time they prepared for the first Thanksgiving, "every family had their portion" of cod, striped bass, and other fish.[11] Because they did learn from Tisquantum and the Wampanoag how to fish and dig eels and gather shellfish even in winter, by the following December the Pilgrims found themselves wallowing in a deluge of seafood: "For fish and fowle, we have great abundance, fresh Codd in the Summer is but course meat with us, our Bay is full of Lobsters all summer, and affordeth varietie of other Fish; in September we can take a Hogshead of Eeles in a night, with small labour, & can dig them out of their beds, all the Winter we have Mussells and Othus at our doores." [12]

Tisquantum taught them another lesson, one that would have dramatic and far-reaching sequels. "He told them," as William Bradford wrote, that unless "they got fish" and planted it as fertilizer with their Indian corn, their crop, particularly "in these old grounds," "would come to nothing." [13] Writing in 1622, after they had the opportunity to observe how other Indians used fish as fertilizer, Edward Winslow told of how "[w]e set this last Spring some twentie Acres of *Indian* Corne . . . and according to the manner of the *Indians*, we manured our ground with Herings or rather Shadds, which we have in great abundance." [14] By the 1630s, this Indian practice had become standard among the New England colonists, as described in Thomas Morton's *New English Canaan*, which told how they used "multitudes" of a fish, "by some called shads, by some allizes," with their "Indian Maize, (which must be set by hands) . . . every acre taking 1000 of them." According to Morton, "An acre thus dressed will produce and yeald so much corne as 3 acres without fish." [15] And Edward Johnson told how "the Lord is pleased to provide for them great store of Fish in the spring-time, and especially Alewives, about the bignesse of a Herring, many thousands of these, they used to put under their *Indian* Corne, which they plant in Hills five foote asunder, and assuredly when the Lord created this Corne, hee had a speciall eye to supply these his peoples wants with it, for ordinarily five or six graines doth produce six hundred." [16]

Other colonists also wrote about learning from the Indians how to use fish as fertilizer. In 1991, anthropologist Stephen Mrozowski actually excavated fish bones in corn hills in a pre-colonial Indian cornfield on Cape Cod. Yet many historians have bought the argument that

Indians in New England did not use fish as fertilizer. Why? Evidently because hardly any historians of this period seem to have ever heard of menhaden or know the origin of the name.[17] Their ignorance is somewhat understandable, given some of the hopeless confusion about fish and the names for fish among the European colonists.

"Herrings," "shads," "allizes," "alewives"—were any of these fish actually menhaden? Almost certainly, yet no colonists could tell us. Why? Because they didn't recognize menhaden as any different from shad, herring, alewives, or various other European fish. In fact, not until the nineteenth century did Europeans or their descendants realize that the menhaden, by far the most abundant of all fish along the Atlantic seaboard, is a distinct species.

As for the Indians of New England, they obviously knew what menhaden were because menhaden were integral to their agriculture—hence the name they gave the fish. The Narragansett Indians called the species *munnawhatteaûg*, as noted by Roger Williams in his 1643 *A Key to the Language of America*, where he defines the word as "A Fish somewhat like a Herring." Later students of this Algonquian language revealed that *munnawhatteaûg* literally means "fertilizer" or "that which manures" or "he enriches the land." As *munnawhatteaûg* became anglicized and corrupted, it evolved into our English word "menhaden."[18] Any remaining doubt about whether the New England Indians used fish as fertilizer should be resolved by the name bestowed on menhaden by the Abenaki Indians of coastal Maine: *pauhagen*, which also means "fertilizer." *Pauhagen* soon became corrupted into "poghaden," which then got shortened to "pogy," one of the more popular current names for menhaden in New England as well as along the Gulf coast.[19]

So the Indians thought of menhaden as "he enriches the land." What they meant by that was simple: used in modest subsistence farming, the fish bequeathed its rich nutrients to the soil. They could hardly have imagined the scene two centuries later, when the fish they had named "he enriches the land" would be converted by the billions into industrial commodities and personal wealth.

THE FISH THEY FOUND

When the Europeans encountered the creatures that jammed the waters of the American coast, they were awestruck. Never in any of their lives had they glimpsed such teeming masses nor such huge sizes, even in the species they recognized. As the Reverend Francis Higginson wrote in his 1630 pamphlet *New-Englands Plantation*, "The abundance of Sea-Fish are almost beyond beleeving, and sure I should scarce have beleeved it except that I had seene it with mine own Eyes."[20]

Cod, halibut, flounder, haddock, some of the skates and hakes, some of the tunas—Europeans knew these food fish, but nothing like here, where forms both known and new seemed to fill the seas. Sure, they were familiar with salmon, but they had never seen hordes, some six feet long, cramming up rivers to spawn.[21] In 1634, William Wood marveled at the twenty-pound lobsters, foot-long oysters, and halibut "two yards long, and one wide; and a foot thicke."[22] Colonists sometimes found themselves in small boats endangered by flotillas of armored sturgeon, up to eighteen feet long and weighing half a ton, surging by hundreds up rivers to spawn.[23] Europeans of course knew mackerel, but they had never seen such gigantic schools or witnessed them driven in heaps onto beaches by equally awesome packs of two voracious predators—bluefish and striped bass, an exotic denizen of this astonishing new marine world. Schools of striped bass weighing up to 140 pounds were so thick that "our Fishers take many hundreds together, which I have seen lying on the shore to my admiration; yea, their Nets ordinarily take more than they are able to hale to Land, and for want of Boats and Men they are constrained to let a many goe after they have taken them, and yet somehow they fill two Boats at a time with them."[24] Boats crossing New York Harbor were accompanied by schools of playful porpoises.[25] Among the giants were the barndoor skate and cownose ray, the basking shark and whale shark, and the spectacular swordfish and sailfish.

Even larger of course were the mammoth whales that cruised the coast and even wallowed in its bays and estuaries. Indeed, until their systematic slaughter began, whales were a hazard to navigation all along the coast. As the *Mayflower* approached Cape Cod, the ship was surrounded by whales. Whales abounded in Chesapeake Bay, and William Penn described the "mighty whales" rolling in the mouth of Delaware Bay.[26] A 1679 sketch shows whales spouting and crisscrossing back and forth in New York Harbor.[27]

But the bulk of animal flesh swimming in these coastal waters consisted not of those marine giants but rather of immense shoals of the small fish that the prized food fish fed upon, what people centuries later were to call "forage" fish. To the northeast, along the southern coast of Newfoundland and out to the Grand Banks, the waters were packed with herring and capelin, well known to the Europeans. Shad and alewives, two cousins of herring, choked the rivers of the eastern seaboard on their spring spawning runs.

Overwhelmed by the awesome profusion of marine life, and amid this deluge of familiar herring and herring-like fish, the colonists failed to notice another member of the herring family. What they didn't see was the single species that perhaps outnumbered and even outweighed all the other fish put together, the fish most essential to the entire marine ecology of the coast—menhaden.

THE FISH THAT'S DIFFERENT

Because the British explorers and colonists had never seen menhaden but were familiar with fish that looked quite similar, they continually confused shad, alewives, herring, and menhaden, thus creating a hopelessly mixed-up fish stew. Remember that Edward Winslow wrote that the Pilgrims used "Herings or rather Shadds" to manure their corn, while Thomas Morton explained that these fish planted with corn were called "by some shads, by some allizes" and Edward Johnson designated these same fish as "especially Alewives, about the bigness of a Herring." It gets worse. John Josselyn cataloged the following names for one native American fish: "Alize, Alewife, because great bellied; Olafle, Oldwife, Allow."[28] Which fish? We don't know. "Alewife" and "oldwife" are still widely used names for menhaden; indeed, until the late nineteenth century, in all regions south of New York the name "alewife" was applied exclusively to menhaden.[29] Writing in 1685 about Pennsylvania, William Penn described "Alloes, as they call them in *France*, the Jews *Allice*, and our Ignorants, *Shads*," thus displaying his own confusion among the Allis (or Allice) shad of Great Britain *(Alosa alosa)*, the North American shad *(Alosa sapidissima)*, and the North American alewife *(Alosa pseudoharengus)*. Penn asserted that the fish greatest both in "Magnitude" and "Number" are "the *Herring*, which swarm in such shoales, that it is hardly Credible; in little creeks, they almost shovel them up in their tubs"; certainly not true herring (pelagic fish that spawn at sea and rarely enter brackish water, much less freshwater creeks), these *"Herring"* were probably some mixture of menhaden, shad, blueback shad *(Alosa aestivalis)*, and alewives.[30] Thus those who tried to identify the swarms of American herring-like fish succeeded only in bequeathing to us a bewildering jumble of names, including at least thirty that are still in use for menhaden.

Because of all this early confusion, menhaden are in various regions still called "herring," "shad," or "hard-headed shad." Elsewhere, perhaps in desperate attempts to escape this mayhem of names, people have just given them monikers based on some specific physical characteristic, such as "bony-fish," "hardhead," "fatback" (because of its profuse body oil and bulging upper body fat when well nourished), or "bug-fish," a reference to a parasitic crustacean *(Olencira praegustator)* found in their mouths in waters from the Chesapeake south.[31]

Captain John Smith, who had lots of experience handling fish and was rather astute at identifying them, was one of the few early British who recognized that menhaden were something different. In his 1608 exploration of the Chesapeake, Smith found astonishingly dense schools of a fish he could not identify. In "divers places" throughout the waters of the Chesapeake, his two-ton barge plowed through "an aboundance of fish, lying so thicke with their heads above the water, as for want of nets (our barge driving among them) we attempted to catch them with a frying pan: but we found it a bad instrument to catch fish with." [32] Some of Smith's contemporaries thought this was a wild exaggeration, and at least one modern writer dismisses it as a tall tale or joke. But in fact it's an accurate description—accompanied by an accurate illustration on the title page of his 1624 *Generall Historie of Virginia, New England and the Summer Isles*—of the solid schools of menhaden that inhabited the Chesapeake throughout American history. That is, until their very recent decimation by modern industrial fishing. [33]

The only seventeenth-century Europeans who actually recognized menhaden as different from other American fish and had an agreed-upon name for them were the Dutch, no doubt because the waters around the city of New Amsterdam in the region of New Netherlands (both of course later renamed for the Duke of York) were frequently so thick with menhaden. But the Dutch confused them with a familiar northern European fish *(Caranx trachurus)* known to them as "marsbanker." So "marsbanker" or "masbank" became their name for menhaden. Jacob Steendam's 1661 poem "In Praise of New Netherland" pictures the "masbank" among the mammoth glut of American fish that "fill the nets to loathing." In their wonderful description of New York Harbor in 1679, two Dutch travelers portray the "marsbancker" amid the predatory porpoises, tunnies, whales, and birds feeding upon them:

> It is not possible to describe how this bay swarms with fish, both large and small, whales, tunnies and porpoises, whole schools of innumerable other fish, and a sort like herring, called there *marsbanckers* . . . which the eagles and other birds of prey swiftly seize in their talons when the fish come up to the surface, and hauling them out of the water, fly with them to the nearest woods or beach. [34]

"Marsbanker" had been anglicized into "moss-bonker" or "moss-bunker" by the time Washington Irving recorded it in his 1809 *History of New York*, which relates the legend of a swimmer drowned in the Harlem River by the devil "in the shape of a huge moss-bonker," causing "moss-bonkers" to be so abhorred that "no good Dutchman will admit them to his table who loves good fish and hates the devil."[35] Thanks to those seventeenth-century Dutch, throughout New York and New Jersey menhaden are still rarely called anything but "moss-bunkers" or, more usually, just plain "bunkers." Growing up in Brooklyn (originally Breukelen, another Dutch name) and now living and fishing in New Jersey, I never called them anything but bunkers before starting research on this book. Indeed, "bunker" is today probably the primary popular name for the fish along most of the eastern seaboard.

It was not until early in the nineteenth century that American scientists began to recognize menhaden as a distinct species. Ichthyologists then debated for about seventy years over whether they were a species of herring, shad, or alewife. Only in the last quarter of the nineteenth century was there general agreement that the American menhaden belong to the genus *Brevoortia*, which also included species in the southern Atlantic off the coasts of Africa and Brazil. By then, menhaden were a major component of the U.S. economy and a growing source of conflict about our relation to the marine environment.

Why was it so difficult, even for ichthyologists, not to mention the colonists, to distinguish menhaden? And if it's so difficult to tell them apart from herring, shad, and alewives, what's so important about menhaden anyhow?

Menhaden are members of the herring family (Clupeidae), but they are not true herring *(Clupea)* such as the Atlantic herring *(Clupea harengus)*, a key forage fish on both sides of the North Atlantic that resembles the Atlantic menhaden *(Brevoortia tyrannus)*, the Gulf menhaden *(Brevoortia patronus)*, the American shad *(Alosa sapidissima)*, and the alewife *(Alosa pseudoharengus)*. Like almost every member of the herring family, all of these species are planktivores. That is, they live on the minute, often microscopic, floating and drifting marine life known as plankton. Each species has a little forest of gill rakers to filter the plankton they feed upon, and all share the family's characteristic deeply forked tail. Indeed, menhaden, shad, and alewives do look very similar. They all have rather dumpy bodies and a similar single dorsal fin and single anal fin. Alewives and fairly young shad are typically about the same ten- to twelve-inch length as mature Atlantic menhaden, and the common alewife and some shad often have a small dark spot behind the head somewhat like that of menhaden.

It's no surprise, then, that the colonists took no special notice of menhaden. What may seem astonishing, however, given all these similarities, is the unique importance of menhaden both in the natural environment the colonists were penetrating and in American history for the next four centuries.

So what makes menhaden so special? Menhaden have four distinct differences from herring, shad, alewives, and other members of the herring family:

1. The first distinction is the crucial one. Almost all the other Clupeidae eat zooplankton, the tiny animals that drift around in the water. But menhaden primarily consume phytoplankton, that is, algae and other drifting bits of vegetable matter. The ecological significance of this difference can hardly be overstated. The actual diet of menhaden was only vaguely perceived in the last decade of the nineteenth century, and its enormous significance for the marine environment was only beginning to be glimpsed in the last decades of the twentieth century. Only in the twenty-first century is there growing awareness that the health of our East Coast bays and estuaries, as well as the vast region of the Gulf of Mexico fed by the entire Mississippi watershed, depends upon these small fish.

2. Because the Atlantic and Gulf coasts of America naturally produce vast amounts of phytoplankton, because menhaden have relatively little competition for this elementary food source, and

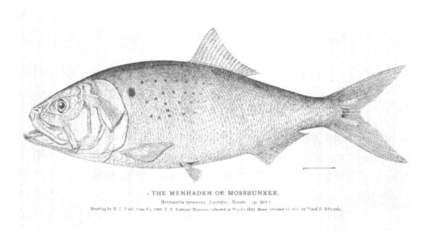

THE MENHADEN OR MOSSBUNKER.
Brevoortia tyrannus (Latrobe), Goode.   (p. 569.)
Drawing by H. L. Todd, from No. 2000, U. S. National Museum, collected at Wood's Hole, Mass., October 11, 1871, by Vinal N. Edwards.

FIGURE 2.1 Atlantic menhaden *(Brevoortia tyrannus)*. From Goode, 1887.

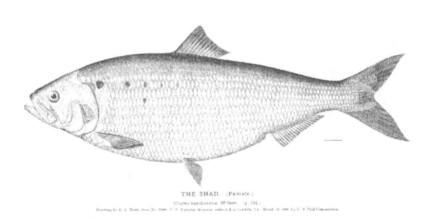

THE SHAD. [Female.]
Clupea sapidissima, Wilson.   (p. 594.)
Drawing by H. L. Todd, from No. 2908, U. S. National Museum, collected at Norfolk, Va., March 19, 1899, by U. S. Fish Commission.

FIGURE 2.2 Shad *(Alosa sapidissima)*. From Goode, 1887. The similarities among menhaden, herring, and shad confused not only the early colonists but nineteenth-century scientists, who classified the shad as a species of herring *(Clupea)*. As opposed to true herring, which spawn in salt water, the various shads spawn in fresh water and are grouped in the genus *Alosa*. To distinguish them from the true herring, the shads are commonly referred to as river herring.

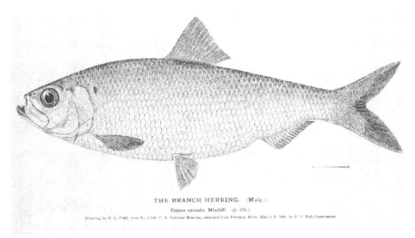

THE BRANCH HERRING. (Male.)

Clupea vernalis. Mitchill. (p. 579.)

Drawing by H. L. Todd, from No. 21430, U. S. National Museum, obtained from Potomac River, March 21, 1880, by U. S. Fish Commission.

FIGURE 2.3   Alewife *(Alosa pseudoharengus)*. From Goode, 1887. Again, Goode classifies the alewife in the genus *Clupea*, or herring, rather than *Alosa*, or shad. The alewife so closely resembles a true herring that its species name is *pseudoharengus*, literally "false herring" (the actual herring species is *Clupea harengus*).

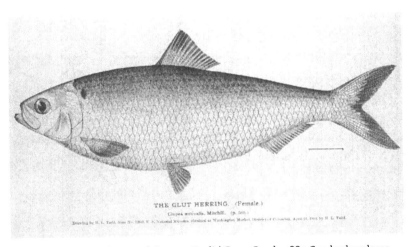

THE GLUT HERRING. (Female.)

Clupea aestivalis. Mitchill. (p. 586.)

Drawing by H. L. Todd, from No. 2868, U. S. National Museum, obtained at Washington Market, District of Columbia, April 21, 1881, by H. L. Todd.

FIGURE 2.4   Blueback herring *(Alosa aestivalis)*. From Goode, 1887. Goode also places this species of "river herring" in the herring genus *(Clupea)* rather than the shad genus *(Alosa)*, where modern science classifies it because it spawns in fresh water.

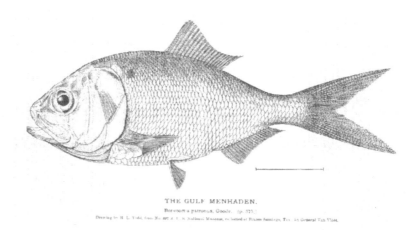

THE GULF MENHADEN.
Bevoortia patronus, Goode. (p. 575.)
Drawing by H. L. Todd, (no. No. 407 t. 1. S. National Museum, collected at Pleasure Anchorage, Tex., by General Van Vliet.

FIGURE 2.5 Gulf menhaden *(Bevoortia patronus)*. From Goode, 1887. Because this species exists only in the Gulf of Mexico, the early English colonists did not encounter it and therefore never had an opportunity to confuse it with herring and shad.

because of their phenomenal fecundity, menhaden were able to become unimaginably abundant, dwarfing the population of any other American fish, possibly exceeding all the fish on both these coasts put together.

3. Because of their stupendous abundance, menhaden were the primary food source for most predatory fish on both the Atlantic and Gulf coasts, as well as many predatory birds and marine mammals. Although all these animals will certainly eat other forage fish, they have a special—almost obsessive—craving for menhaden.

4. We humans, on the other hand, don't like to eat menhaden, although many other members of the herring family have long been major food fish or even delicacies. Their bony head is very large, the rest of their body is full of bones, they are oily inside and slimy outside, and they smell awful. This is not to say that they are inedible or have never been eaten (even with pleasure,

according to some early accounts!). But given a choice in nature's extravagant bounty of American fish, who would choose to dine upon menhaden?

These four distinctions interact in a complex synergy.

Paradoxically, our distaste for menhaden contributes to their most significant roles in American history. Because they are not appetizing cuisine, the Indians named them "fertilizer" and used them to enrich the difficult soils of New England. Because the Indians used them as fertilizer, the colonists did too. Because they were so phenomenally abundant and easily available, their use in the colonists' small-scale, mainly subsistence farming would eventually morph into their first avatar as an industrial commodity, fertilizer for nascent agribusiness, and then into a shifting variety of other industrial commodities in the nineteenth, twentieth, and twenty-first centuries. Since they were not a food fish, at first nobody seemed to care, hence their reckless wholesale slaughter in the wild days of industrial capitalism, especially from the close of the Civil War through the epoch after the Second World War. This slaughter led to disastrous consequences, which in turn led to the birth of a specific ecological consciousness in the second half of the nineteenth century, perhaps the very first based on an awareness of the interdependence of species.

Thus as menhaden's roles in America's economy and history have kept evolving, this fish has also played a leading role in deepening America's consciousness about the marine environment and our relationship to it. To comprehend this complex and quite surprising economic and cultural history, we need to know more than the Indians, the colonists, and our other predecessors knew. So let's first get to meet the fish face to face and then plunge with it more deeply into its world.

Meeting Menhaden: In Our World and Theirs

F ACE TO FACE

Blunt head, lower jaw sticking out in front of a large, gaping, toothless mouth, pudgy body—a menhaden sure doesn't look like the superstar of coastal ecology. The relatively massive, scaleless head constitutes a full third of the body's length and close to half the total weight. Since the remaining flesh is filled with bones, it's no surprise that menhaden are not a favorite food fish for humans. But this large head, often trailing a stream of guts, is a main course for other predators in that bountiful banquet left by ravaging bluefish after they have chopped off the rest of the adult fish.

The head has to be large to accommodate the unusually complex gill structure, which has a dual function. Fish generally get their oxygen from water pouring through their mouths and flowing out through their gills—their equivalent of lungs: as blood circulates in the gills, it absorbs oxygen and expels carbon dioxide. Menhaden also have a net-like thicket of bony gill rakers that extract tiny particles of phytoplankton and detritus from the water continually swirling into their mouths and out their gills. As an adult menhaden filters four to eight gallons a minute through these gill rakers, it is simultaneously breathing (the dissolved oxygen) and eating (the minute suspended particles).

Their coloration is attractive as well as beneficial to the menhaden. The top of the body can be a variety of fairly dark olive greens or blues mixed with gray or brown; seen from above, the body blends in with marine waters, obscuring the fish from aerial attackers. The sides and belly are silvery yellow or brassy; seen from below, the body blends in with sun and sky, concealing the fish from underwater attackers. The large, opalescent scales have a pearly appearance and have been used for human ornamentation. A prominent dusky round spot behind the gill plate and irregular rows of smaller dark spots are key identifying marks. The tail is deeply forked like that of the other members of the herring family. It also resembles the deeply forked tail of one of menhaden's most insatiable predators, the bluefish, thus possibly serving as a survival mechanism. Picture the chaos in the midst of a panicked school of menhaden as the marauding bluefish try to target menhaden rear ends amid a jumbled mayhem of forked tails.

Unlike the keen eyes that predatory fish use to spot their prey, the eyes of menhaden have a thick, glazy covering that gives them a sleepy look. But they have another sensory system, the lateral line that runs from the gill plate almost to the tail. Extremely sensitive to disturbances in the water or changes of pressure, the lateral line helps the fish coordinate with the school. It also detects the presence and movement of predators, even when they approach from behind.

Pick one up. Your hands are now coated with thin, slimy mucus. Even if the fish is alive, your nostrils are assailed by a distinctive foul odor, much more pungent if the fish has been dead awhile. You may not be able to get this smell off your hands, even with repeated washings, for many hours. Unlike the stench of skunks, the scent of menhaden is not a defense mechanism, but paradoxically quite the opposite. Indeed, perhaps the only predator that finds this smell repellent is Homo sapiens. Most marine predators and scavengers seem to find it irresistible. That is why menhaden in almost any form—dead or alive, whole bodies or small chunks, ground-up mush, oil, or even the scent itself—are used for bait.

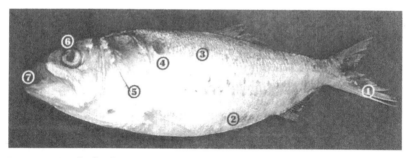

FIGURE 3.1 Menhaden features

1. Hydrodynamic propeller: Flapping a deeply forked tail, menhaden traveling in schools may cover two miles a day. The tail is also used to flip the fish out of water to escape attack.

2. Oceanic camouflage: A predator approaching from below might mistake the narrow silver belly of a menhaden for the glint of light on the water's surface. A predator approaching from above is presented with a dark-bluish dorsum, with an occasional golden tint, that tends to blend in with the water column.

3. Invisible feelers: A subcutaneous sensory system called a lateral line, which runs along the flanks, helps a menhaden feel other fish to maintain its position in the school and sense the presence of predators.

4. Signature markings: A dark spot behind the gill flap, followed by two or three rows of smaller spots, may make a menhaden more visible in turbid water to other menhaden.

5. Breathing apparatus: The menhaden uses gill filaments to pull dissolved oxygen from the water. Special cells in the gills also control the concentration of salt in the body.

6. Dim peepers: Unlike predatory fish that depend on keen eyesight to spot prey, the menhaden is a forager with thick, glazy coverings over its eyes that give it a sleepy look.

7. Vacuum cleaner: A menhaden swims with its mouth open, filtering four to eight gallons of water per minute through rakers on the inside of gill arches that sieve plankton.

BAIT

Although most Americans have never touched a menhaden, many have. As bait.

Summertime vacationers flock to bait-and-tackle stores to buy frozen menhaden that they then painstakingly attach inside crab traps for themselves or their children. Seasonal sounds along the Atlantic coast include the shrieks of delighted kids hauling up their little wire traps, thrilled at the sight of crabs that couldn't resist the seductive stink of the rotting menhaden still stubbornly clutched in their claws.

What's fun for the kids has long been hard labor for others. Menhaden have been for centuries the main commercial bait for Atlantic lobsters and crabs. Even today, the innumerable lobster and crab traps of commercial fishermen are baited, whenever possible, with bunker carcasses or heads.

The Atlantic coast game fish most accessible to people of modest means and limited time is the menhaden-lusting bluefish. If you want to catch large bluefish and you don't own your own boat or have access to someone else's or have enough money to charter a boat, you pay a reasonable fixed fare on a large "party boat" (also known as a "head boat" or "open boat"). From late spring through fall, many thousands of anglers are packed elbow to elbow along the rails of these boats as they plunge into the Atlantic, loaded with barrels of dead menhaden that will be converted by the crew into spectacularly effective bait for bluefish. It would be quite a surprise to both the crew members and the anglers to learn that almost every detail of this form of recreational pursuit of bluefish comes straight out of a form of commercial fishing developed in the New York–New Jersey area during the Civil War.

It sure surprised me when I came across "Blue Fishing for Market: A Cruise on a Fulton Market Smack," an 1877 *New York Times* article that describes this method of bluefishing and how it originally developed. The *Times* writer pokes fun at the "sportsmen" who spend up to "$30 per pound" for the bluefish they catch by hiring yachts and who cannot understand how the fish dealers in Manhattan's Fulton Market can make a profit selling them for "6 to 8 cents per pound."[1] These "amateurs" believe that the commercial fishermen must "catch them in nets." But they're wrong. The secret is menhaden. From late spring through early fall, the masses of bluefish in the Fulton Fish Market were being caught not with nets but "in the good old-fashioned way with hook and line," thanks to a relatively recent method of baiting with menhaden. Around 1862, a single commercial sailing vessel began "chopping up the menhaden to attract the fish, and then using pieces of the same as bait to catch them. . . . When they returned to market they brought in such a lot of blue-fish as amazed the oldest inhabitants." Although the crew tried to keep this secret, it gradually leaked out, and "very soon that was the only mode in use, and the market was glutted with this choice product of the sea."

Eager to see for himself how this is done, the *New York Times* writer signs on for a three-day bluefish cruise on a forty-nine-ton schooner smack, a sail ship crewed by a captain, a mate, a cook, and four other men. The ship first loads up with tons of ice from an East River port in Brooklyn and then sails into Raritan Bay, between New Jersey and New York, where the captain buys about ten thousand fresh "menhaden, or 'moss-bunkers,' or 'alewives,' or 'bony-fish,' for they bear all those names in different places." Finally the schooner heads out to fish in precisely the same ocean sites off the New Jersey shore where hordes of recreational anglers, myself included, still go to fish for blue-fish using menhaden as bait. Loads of menhaden are then ground up by a mill on board into "a disgusting looking mess" they call "stosh" or "chum." Other menhaden are cut up into baits for the hooks, either by "slivering" the sides into strips or by cutting the fish "across in three or four fragments, throwing away only the head"—the two techniques still in use. Also still the same are the fishing rigs, "with stout wires connecting their hooks with their lines, wires which the ferocious blue-fish cannot bite off." The only procedure significantly different from those on a twenty-first-century diesel-powered party boat, where everybody stays on board, is that this nineteenth-century commercial sail ship then deployed its anglers, one per vessel, in five rowboats. Both then and now, the next steps are anchoring the fishing vessels, splashing ladlefuls of the ground-up menhaden overboard to attract the bluefish, baiting the hooks with the menhaden pieces, floating the line into the menhaden-laden water, hooking the bluefish, and fighting them on board. The man who caught the most fish—known then as the "high line" (today called the "high hook")—hauled in 127 fish in one night, a number that would amaze anglers of today's depleted seas.

Yet even in these relatively barren waters, the menhaden have an almost magical effect. As soon as a modern party boat anchors at an ocean site sometimes prowled by bluefish weighing up to twenty pounds, the mates begin to ladle globs of chum into the sea. As the bits of chum float and sink, the menhaden oil begins to form a noticeable slick on the surface that spreads out and away with the current. Gulls are usually the first to arrive, diving and floating to pick out tidbits. The anglers feed out their line, trying to keep their baited hooks in the chum slick. Before long, in perhaps twenty or thirty minutes, the calm is abruptly broken as someone suddenly feels the rod almost snatched out of his or her hands and excitedly yells, "Fish on!" Soon hordes of bluefish arrive and begin to go into one of their characteristic feeding frenzies, initiating an equally frenzied scene on the boat as anglers battle their quarry amid tangled lines and shouts and bloody fish flopping on the deck. Sometimes the chum also draws other predators dependent on menhaden, such as the small tuna variously known as bonito, little tunny, or false albacore.

On one such boat, I witnessed a striking display of menhaden's allure. In the late-evening dusk, a large shark surfaced just a few feet from the boat and began feeding on tiny morsels in the chum. Four or five black-backed and herring gulls pounced on the shark's back and began pecking it, driving it down. Shark, birds, bluefish, humans—all seemed to be pulled by the menhaden into the ocean's dark ferocity.

Menhaden are also a choice bait for striped bass, weakfish, fluke, drum, and other favorite food and sport fish. In the fall, many of these highly prized fish feed voraciously on schools of four- to six-inch juvenile menhaden known as "peanut bunkers" or just plain "peanuts" as they pour out of rivers and creeks to begin their first journey into the ocean. Some of the peanuts are snared in small cast nets by individual anglers and charter boat captains, and then put on hooks, where they draw savage strikes from the hungry predators. Almost as effective are artificial soft plastic lures designed to look like the baby menhaden, swim like them, and even smell like them, thanks to menhaden oil sometimes impregnated into the plastic. I write this paragraph the morning after filleting dozens of bluefish and a few striped bass that three friends and I caught on a late fall day, from a small boat in the ocean just off the northern New Jersey shore, in the same site fished by that 1877 schooner. The boat's deck had soon gotten hazardous from slippery layers of baby menhaden spat up by the bluefish. The bellies of the fish, which we caught on rubbery plastic artificial bunkers that we cast under birds preying on the juvenile menhaden as they were being attacked from below, were stuffed with peanut bunkers in various states of digestion.

In the spring and summer, adult menhaden are the most successful bait for the largest striped bass. When a menhaden head is used, it tends to discourage roving bluefish while enticing stripers, probably because they are accustomed to gobbling disembodied heads that drop down as bluefish gorge above on the bodies they have severed. The largest stripers, however, usually prefer to swallow whole menhaden.

Menhaden swarm in dense schools and cram together even more tightly when under attack. This is a fine defense against their natural predators, giving the species an evolutionary advantage that must have led to a tendency to ever greater cramming. But it is the worst possible defense when faced with the ultimate predator, men in boats with nets designed to capture entire schools. It's not even a good defense against individuals from this predatory species intent on capturing just a few adult menhaden to use as bait for big striped bass. Taking advantage of the density of the packed menhaden, they cast a "snagger," a lead-weighted treble hook, into the school, let it sink, and then retrieve it with quick jerks. The menhaden are so thick that one can feel the snagger bumping through the school, and each cast has a good chance of snagging a ten- or twelve-inch bunker, the favorite dish of yard-long and even bigger striped bass.

Sometimes the bunker doesn't make it to the fishermen's boat because its thrashing attracts a bluefish that chops off half the unfortunate fish, leaving its telltale dental signature on the mutilated remnant. At other times the striper fishing unexpectedly begins while the snagged menhaden is being reeled in. A mammoth striped bass lurking under the menhaden school, unable to resist the sight of the wounded bunker, may grab the struggling fish in its toothless mouth and begin swimming away to swallow it, suddenly peeling off many yards of line from the reel of the startled angler.

A spectacular example was recently witnessed by beachgoers on Long Beach Island, New Jersey, one early evening in June. Fourteen-year-old Bobby Capri, Jr., who had seen a menhaden school just beyond the surf, borrowed his uncle's ten-foot kayak, paddled out, and snagged a bunker on his very light rod and twelve-pound test line. The next thing he knew, his kayak was being towed around in giant circles past two jetties. Because the striper wore itself out towing the kayak, Bobby eventually managed to bring it on board, but the fish was so heavy that it kept the bow under water. Knowing that he was inevitably going to be spilled out in the surf, the young angler put his arm through the gill plate of the striper and somehow got his catch, the kayak, and himself onto the beach. In the stomach of the striper, which weighed in officially at fifty-two pounds and eight ounces, were five undigested whole adult menhaden.[2]

Menhaden's ecological role as food for other marine animals is demonstrated by its fatal attractiveness as bait. In the 1870s, its value as bait led to a dangerous altercation between the United States and Britain, because the livelihood of many Canadian fishermen depended on having adequate supplies of this exclusively American species. Canadian officials recognized that menhaden as bait is so "far superior to any which can be secured in this country" that Canadian fishermen "have no chance while an American schooner is fishing near them," and that menhaden "is so much the favorite bait that one fishing vessel having this bait on board would draw a whole school of mackerel in the very face of vessels having an inferior bait."[3] As we shall see in chapter 5, menhaden's roles as food and bait for other fish would lead to the birth of a marine ecological consciousness as well as conflicts lasting for centuries.

The School

An individual menhaden is just a fish, a rather ordinary-looking fish, one that hardly inspires any profound emotional response. But the individual menhaden is merely a unit in something much greater than itself: the school. Nobody will ever write a *Moby-Dick* about a menhaden. Yet a school can weigh as much as the largest whale—and behave like a single organism. Watch an acre-wide school creating flashes of silver with flips of forked tails and splashes, whirling swiftly through three dimensions in moves more dazzling than those of a modern dancer or kung fu artist, as it seeks escape from hordes of bluefish and striped bass pursuing it from below and gulls, terns, gannets, and ospreys diving from above—and one is not so sure there's no epic story here.

Watching a school of menhaden in action can indeed be a breathtaking experience. Maybe large numbers of people will never travel long distances and pay lots of money to watch a menhaden school, the way they do now for a chance to watch a whale, but perhaps they should. While they can.

To see a large school of most other fish, you have to go underwater or at least look through the transparent bottom of a boat in very clear water. But a menhaden school often makes itself quite visible, even in

FIGURE 3.2 Menhaden school underwater. NOAA photograph by W. F. Hettler.

the kind of water it prefers, water so richly loaded with life that it's more translucent than transparent. Of course you can't get to see a whole school, because it's too dense, too deep, and often too wide. Then again, whale watchers rarely get to see a whole whale.

How do you know where there's a school? And what do you see?

Sometimes the only evidence of the school is an oily slick on the surface. If you are high enough above the surface, you can see a large purplish or reddish patch, a color somehow projected from the tops of the densely packed school and quite distinct from the blues and greens of the sea.

Often the surface of the water becomes all dimpled, as if it were being pelted with hail. Or the water may be rippled, especially when the topmost fish are swimming with their dorsal fins protruding slightly above the surface. In deep water, on the other hand, the school's presence can be announced by an unusually calm area, formed because the fish are massed so thickly that they actually still the ocean's waves. But if the school crowds into relatively shallow water, sometimes the surface becomes an undulating thicket of tails and dorsal fins, looking almost solid enough to walk across. At other times, the top layer of the fish are swimming with their mouths partly out of the water, just as Captain John Smith observed in the Chesapeake.

Sometimes you hear the school before you see it. If you are in a boat on a calm day, you may detect a rustling or whispering sound, like a broom sweeping pavement, as the school approaches. A school under attack makes a much noisier sound, as many of the fish hurl themselves out of the water to escape their predators and fall back with a staccato of splashes. In a characteristic behavior that mystifies many observers, a school not under attack also sometimes has hundreds of the fish flipping themselves sideways out of the water and falling back in with loud splashes. The noise from this flipping can be heard for long distances over the water. Why do they do this? Nobody knows, but almost everybody has a theory. Perhaps they are aerating the top layer of the water. Maybe they are just so crowded that some of the top fish are almost forced into the air. Some charter boat captains in Raritan Bay, a prime bunker spawning area, believe that these are females accelerating the discharge of their roe.

Maybe they are changing places in a kind of ritualized dance. As the flippers leave the water, this must move them back in the pack, which is continually swimming forward. So perhaps the pressure of the masses forces some of the leaders into losing their privileged places. After all, if the fish always maintained their same positions in the school, all but the ones in front would be eating mainly the feces of their leaders.

The school always seems to be on the verge of panic, ready to flee or dive at the sight of even a single predator. Yet they often treat a small boat as a harmless inanimate object, even when the people inside it are making the loud water-borne noises of talking or walking on the deck. On many occasions, I have been fishing with three other noisy men in a boat right in the path of an oncoming school evidently intent on slurping up plankton and detritus. Our boat might as well have been a person standing in the way of an elbow-to-elbow crowd leaving a sports stadium or a rush-hour subway car. Looking down, we could see the almost solid mass of shimmering bodies rushing past with flashes of silver underneath and on all sides of the boat. And all during the time that we were amid the onrushing school, we could feel and hear the continual thump-thump-thump of fish bumping into the hull.

In his classic book *The Bay*, naturalist Gilbert Klingel, who built a diving bell in the 1940s to witness life in the Chesapeake Bay, described the experience of seeing menhaden in their own medium. Menhaden, "those dull things of tarnished silver," underwater "become glittering objects of coppery gold":

> To see one of these hordes of menhaden underwater is a never-to-be-forgotten sight. I have been completely surrounded by their massed golden-hued shapes. Packed in serried ranks, head to head, tail to tail, they have poured past my helmeted body in a deluge of finny forms. Nearly always they are in a state of high nervous tension. The slightest motion will cause them to break into terror-stricken flight; instantly the mechanisms of fear take hold of the entire school and the hysteria is communicated from one individual to another until the entire mass is transformed into a blurred deluge of frenzied fish.[4]

The most spectacular, the most awful, and the most wondrous sight is the school under assault by predators, a scene I have tried to describe in the opening paragraph of this book. There are few scenes in nature that reveal so intensely and thoroughly its bountiful, pitiless, savage, and efficient ecology. Dozens of written descriptions since the early nineteenth century have focused on the viciousness and frenzy of the bluefish as they slash chunks out of the living bunkers and then often vomit undigested pieces so they can keep on killing and eating. As we shall see, these continual unrestrained onslaughts by bluefish have been used since the 1870s as an argument that human predation on menhaden is relatively trivial in comparison. But any such argument misses the ecological economy of these horrendous and marvelous scenes.

Think of the menhaden school as a seething mass of delicious nutrition concocted by nature's cookery out of unappealing ingredients. Indigestible minerals and chemicals in soil and water were first transformed into algae and other phytoplankton. Then menhaden transformed the phytoplankton into animal flesh, loaded with omega oils and other essential nutrients. Enter the bluefish. If the bluefish listened to their mommies and daddies and finished everything on their plates, never wasting an ounce of their food, all the menhaden would be converted into bluefish. But because the killing and eating frenzy of the bluefish leaves the water filled with mangled, bleeding fish, severed heads, bloody slicks, entrails, and disgorged chunks, the menhaden also get converted into striped bass, weakfish, fluke, crabs, lobsters, sharks, seals, porpoises, gulls, terns, gannets, ospreys, and many other animals drawn to the gory smorgasbord.

As for the school itself, here one sees its own wondrous life as an organism. Besieged and attacked from above and below and on all sides by this host of diverse predators and scavengers, the school usually draws together even more densely and begins to execute graceful high-speed maneuvers that make a destroyer or a submarine or even a jet fighter look like a clumsy contraption. It may suddenly dive and swerve simultaneously, then surface and dart erratically, racing from one direction to another. It may elongate and whip back and forth like a fleeing snake. It may scatter into smaller units and then quickly reform itself. Amazingly enough, these maneuvers often seem to work. The birds give the sign that the predators have lost contact with the school, as they begin circling and scouting in different directions, desperately trying to locate the fish again.

When a predator attacks a segment of the school, it is by no means assured of catching any prey despite, or even because of, the density. How is this possible? The Monterey Bay Aquarium has an exhibit that shows how difficult it is for a predator to catch a fish inside the swirling chaos of a frenzied school. As you become the predator dashing into a video of an actual school under attack by an actual predator, you find it virtually impossible to target an individual fish, because they writhe with astonishing speed and complexity into an indistinguishable jumble. In a second video of the same scene, you find that you can catch a fish, one that has been given a distinctive color. Before I saw that exhibit, I could never understand why a striped bass or bluefish would snatch an artificial lure cast into a school of real living bunkers.

Despite all its defenses, the school of course always suffers considerable losses. If an animal the size of a menhaden school had bits and pieces bitten off by predators, it would eventually die. For example, several years ago a group of oceanographers watched a pod of sperm whales being slaughtered by relatively diminutive orcas that killed their giant prey by nipping and slashing them with a prolonged series of high-speed attacks. But the organism that is the menhaden school does not succumb to its losses, because there is no vital organ, its numbers are immense, and whatever members survive still constitute the whole entity.

Indeed, the school is such a marvelous natural defense that it is virtually invulnerable to natural predators. But menhaden's role in the history of America revolves around the fact that the school is precisely what makes menhaden so vulnerable to human predators.

The World of the Drifters and Swimmers

Although we call it Earth, our world is a planet of oceans. That's why, as we now know ever since we got to view it from space, it's the Blue Planet.

The living world is even more oceanic. Not only do the seas occupy almost three times the surface area of those shifting islands we call continents, but their zones of life are much more vast in both space and time. Life began in the ocean. Plants and animals first emerged from the sea only about 400 million years ago, billions of years after the formation of our planet. We humans, like other land vertebrates, have bones and organs and cells originally evolved in the sea, and we can live out of the water only because we still carry the ocean—our blood—

within us. Just as the oceans form 71 percent of the earth's surface, 71 percent of our bodies are salt water, exactly as salty as the sea.[5] Yet terrestrial life is so profoundly different from the life of the seas that it is almost as though we live on an alien planet, quite foreign from the home world of our marine ancestors. To understand menhaden and their life, we need to project our imaginations back into that strange home planet from which those ancestors voyaged 400 million years ago.

Imagine a world in which the effects of gravity are so weak that we can move ourselves up and down in three dimensions with less effort than it now takes us to walk or crawl in two dimensions. That may not require any great stretch of the imagination for those of us who have swum, but swimming gives us only a tiny glimpse of life in a marine environment. Relatively few of the life forms in the ocean can swim strongly enough to resist the currents and tides, and most can at best control only their vertical movement in the water column. The true swimmers, what scientists call the nekton, are one of the three basic life forms of the seas, but they are in the minority.

Gravity is so weak in relation to other forces that the vast majority of the ocean's life forms just drift around without any volition of their own. These drifting plants and animals are plankton, the second basic form of marine life and the true elemental life of the ocean.

Although we don't have roots, we terrestrial slaves of gravity are forced to spend most of our lives attached to the ground or some other firm bottom. Even when we fly in airplanes or sail in boats, we pretty much stick to the bottom of the vessels. So we are most like the third category of marine life, the benthos, the bottom dwellers, and in that sense our closest marine counterparts are not mammals but the crabs and lobsters and snails and worms crawling around on the floor of the ocean (though even crabs and lobsters can soar off swimming at will). Except in the few hours when we swim, we do not share much experience with the nekton—the fish, marine mammals, and other active swimmers of the seas. The organisms most alien to our mode of life are those plankton, the animal and vegetable life that drifts with little or no control of its own locomotion. Indeed, in our environment there are few life forms that spend their entire existence drifting around. Unlike seawater, which is dense enough to buoy massive objects and which is filled with minerals and potentially nutritious chemicals, air does not support a massive population of drifters, like the plankton that fills the seas.

Most of the plants in the sea world spend their entire existence in such a drifting state. This vegetable plankton, or phytoplankton, can be as large as great masses of rootless seaweed. But most of it consists of much smaller algae, including spectacularly varied forms of one-celled plants, that permeate the upper levels of the ocean's three-dimensional environment. This is what menhaden are designed to eat.

Animal plankton, or zooplankton, has myriad forms: microscopic creatures, eggs and larvae of most fish, countless tiny crustaceans including vast clouds of krill, and even shoals of jellies. Menhaden, like most fish, begin their lives as zooplankton, helpless prey carried wherever by tide, wind, and current.

Evidently, the earliest forms of fish were mainly planktivores, swilling rather than chomping their food, since no fish developed jaws until the Silurian age, also 400 million years ago. Most of the zooplankton today are themselves planktivores, consuming organisms even smaller than they are. Feeding on tiny drifting particles of life, however, does not limit size. The largest sharks—the whale shark and the basking shark—are planktivores. Baleen whales, such as the humpback, the right whale, and the finback, are planktivores. The blue whale—the largest known animal ever to live on our planet, more than twice the size of the largest dinosaur—is a planktivore. Although an individual menhaden is tiny compared with the giant planktivores, a school of menhaden can be heavier and far larger than a blue whale.

Most of the swimming planktivores live on zooplankton, that is, other animals. Adult menhaden, on the other hand, live mainly on phytoplankton and miscellaneous suspended detritus. In the larval stage, before they are equipped for this diet, they too are consumers of zooplankton. But then they transform into creatures with a radically different relationship to the marine environment. Consuming mountainous quantities of phytoplankton is the fundamental fact of the adult menhaden's existence and importance in the ecological scheme.

All animals, even those that eat nothing but the meat of other animals, in the final analysis depend on plants to convert vital inorganic substances into digestible food. Pure carnivores don't have to be nagged to eat their vegetables because they usually get all they need by eating herbivores or, somewhere down the line of consumption, other carnivores that have eaten herbivores. This seems obvious on land, where there are far more varieties and numbers of herbivores than carnivores, and where the few strict carnivores such as lions have the option, in the natural environment, of feeding exclusively on herbivores, such as the herds of antelope, zebras, and giraffes among which they live. But the sea abounds in carnivorous fish, eager to devour almost any other fish that they can. Hence our familiar image of the big fish eating the medium fish eating the small fish. That image, however, presents a somewhat skewed and misleading picture of the consumption that goes on in the sea, because all that stupendous volume of animal flesh in the world's oceans must still somehow depend on plants for basic nutrition.

With that in mind, we can begin to comprehend why there are so many menhaden and why all those predatory fish, birds, and marine mammals go wild in their insatiable desires to consume menhaden. For menhaden are certainly prime contenders for the global championship in phytoplankton consumption. And thus they form an extraordinary link in the marine food chain.

Like other large land animals, we humans feed on plants that are rooted in the soil and on other animals that also feed on rooted plants. Indeed, much of our terrestrial environment is defined by different kinds of rooted plants—grasslands, brush lands, forests, high meadows, bogs—each supporting hosts of animals with its own vegetable products. But the fundamental source of animal food in the ocean is phytoplankton, that inconceivable mass of rootless plants that drift about in the sea with little or no control of their own locomotion. Indeed, all ocean life, except for some of the recently discovered life forms thriving in thermal vents on the deepest ocean floor, ultimately owes its existence to phytoplankton. This phytoplankton consists fundamentally of a dizzying kaleidoscope of the innumerable varieties of algae—microscopic diatoms, slimy colonies, toxic dinoflagellates once classified as animals, phosphorescent conglomerates, one-celled plants that bloom into great masses defined by each one's distinctive color and effects—all formed of the nutrients in the waters of the sea and the energy of the sun.

Because intricate networks of rivers and other drainage flood nutrients into estuaries, bays, and wetlands along the low-lying Atlantic and Gulf coasts of North America, these coastal waters have a natural superabundance of algae and other phytoplankton. Left unchecked, this bonanza of growth could block sunlight, reduce oxygen, and possibly create the kind of swamp ecology most dramatically evident in the Everglades. But taking advantage of these conditions, a humble species of fish—menhaden—evolved ages before the arrival of humans to play that dual role in marine ecology perhaps unparalleled anywhere in the world.

All along the Atlantic coast from mid-Florida to northern Maine, and all along the Gulf coast from mid-Florida to Veracruz in Mexico, immense schools of menhaden filter-fed on algae, cellulose from rotting vegetation, and various forms of detritus, all largely indigestible or even toxic for other animals, thus maintaining a clean, sun-drenched, and thoroughly oxygenated environment hospitable to a great diversity of fish and shellfish. Probably at one time a single species, menhaden, evolved into two major modern species, the Atlantic menhaden *(Brevoortia tyrannus)* and the Gulf menhaden *(Brevoortia patronus)*, separated from each other by a gap around southern Florida.[6]

Why were these two species so astonishingly abundant? One obvious answer is that both are extremely fecund breeders. Mature female Atlantic menhaden, for example, contain so many eggs that they have to keep intermittently spawning throughout much of the year because if all these eggs ripened to full size, the fishes' bodies couldn't hold them. But this cannot account for their superabundance because, in a principle fundamental to Darwin's analysis, even the slowest breeders have the potential to overrun the planet. What limits most species to reasonable proportions is usually some combination of predation and competition, especially for food. Menhaden achieved their phenomenal abundance, despite being the favorite food of innumerable hosts of predators, because they have never had any significant competition for their phytoplankton food source, which is virtually unlimited. Thus, unimaginable quantities of particles of vegetable matter were converted into equally unimaginable quantities of living animals, schools of menhaden that once thronged the Gulf coast and flowed in a river of flesh along the Atlantic seaboard extending for miles into the ocean.

The schools that today still give up billions of fish annually to the reduction industry are just the remnants of this river of flesh. The fish were "frequently seen in immense shoals, fairly blackening the water for many miles." Sea captains gave reports like this: "I saw a school of menhaden out at sea, when I was going to Portland, that was two miles wide and forty miles long."[7] Even after the wholesale slaughter had been going on for more than a decade, the river flowed on. As they approached the northern limits of their range in Maine in·early summer, "the fish extend from the surface two or three fathoms deep, more or less, as far at least as can be seen, in a compact mass, either lying perfectly still or moving slowly with their heads all pointed one way as if intently gazing at some object before them." As they leave in the fall, "the withdrawal is nearly simultaneous, but in a body so immense that the vanguard reaches Cape Cod before the rear has left the Maine waters."[8]

SURVIVORS?

That living river of menhaden flowed with the seasons north and south along the coast. Many miles wide along the coast, it yet filled bays and estuaries from Florida to Maine with almost solid flesh. Throughout the length and breadth of this almost unimaginable mass of a single species fed hosts of predators. Bluefish, tunny, dogfish, weakfish, drum, cod, and fluke tore at their flesh from below. Striped bass, porpoises, seals, tuna, swordfish, toothed whales, and sharks gulped them whole, sometimes by the dozen. Their presence was marked by the clouds of gulls, terns, gannets, pelicans, ospreys, and sometimes loons and eagles ravaging them from above. It is easy to see why G. Brown Goode concluded that the "mission" of menhaden is to be eaten.

Whether it's a four-inch-long peanut or a one-foot-long adult, a menhaden is subjected to so many mortal risks, even without the industrial fishery, that none could ever buy a life insurance policy at any price. Just getting to be a juvenile menhaden is almost a miracle.

Atlantic menhaden spawn as they migrate. From late spring until late summer, they spawn in coastal waters, bays, and estuaries from northernmost New Jersey well into New England. From fall through winter, most of their spawning takes place progressively farther off-shore; by the time they move south of Cape Hatteras, some spawning occurs far from land.

The eggs are transparent, each about the size of the period at the end of this sentence. Inside is a small globule of oil, a flotation device that will also provide food for the larva. Unless eaten, defective, or destroyed by the elements, the egg will hatch within forty-eight hours. The hatched larva is almost transparent, incapable of purposeful swimming, and less than half the size of an uncooked grain of rice. At first the larva has nonfunctional eyes and no mouth. Within about two to six days, however, it will begin feeding on tiny bits of plankton.[9]

Since both the eggs and the larvae are themselves forms of

zooplankton, they are prey to all the innumerable planktivores of the ocean. They can be wiped out by one of the vast swarms of comb jellies drifting through the sea. They could be slurped up in the cavernous mouth of a gigantic cruising planktivore, such as a basking shark or a whale shark or one of the baleen whales such as the humpback whale, right whale, fin whale, or blue whale. A large school of any of their zooplankton-devouring cousins in the herring family, such as herring, shad, or alewives, could easily destroy an entire brood. Drifting on or near the surface, they are also an easy meal for flocks of hungry sea birds.

The larvae that hatch in the ocean, with little significant locomotion power of their own, float at the will of winds, tides, and currents. If they are to become juvenile menhaden, the vagaries of these forces will have to propel them somehow into creeks and tributaries of bays, sounds, and estuaries. But many of these forces, including the surging Gulf Stream, conspire to drive them away from the shore they must reach in order to survive and mature.

As larvae, menhaden do not have the ability to digest phytoplankton, so they eat whatever zooplankton they can. Unlike adults, which feed as a school filtering whatever is in its path, the larvae feed as individuals and selectively. If a larva gets close enough to an individual zooplankton small enough to eat, it will snatch the tiny little animal in its mouth.[10]

The infinitesimal proportion of the larvae that actually make it to a hospitable environment, often a saline creek, now metamorphose into juvenile menhaden. As they grow in size, they develop the complex network of gill rakers, a gizzard-like stomach, and other intestinal apparatus they will need for a lifetime of filtering and digesting phytoplankton, cellulose, and detritus. Because in this early stage they are often living in marshy waters abounding in detritus and bits of cellulose from rotting vegetation, all this natural trash is often a significant part of their diet. Many animals (including humans) cannot digest cellulose (wood and the other cell walls of plants), and those that can—

such as termites, carpenter ants, cows, and other ruminants—harbor colonies of bacteria that do the actual digestion for them. Marine biologists point out that this unusual ability to digest cellulose and detritus must have been part of the menhaden's evolutionary development since "they don't need all that digestive apparatus just to eat phytoplankton."[11] While they are growing, they are of course a favorite food of innumerable birds and fish and mammals foraging in these relatively confined waters. Depending on when they were spawned and the conditions where they metamorphosed, these juveniles, designated "young of the year," are ready for oceanic existence in about ten to eighteen months. That is when they begin to stream out of the creeks and rivers and bays on that first journey to the sea and their first coastal migration.

The entire fall route of the northern juveniles to the ocean and down the coast is, even today, when the schools are much smaller than in the past, highlighted by spectacular shows, often visible from the shore. Predatory fish and birds are also on their fall migrations, and the menhaden schools offer just the high-lipid diet the predators require to sustain their continual high expenditure of energy. Bluefish and striped bass keep driving the juveniles to the surface, where they attract ravenous flocks of birds. Unlike in the spring, when the gulls and terns were dependent on bluefish to chop up and regurgitate bite-size pieces of adult bunkers, these birds now can swoop down on babies small enough to be eaten whole. And now they are also joined by gannets, folding their six-foot wingspan to vertically power-dive at high speeds and then crash explosively through the surface to pursue the fleeing peanut bunkers underwater.

The surviving juveniles from the north, from the Chesapeake, and from the southern states now winter somewhere in the ocean, still under continual predation. As they grow, they become no less appealing and no less vulnerable to all the many species of predatory fish, birds, and mammals that evolved as dependent on menhaden as wolves and cougars are on herbivorous animals. If the juveniles are to create new generations of menhaden, they will have to survive until age three for Atlantic menhaden or age two for Gulf menhaden, when they become capable of spawning.

Preyed upon throughout their lives by fish, birds, marine mammals, and now people, menhaden today face another hazard that annually causes the death of millions. Because the most plentiful supplies of their food are near the surface, menhaden evidently evolved to live in quite aerated waters, where they can depend upon high levels of dissolved oxygen. Their intolerance of low levels of dissolved oxygen is demonstrated by the inability of even a single fish to survive very long in a container of seawater unless it is kept thoroughly aerated. This contrasts strikingly with some fish accustomed to living in deep water, such as the tautog (blackfish), which can survive for hours in a small pail of water even crammed with other fish. Since each individual menhaden needs an ample supply of dissolved oxygen, a dense school is quite vulnerable to oxygen depletion. Because the bays and estuaries they inhabit now often have very low levels of dissolved oxygen—due to pollution and, ironically enough, overgrowth of phytoplankton because of the reduced menhaden population—huge kills of millions of the species are routinely reported every summer along the Atlantic and Gulf coasts. The fish are frequently even drawn to their doom by following their natural instincts toward the most algae-filled waters, precisely where the oxygen content is most depleted. But though wildly multiplied and exacerbated by the current poor conditions of coastal waters, some massive piles of dead menhaden along beaches and coves were evidently part of the natural order long before large-scale human pollution and even humans themselves arrived in North America.

In their wild appetite for menhaden, bluefish and other predators attack the schools in such frenzy that they often drive the panicked bunkers into areas of shallow water where there is not enough dissolved oxygen for so many fish to breathe. Sometimes the assault is so savage that large schools are actually driven onto a beach, where they rot by the millions. One such beaching in seventeenth-century New

England was recorded by British voyager John Josselyn (who refers to the menhaden as *Herrin*): "The *Herrin* which are numerous, they take of them all summer long. In *Anno Dom.* 1670. they were driven into *Black-point* Harbour by other great fish that prey upon them so near the shore, that they threw themselves (it being high water) upon dry land in such infinite numbers that we might have gone up half way the leg amongst them for near a quarter of a mile."[12] This seems to have been an annual occurrence in parts of eighteenth-century Virginia, according to Mark Catesby in his 1771 *Natural History of Carolina, Florida, and the Bahama Islands,* in which he tells how the "small fish called a *Fat-back*" is driven "on shore by the pursuit of Porpesses and other voracious fish": "The most extraordinary inundation of Fish happens annually a little within the Northern Cape of *Chesapeck* Bay in *Virginia,* where there are cast on shore usually in *March,* such incredible numbers of fish, that the shore is covered with them a considerable depth, and three miles in length along the shore."[13]

But menhaden had one great survival advantage: their almost miraculous fecundity. With an almost unlimited source of food in the profuse phytoplankton of the nutrient-rich Atlantic and Gulf coasts, and with a mature female able to release millions of eggs in each spawning and the ability to spawn multiple times each year, they were exceptionally well fit to survive. Despite all the carnage and other natural hazards, menhaden kept flourishing in their countless trillions.

They could even thrive undiminished through the many centuries of human use of nature's marine bounty before Europeans came and for a few centuries after. But then came industrial capitalism.

Whales, Menhaden, and Industrialized Fishing

c h a p t e r   4

FERTILIZER: FROM INDIANS TO INDUSTRY

What happened to those miles of dead menhaden that Mark Catesby observed on the shore of Chesapeake Bay in the late eighteenth century? He described how people flocked to put many to use while the rest just rotted: "At these times the inhabitants from far within land, come down with their carts and carry away what they want of the fish; there remaining to rot on the shore many times more than sufficed them. From the putrefaction that this causes, the place has attained the name of *Magotty Bay*." Whether they ate these dead fish or, as is more likely, used them as fertilizer, Catesby does not tell us (though he does enthuse about these "excellent sweet fish" that are caught in "infinite numbers" by the "inhabitants," who savor their "excessive fat" and "delicacy").[1] In any case, we do know that in eighteenth-century New England and Long Island, the use of menhaden as fertilizer was expanding, evolving, and laying the foundation for the nation's first menhaden industry.

The earliest seventeenth-century colonists used menhaden Indian style, burying the fish hill by hill with their seed corn. But the colonists' agriculture rapidly reverted to European methods. As soon as draft animals such as oxen arrived from England, farmers were able to plow large fields, making it possible to plant the Indian corn not simply as a subsistence crop but as a market commodity. The European plow agriculture suitable for grains such as wheat, rye, and barley was now also being used for corn, a crop the Indians had developed for cultivation with hoes. Because of its exceptionally high yield and resulting profits, corn tended to lure farmers into monoculture, quite unlike the Indians' ecologically sound methods of mixing plants, such as using corn stalks as bean poles for legumes that held nitrogen in the soil. Corn demands an extremely rich supply of nutrients, especially nitrogen to stimulate fast growth of the lush stalks (particularly in the short northern growing season) as well as phosphorus and potassium to make the stalks and roots firm enough to hold the cobs. One way the Indians met this need was by planting the corn in new grounds, which they could do simply by moving the farm, a solution unavailable in a European system based on private ownership of the land.[2] When they used old grounds, the Indians fertilized the corn hills individually with fish, usually menhaden, shad, or alewives. This is precisely what Tisquantum was talking about when he told the Pilgrims that "in these old grounds" it was necessary to bury fish with their corn, or their crop "would come to nothing."[3]

The colonists' depletion of the soil was already beginning to be a problem as early as the 1630s.[4] By the late eighteenth century, many of the farms in New England and Long Island were suffering from severe soil exhaustion. Amid these ominous conditions and the bleak outlook for farming, there emerged the New York Society for the Promotion of Agriculture, Arts, and Manufactures. In the first volume of the

Society's *Transactions*, published in 1792, appeared a portentous article by Ezra L'Hommedieu about menhaden's potential as a fertilizer. Although menhaden had been sporadically used as a fertilizer ever since those early colonial days, there was little public awareness of this and even less thought of using the fish more systematically. The prominent statesman L'Hommedieu, who had served five terms in the revolutionary Continental Congress and was then a New York state senator, was also an amateur scientist and gentleman farmer from Southold, Long Island, adjacent to Peconic Bay, which annually filled with menhaden from May through September. With enthusiasm, L'Hommedieu wrote:

> Experiments made by using the fish called menhaden, or mossbunkers, as a manure have succeeded beyond expectation, and will likely become a source of wealth to farmers living on such parts of the sea-coasts where they can be taken with ease and great abundance. These fish abound with oil and blood more than any other kind of their size. They are not used for food, except by negroes, in the English West India Islands; and the price is so low that it will not answer to cure them for market.[5]

L'Hommedieu went on to give examples of various methods of use, from burying the fish hill by hill with corn in the Indian manner to spreading it over acres of land preparatory to sowing grass crops or planting vegetables. He also noted, "On some part of Long Island those fish are taken in seines, and carted six and seven miles for the purpose of manure, and is found to be very profitable business."[6]

In the wake of L'Hommedieu's article, a mass conversion of menhaden to manure began to take off. When the president of Yale, Timothy Dwight, visited eastern Long Island in 1804, he was amazed by how farmers had managed to revitalize their exhausted soil by covering their fields with "immense shoals" of menhaden netted in Long Island Sound, causing "prodigious" improvements to their crops:

> The number caught is almost incredible. . . . [O]ne hundred and fifty thousand have been taken at a single draught. Such upon the whole have been their numbers, and such the ease with which they have been

obtained, that lands in the neighborhood of productive fisheries are declared to have risen within a few years to three, four, and in some cases to six times their former value.

"No manure is so cheap as this where the fish abound," he wrote, and "none is so rich," increasing the yield per acre from scarcely ten bushels of wheat to forty. Dwight had reported finding the same results in 1800 in various townships along coastal Connecticut, where this "species of herring remarkably fat and so full of bones that it cannot conveniently be eaten" is "caught with seines in immense multitudes" from Long Island Sound and then applied, at the rate of ten thousand per acre, as a "rich dressing" for the land.[7]

Who caught all these fish? Farmers themselves.

In the early days, nets were made from twine manufactured by the farmers' wives from flax grown upon the farms. Later, farmers used cotton twine to make seines nearly a mile in length. Informal cooperatives were instituted, and soon in coastal areas nearly every farmer shared rights to a seine and a boat. Men would work on their farms until a lookout posted on the shore signaled that he had spotted a school of bunkers, and then these farmers would dash for their boat and net, stored in a wood shack on the beach. With coves and bays packed with dense schools of bunkers, filling the nets was easy. The hard problem was hauling a seine bulging with perhaps hundreds of thousands of fish, weighing fifty tons or more, to the beach. A diary entry records one epic struggle when two boats joined their nets to drag more than 1.2 million bunkers to land in a single haul. As the demand for menhaden soared, groups of farmers now turned their informal associations into small "companies"—with jaunty names like Coots, Fish Hawks, Eagles, Pedoodles, and Water Witches—that owned the multiple boats, huge nets, and draught horses needed to catch, haul, and market these untold millions of fish.[8]

The beaches of Long Island, Rhode Island, and Connecticut soon featured giant reels drying huge menhaden seines, along with horses of the menhaden companies harnessed to massive black cast-iron capstans. When a bunker school was spotted, men rushed to their boats, loaded the seine, and rowed out to trap the school between their net and the shore. Then a heavy line from one end of the seine was secured to the capstan on the beach, and a lumbering horse was made to trot around and around, turning the capstan and thus inexorably pulling the net, with its thrashing masses of fish, toward the beach. As hundreds of thousands of writhing and dying menhaden piled up on the sand, eager farmers from the surrounding area came to watch the spectacle, purchase some of this cheap manure, and truck it back in their horse-driven wagons for their own fields.[9]

Within a few decades of Ezra L'Hommedieu's 1792 article, menhaden had become an industrial-scale fertilizer for the coastal farmlands of New England and the mid-Atlantic, with countless rotting fish spread out over many thousands of acres to prepare the land for crops. Although this use of raw fish as manure did indeed rejuvenate much of the worn-out soil, revitalize many dying farms, and bring wealth to coastal communities, it had some unpleasant consequences. Despite his enthusiasm, even Timothy Dwight complained about the "almost intolerable fetor" from the rotting fish, a stench that farmers seemed accustomed to but one "extremely disgusting to a traveler."[10] Unfortunately, the smell had quite an opposite effect on animals, which sometimes dug up fields to get at the fish. (This problem led the town of Ipswich, Massachusetts, to pass a law in 1644 requiring dogs to have one leg tied up: "If a man refuse to tye up his dogg's legg, and hee bee found scraping up fish in a corne-field, the owner shall pay twelve pence damage beside whatever damage the dogg doth.")[11] More ominous, however, were some unintended effects on the soil that derived from one of the very qualities of menhaden that made them so invaluable to marine predators and would soon make them almost as precious to human predators: their profuse oil. Writing in the late nineteenth century, G. Brown Goode lamented that the practice of manuring fields with "the entire fish, in a raw state" continues "to a great extent, even to the present day," even though it has been shown to be "injurious":

FIGURE 4.1 Horse turning capstan to tighten the haul net. From Goode, 1887

The oil thus introduced with the flesh into the earth is entirely useless as a fertilizer, and permeating the soil renders it peculiarly liable, first to become soggy and heavy, and then to bake and crack with the heat of the sun. Many farms in Connecticut and Long Island are pointed to as having been ruined by this mode of planting.[12]

By the time this was written — 1880 — catching menhaden and converting them into industrial commodities had become a major U.S. industry, far exceeding the whale fishery in importance. One of these commodities was a mass-produced fertilizer that was somewhat deodorized (and thus not repulsive to people), easily transportable, and extremely important for emerging American agribusiness. Farmers would no longer have to worry about the oil, which was being cooked and pressed out of the fish before they were ground up and then processed into a cheap substitute for many industrial oils. By this time, Peconic Bay was surrounded with modern menhaden processing factories, including one in Southold, Ezra L'Hommedieu's hometown.

How Menhaden Dwarfed the Whales

The first industry in which the United States became the undisputed global leader was whaling. By 1846, almost three-fourths of the approximately one thousand whale ships in the world were American. In a nation that was industrializing at a frenzied pace, whale oil flowed like petroleum today into illumination, lubrication, and a multitude of manufactured products. And baleen (the brush-like filter in the mouths of planktivore whales) was "the plastic of its age," used in everything from corset stays to buggy whips.[13]

Yet within three decades, the whale industry would be dwarfed by the menhaden industry. By 1874, the production of menhaden oil, which was rising, was already 50 percent greater than the production of whale oil, which was declining.[14] By 1876, half a billion menhaden were being processed each year in ninety-nine factories up and down the eastern seaboard.[15] By 1880, the number of menhaden ships (456) was well over two and a half times the number of whale ships (171).[16]

In *Moby-Dick; Or, The Whale*, published in 1851 during the peak decade of the whale industry, Herman Melville wrote: "Nowhere in all America will you find more patrician-like houses; parks and gardens more opulent, than in New Bedford. Whence came they? . . . Yes; all these brave houses and flowery gardens . . . were harpooned and dragged up hither from the bottom of the sea."[17] Twelve years later, a New Bedford newspaper would be drooling about "the almost fabulous profits" being made elsewhere in the "Menhaden fishery" and hoping that New Bedford would be able to catapult into the business with its brigs fitted up with "try works similar to those of a whaler."[18] By 1884, owners of menhaden companies would be "the richest to be found in the provincial towns of New-England and on Long Island," constituting, as the *New York Times* put it, "the bony-fish aristocracy of the country."[19] That world-famous whaling port of New Bedford, which indeed then did have the highest per capita income in the nation, would soon yield this distinction to Reedville, a town on isolated Cockrell's Creek in Virginia's Northern Neck, founded as a menhaden port by a Yankee sea captain who sailed into the creek in 1868. Reedville would soon become the nation's second-largest fishing port by tonnage; today it remains the third largest by tonnage. The opulent Victorian mansions that still line its streets, like the town itself, were all built by the billions of menhaden hauled up from the sea and the waters of the Chesapeake.[20]

Not since the nineteenth century has whaling been a significant American industry, while menhaden is still the nation's largest fishery in numbers of fish caught and second only to Alaska pollock in tonnage. Fortunately, today money flows into the American economy from watching whales rather than killing them, from whaling museums, and from whole libraries of books published about whales and the whaling industry. Yet only two books about menhaden have been published since the 1880s, and these don't have collectively as many pages as *Moby-Dick* (not to mention the dozens of books about *Moby-Dick*).[21]

Nineteenth-century American whaling was also the first truly industrialized fishery. This is not to deny that tools and methods for catching fish and marine mammals had been evolving throughout human history (the American Indians themselves had fairly advanced fishing technology). Certainly, the European fish and whale ships that had been sailing for centuries on hunts far into the north Atlantic had developed equipment and techniques to process and preserve, as well as kill, their quarry, which were destined to become large-scale marketable commodities. What made the nineteenth-century whale fishery different was the intense and rising demand for industrial oil, coupled with the astonishingly long voyages of the typical whaler. Half the Yankee ships sailing from New Bedford fished in the Pacific Ocean, necessitating many months of travel to and fro, as well as years of hunting on a single voyage. This meant that the dead whales had to be butchered alongside and on board the ships, passed through the industrial process known as "trying out," and then stored as barrels of oil or baleen. To do that, the factory that manufactured the oil had to be brought on board. Thus the typical Yankee whale ship became a floating factory and its crew became factory workers. At the center of that floating factory was the "try-works."

Moby-Dick is, among many other things, the first great American novel set largely inside a factory and describing in precise detail the tools, machinery, and methods of industrial labor. Its preeminent factory scene is the "Try-Works" chapter (96), which begins with a description of the massive try-works, "planted between the foremast and mainmast, the most roomy part of the deck": "The timbers beneath are of a peculiar strength, fitted to sustain the weight of an almost solid mass of brick and mortar, some ten feet by eight square, and five in height." Inside are the two "great try-pots," "each of several barrels' capacity." Directly underneath the pots are "the two iron mouths of the furnaces":

> These mouths are fitted with heavy doors of iron. The intense heat of the fire is prevented from communicating itself to the deck, by means of a shallow reservoir extending under the entire inclosed surface of the works. By a tunnel inserted at the rear, this reservoir is kept replenished with water as fast as it evaporates.

The night after killing a sperm whale, cutting into the body, and hauling the huge strips of blubber aboard, the crew fires the *Pequod*'s furnaces. As the harpooners feed the blubber into the try-pots, the ship, plunging into "the wild ocean darkness," belching smoke and stench, lit by the red fires of its furnaces, and sloshing with boiling whale oil, becomes at once an inferno, a hallucinogenic vision of hell, a symbol of its mad captain's quest for revenge against nature, and a realistic representation of the factories converting the bodies of animals and the labor of people into dollars.

The very year that *Moby-Dick* was published, industrial methods were being developed simultaneously in Maine, Connecticut, and New York for trying out oil from menhaden. In the prominent whaling port of Greenport on the eastern end of Long Island, whalers' try-pots were actually the vessels being used to separate the oil from menhaden bodies, and a successful factory was just beginning operations. By 1867, the menhaden fishery had entirely eclipsed the whale fishery in Greenport, around which clustered twenty menhaden factories processing the teeming bunkers of Peconic Bay and Gardiner's Bay.[22] The

FIGURE 4.2 Menhaden sloops and steamers in Gardiner's Bay, Long Island. From Goode, 1887.

Long Island Rail Road, which had previously been extended to Greenport in order to transport whale products, now filled its trains with menhaden products instead.

Why did the whale fishery collapse and the menhaden fishery arise from its ruins? Several factors converged to hurl the whale industry down from its peak in the 1850s.

Up to this time, whale oil was a primary source of illumination, but this role was being rapidly usurped by new sources of lighting, including kerosene derived from coal and, more important, natural gas, which was soon flowing through networks of pipes to inaugurate the gaslight epoch of late nineteenth-century urban America. Whale oil's second major role, lubrication, was also threatened by kerosene and soon, far more decisively, by petroleum. In 1859, in Pennsylvania, came that event still rocking the world: oil gushing from the first commercially viable well. Whale oil's other main uses, as a constituent of industrial processes like tanning and as a component of such

FIGURE 4.3 Fleet of menhaden steamers heading to south shore of Long Island. From Goode, 1887.

industrial products as paints, soaps, and cosmetics, would soon have a cheaper substitute — menhaden oil, which was also even cheaper than petroleum.

Then came the Civil War, which was a disaster for whaling and a golden opportunity for the menhaden reduction industry. Forty-six slow-sailing whale ships were captured or destroyed by modern Confederate cruisers such as the *Alabama, Florida*, and *Shenandoah* (all built in England and crewed mainly by British seamen). Another forty, whose owners were now eager to get out of the whaling business, were bought by the federal government, filled with stones, and sunk in a futile attempt to block southern ports.[23] With whale oil scarce and war industries consuming more and more oils, demand and prices for menhaden oil soared.[24] In the wake of the war, an 1867 *Scientific American* article titled "The Menhaden Oil Mania" could refer to this as "a mania second only to the petroleum excitement."[25]

By 1871, *Scientific American* was lamenting the fate of Sag Harbor,

Long Island, "once one of the largest and most important of the whaling towns," which "now does almost no business in that line" because its place has been taken by the menhaden industry, which "has grown into enormous proportions, and is immensely profitable."[26] Later that year, famed New York City artist Gilbert Burling visited the Long Island factories, sailed with the bunker fishermen, and then wrote a fascinating account, illustrated with thirteen of his own fine drawings of the scenes, for *Appleton's Journal of Literature, Science and Art.* Burling began with these revealing words:

> Not hundreds of feet below the surface of the soil, shut up in crevices of rocks, but in the surrounding waters, are found the oil-supplies of Long Island. Comparatively a few years ago, the eastern end of it was built up by adventurous whalemen, who then established the principal villages of Sag Harbor, Greenport, and Orient. Their occupation gone with the almost extinct whales, these hardy fishermen left to their sons a gentler livelihood, gained by netting a finny prey they would have despised — for the moss-bunker, menhaden, or bony fish, is a little creature of something near a pound only in weight — to the great whale, what a fly is to an ox.[27]

The postwar menhaden reduction industry had obvious competitive advantages over whaling. Why chase a decimated whale population halfway around the globe when what was called "the miniature whale" was cramming the whole coast?[28] In a single week a menhaden vessel might be able to bring in as much oil as a whaler on a multiyear voyage — and without the frightful risks of whaling. After all, of 787 whale ships in the New Bedford fleet during its peak years, 272 were lost on whaling voyages.[29] Moreover, except for the extracted oil and baleen from the planktivores, the meat and the rest of the whales' bodies were discarded as valueless.[30] But the dried-out bodies of the bunkers — stripped of the oil that corrupted the value of the raw fish as fertilizer, then dried, pulverized, and conveniently packaged for transport and storage — were thus transformed into further wealth for the owners of the menhaden factories.

As soon as those first factories began operations in the early and mid-1850s, they were immediately hailed as rescuers of America's depleted soils and liberators from dependency on Peruvian guano. Desperate for nitrogen and phosphorus, America's farmers had been forced to import large quantities of guano all the way from Peru, and these droppings of sea birds were quite pricey by the time they were shipped around Cape Horn, unloaded in U.S. ports, and transshipped to the farms. In "Manure from the Sea," an 1855 article reprinted in the *Southern Planter*, the *Maine Farmer* enthused about how the ocean has thus become "a vast reservoir" from which "may be taken an almost unlimited supply of material, by which to replenish the exhausted fertility of the earth." Instead of the "nauseous stench" from rotting raw menhaden used as manure, these modern factories can give the fish "a proper and suitable preparation" so that the product can "be transported to a distance and used at pleasure."[31] In "Artificial Guano from the Sea," *The Cultivator* recognized that "millions of fish can be obtained at a trifling cost" and trusted that this "artificial fish-manure" "can be manufactured so cheap as to drive the foreign guano from the market."[32]

Just as menhaden oil was pouring into American industry, menhaden "guano" or "scrap" was feeding American agriculture. Trainloads of this "artificial fish-manure" were soon steaming from the ports and factories of New England, Long Island, and New Jersey to inland states and, briefly before the Civil War, to the South. But the southern fishery itself was about to explode, thanks to the Chesapeake Bay and the rich waters off the coast of Virginia and North Carolina, where menhaden could be hunted all year round.

Perhaps, like Captain John Smith two and a half centuries earlier, Union soldiers had observed the incredible density of menhaden in the Chesapeake.[33] In any case, within months of the end of the Civil War in 1865, New Englanders in the menhaden business were rushing to check it out for exploitation. "A party of New London manufacturers, visiting the Chesapeake in 1866, found menhaden in almost incredible quantities," G. Brown Goode reported. What met their ears, as well as their eyes, was breathtaking: "They were so thick that for 25 miles along the shore there was a solid flip-flap of the northward-swimming fish." These Yankee businessmen got so carried away that "one enthusiastic member of the party jumped into the water and with a dip-net threw bushels of fish upon the beach."[34] Maybe John Smith and his crew were not so goofy after all when they tried to catch them in frying pans.

In December of that year, one of the thriving menhaden industrialists of Greenport, Long Island, dispatched his steamer *Ranger* to fish the Chesapeake region. Emulating the whale ships, the *Ranger* was a factory ship fully equipped with the furnaces, boilers, and the rest of the industrial apparatus necessary to process the menhaden and store the products. Evidently it took only eleven days of fishing for the *Ranger* to fill to capacity (in stunning contrast to a typical whaling voyage), and the ship was sent back for repeat performances the next two years.[35]

To fish this far from a homeport, a ship would need to be a floating factory because otherwise the menhaden would rot before they could be processed. But factory ships were not the wave of the future, and the short-lived experiments with them may have yielded little more than a failure to think outside the whale-fishery box. Instead of sending ships on long voyages to hunt an elusive quarry, it made more sense to berth the ships and set up the factories right next to where the quarry conveniently packed themselves.

That's just how they were doing it in the post–Civil War menhaden boom in Maine (where the fish were, and still are, known as "pogies," the local corruption of the Abenaki Indian word *pauhagen*). Elijah Reed, a forty-year-old former sea captain, was then thriving on pogy fishing in the teeming waters around Penobscot Bay, right out of his hometown of Brooklin, Maine. Having seen the Chesapeake himself, and perhaps sensing that Maine waters were already being overfished, Reed packed his menhaden reduction machinery onto two schooners and set sail for Virginia in the summer of 1867.[36] It was to prove a momentous voyage.

After trying a couple of other Chesapeake locations, Reed finally established his business in a sheltered harbor of Cockrell's Creek. Within twenty years there would be dozens of menhaden oil and guano factories around this site, which would become known as Reedville, a small town and major U.S. fishery port named for its Yankee founder.[37] As the northern fisheries succumbed to overfishing, menhaden reduction would become mainly a southern industry, with Reedville as its core.[38] And then, as the great schools of menhaden along the southern coast were destroyed by overfishing in the second half of the twentieth century, the entire East Coast industry would shrink, except for one small independent operation in North Carolina, into Omega Protein, a single monopolistic corporation with its lone Atlantic plant and its fleet of oceangoing vessels and aircraft all at Reedville.

Although nineteenth-century whaling was an industrialized fishery, the post–Civil War menhaden fishery was a far more blatant and integrated component of an industrialized society. Hundreds of menhaden factories belched their black smoke and stench along the nation's coast, not, like Melville's ship, somewhere out in the middle of the Pacific Ocean. While the youthful Herman Melville in search of romance and adventure chose to become a crewman on a whale ship, there was nothing that could be viewed as romantic or adventurous about the grueling lives of the workers who labored long hours inside the reeking menhaden factories, their bodies permeated by the stink of cooked and ground bunker. One of the worst fates for Jurgis, the protagonist of Upton Sinclair's 1906 naturalist novel *The Jungle*, is having to work in a fertilizer plant amid the Chicago stockyards and slaughterhouses, making him stink so bad that nobody can tolerate being near him. An 1879 visitor to a "fish guano" factory wonders "how persons stand" the smell "who have to work among it" and notes that anyone who works there a week carries so much of its "perfume" with him that "he is debarred from all social relations with the outside world." Even when guano was put outside to dry, "the windows of a church two miles away had to be closed."[39]

The menhaden factories were such awful polluters that they were often "driven away as a public nuisance" from settled areas and forced to relocate in some "desolate spot" like "Promised Land" out toward the eastern tip of Long Island, as described in "The Menhaden Fishery and Factories" in *Lippincott's Magazine of Popular Literature and Science*:

> Its salient features are six great brown-and-red factories, with black chimneys . . . and long docks thrust out like antennae into the waters of the bay. About these are grouped the frame dwellings that shelter the workmen and their families. These workmen are almost entirely Virginia negroes, who return South at the close of the fisheries in autumn.[40]

What kinds of working conditions and pay would lead owners to bring black workers from the South, especially with a large immigrant labor force available in nearby New York City? The author doesn't say, even when he finds the same labor force of "sleek Virginia negroes" elsewhere in his tour of the menhaden factories lining both the north and south shores of Long Island as well as Connecticut. On Barren Island, located right on the edge of New York Harbor, he finds "three hundred sleek and oily negroes" "spreading and raking on wide board platforms the shredded remnants of what yesterday was darting in life and beauty through the water."[41]

The steamship, that terrible new weapon that marked the doom of the sail ship during the Civil War, became soon after the war an equally ominous weapon when aimed at those teeming masses of fish that had once seemed so inexhaustible. No fish or school of fish could swim fast enough or far enough to escape the range of the modern fishing vessels being fabricated in the postwar shipyards. As long as the bunkers continued to pack themselves conveniently in bays and estuaries, sail ships were quite adequate for catching and unloading hundreds of thousands

FIGURE 4.4 Steamer offloading menhaden at oil and fertilizer factory, Tiverton, Rhode Island. From Goode, 1887.

of fish in a day. But these inshore schools in northern waters were soon decimated, and so in that region the menhaden fishery had to move out to sea.[42] As it became necessary to chase fast-moving oceanic schools, the steamship became indispensable to the industry—until it was replaced by diesel-powered warships after the Second World War.

FIGURE 4.5 Dumping fish into pens on top floor of factory. The fish are led through a trough to the cooking tanks. From Goode, 1887.

PURSING THE SEAS

One particular American invention revolutionized the menhaden industry during the 1860s and thus would have profound and unforeseen consequences. This was the purse seine.

Unlike all but the tiniest finned fish sought commercially, the bunker cannot be caught with bait, hook, and line. Its usual food is too small to be seen, and it feeds not individually but as a school. As noted earlier, its huge, incredibly dense schools are a fine group defense against its natural enemies, the predatory fish that can pick off only individuals making up a small percentage of the mass. Although people have been amazed by the numbers of bunkers consumed in a single gulp of a shark or whale, even the largest shark or whale is actually grabbing only hundreds of a school often numbering in the

FIGURE 4.6 Menhaden oil and fertilizer factory, Milford, Connecticut. Steamers unloading fish at the wharf. Incline railway for carrying fish to upper floor of factory. Oil tanks and storage sheds in foreground. Elevated railway takes fish to platform for drying scrap in rear of factory. From Goode, 1887.

hundreds of thousands and sometimes in the millions. But that very defense is what made menhaden so vulnerable—and therefore attractive—to the most efficient predator on the planet.

The purse seine was designed precisely to do what no other net could do: consistently capture entire schools of fish. The haul net used by those fishermen-farmers to gather fertilizer in the early nineteenth century could ensnare a big portion of a large school but not the whole school itself. The purse seine, however, could accomplish this routinely by turning the menhadens' main defense, their tendency to mass and pack as close as possible when under attack, into the instrument of their doom.

As its name implies, the design is aimed to enclose the school completely inside a purse. From the 1860s to the present, the form and method of use have not changed fundamentally. Two boats next to each other share the seine and then begin to move, whether by oars then or motor now, in opposite directions. They encircle the entire school, paying out the net as they go. The net has floats at the top to keep one edge on the surface and weights on the bottom to keep the other edge deeper than the school. Thus the net forms a wall encircling the fish. On the bottom edge of the net are rings, through which run lines. When these lines are tightened, they purse the net—just like the strings on a handbag. Previously unaware of the danger below them, the panicked fish, which were all trying to find an exit through the sides of the net, can now no longer escape by diving below it. The school has literally been bagged.

The boats now move toward each other, hauling the net tighter and tighter as they go, concentrating the fish into a mass just as solid as the proverbial sardines in a can. Then the bunkers are transferred to the ship. The only real difference between the practice in the nineteenth century and now is in the means used to haul the net and get the fish on board the ship. Then the workers used only muscle to tighten the net, a backbreaking job demanding large boat crews with almost Herculean strength and endurance. Next, hand-powered dip nets were lowered from the ship, soon to be replaced by nets lowered and raised by steam-powered donkey engines. Eventually power blocks and hydraulic winches eliminated the need for all that muscle, and today gigantic power tubes suck and pump the trapped bunkers from the purse seine to the hold of refrigerated ships capable of holding more than a million fish.

The menhaden reduction industry was the vanguard of the overall industrialization of fisheries in post–Civil War America. The purse seine itself was adapted for other densely schooling fish, such as mackerel, sardines, and herring, with disastrous consequences. The deadly efficiency of the purse seine also inspired rapid technological development, as well as industrial production, of other means of catching fish. The scale of the menhaden fishery and its integration with its factories and markets served as an industrial model to be emulated. By 1874, an article in the *New York Times* could boast that "the methods by which fish are captured in the United States are superior to those in use in all other countries," thanks to "what may be called industrial fishing." It then went on at length to describe, with great enthusiasm, various modern "apparatus" well designed for "the wholesale destruction of

FIGURE 4.7 Gang of men using dip nets to offload fish from hold of steamer. From Goode, 1887.

fish": a seine "a mile in length, hauled in by a windlass worked by the power of horses or oxen or by a steam engine"; the gill net (designed specifically to entangle fish by their gills); the drift net (which floats unattended and freely, enveloping whatever fish it encounters); shoulder-fired harpoons; torpedoes; "traps, pounds, heart-nets, weirs, and fykes" (fixed nets, some of which were capable of catching all fish entering a body of water); and the "trawl-line," "trot-line," or "long line" often "several miles in length."[43] Thanks to "the marvels of American industry," boasted an 1882 magazine article ballyhooing the industry, a "season's catch with present appliances" can reach four billion menhaden.[44]

The fisheries in the period after the Civil War were continually increasing the efficiency of their tools and equipment, as they had been

FIGURE 4.8 One man at pump offloading fish from modern fishing ship. Southport, North Carolina, 1969. NOAA Photo by Bob Williams. Courtesy of NOAA.

doing for centuries and would continue to do until they had annihilated all but a tiny percentage of the fish they sought. The lone fisherman in his dory, skillfully using bait, hook, and line to make his living, was on his way to becoming merely a figure of myth, poetry, and song. The old man of Ernest Hemingway's *The Old Man and the Sea* can't even bring his one great fish to shore, and even though Billy Joel's Downeaster *Alexa* is diesel powered, its skipper, who "worked my fingers to the bone, / so I could own my own," has to lament:

> I've got bills to pay and children who need clothes
> I know there's fish out there but where God only knows
> They say these waters aren't what they used to be

They aren't what they used to be because the single hook and line of the past has been replaced by the long line extending for miles and baited with thousands of hooks, industrial production has kept turning out new and huge forms of nets and other deadly contrivances, power winches have replaced muscle power, and industrial capital has been financing fleets of ever more efficient ships. In short, American fisheries have become industrialized—with the menhaden reduction fishery always leading the way.

The Death of Fish and the Birth of Ecology

c h a p t e r   5

> I believe, then, that the cod fishery, the herring
> fishery, the pilchard fishery, the mackerel fishery, and
> probably all the great sea fisheries, are *inexhaustible*;
> that is to say, that nothing we do seriously affects the
> number of the *fish*. And any attempt to regulate these
> fisheries seems consequently, from the nature of the
> case, to be useless.
>
> Thomas Henry Huxley, 1883[1]

SCIENCE WADES IN

With the menhaden fishery in the vanguard and the press occasionally cheering the onslaught, industrial fishing was happily sweeping the seas after the Civil War. But every now and then a troubling question kept arising: Where have all the fish gone?

The question was not entirely new. The depletion of fish was one inspiration for George Perkins Marsh's 1864 *Man and Nature*, considered one of the founding documents of American environmentalism.

Even earlier, Marsh had been commissioned by the Vermont legislature to determine whether the depleted stocks of fish could be restored by artificial propagation; he concluded that he "can only recommend perseverance in experiment."[2] In *Man and Nature*, republished in 1874 with the more ominous title *The Earth as Modified by Human Action*, Marsh raised the question of the extinction of marine species and cited the prodigious slaughter of menhaden as evidence of man's "destructiveness."[3]

Commercial food fishermen on the sea claimed that the main destroyers of fish were the same "traps, pounds, heart-nets, weirs, and fykes" acclaimed as wonders of American technology in that *New York Times* hymn to American industrial fishing published in 1874, the very year Marsh was warning of how we were modifying our environment.[4] Each of these devices is a kind of net or trap fixed in place and usually connected to the shore. Some had actually been developed and used on a modest scale by the Indians, who had even taught colonists how to construct weirs. But they had evolved into monstrous contraptions sometimes a thousand feet or more in length, often stretching across and even completely blocking waterways through which the fish had to pass to feed in bays or spawn in rivers. Unlike fishing vessels, these nets and traps caught fish twenty-four hours a day, indiscriminately and prodigiously.

The bays, sounds, coves, and estuaries of New England, Long Island, and northern New Jersey no longer swarmed every summer with striped bass, sea bass, weakfish, bluefish, drum, and scup. The hook-and-line commercial and recreational fishermen, as well as the factory and office workers who supplemented their income and lightened their lives by fishing from shore, began to wage vigorous battles in their state legislatures to banish or at least restrict these fixed nets.[5]

Who owned these fixed nets and traps? The wealthy owners of shoreline property, including the owners of the menhaden factories, did. Thus the political fights took on a distinct class character.

The nets and traps were opposed by another contingent in addition to saltwater commercial and recreational fishers: the people who fished the rivers for the surviving anadromous fish, those oceanic inhabitants that must return to freshwater to spawn. These mechanisms were wiping out what was left of the salmon, shad, and alewives that had once filled the rivers of the northeast in their spawning runs.

Even before the Civil War, nature's stupendous bounty of these fish had been almost annihilated by industrialism's dams and pollution combined with overfishing. The preeminent victims were salmon. These magnificent fish had once filled Long Island Sound and were so abundant throughout the Connecticut and Merrimack river systems that they too were often used as fertilizer. Fishmongers gave them away for a token price. Some bondservants in eighteenth-century Connecticut even threatened to go on strike if their ration of salmon was not reduced.[6] By the early 1800s, salmon had virtually disappeared from Connecticut and New York. One day in 1872 at Old Saybrook on the Connecticut River, a fisherman was startled to find in his net a strange fish he had never seen before. He asked the other fishermen what it could be. Nobody knew. Nor did anyone else around town, because no one had ever seen a salmon. At this very spot a century earlier, it was not unusual to catch more than three thousand salmon in a single drift of a net.[7] By the 1840s, there were virtually no salmon left south of Maine. Henry David Thoreau in 1849 mourned the loss of the "miraculous" abundance of "Salmon, Shad, and Alewives" in the Concord River and ruefully hoped "Perchance, after a few thousands of years, if the fishes will be patient, and pass their summers elsewhere," "nature will have levelled" the dams and factories, and the river "will run clear again."[8] (Today, of course, the Atlantic salmon of the United States are essentially extinct—except for those being industrially produced with a diet consisting largely of cooked and ground menhaden.)

With commercial food fishermen and recreational anglers allied on one side and menhaden companies and greedy coastal property owners with their fixed nets on the other, more and more heated clashes raged in the northeastern states over the fate of the disappearing fish. Finally the crisis seemed ominous enough to propel the federal government into action. So in 1871, a joint resolution of Congress established the U.S. Commission on Fish and Fisheries, the first federal conservation agency and the direct ancestor of today's National Marine Fisheries Service. Congress gave the commission a mandate to determine whether a "diminution in the number of food-fishes of the coast and lakes of the United States has taken place; and, if so, to what causes the same is due; and also what protective, prohibitory, or precautionary measures should be adopted."[9] Selected to head what is commonly called the U.S. Fish Commission was the man who had adroitly worked behind the scenes to engineer its creation, Spencer Baird, a key administrator of the Smithsonian Institution and founder of the Woods Hole marine research center, who would prove to be a formative force in the history of American ichthyology. Baird managed to convince Congress year after year to fund research, publications, and programs designed to maintain and restore America's saltwater and freshwater commercial fisheries as well as the freshwater fish that were sought largely by recreational anglers. Baird himself had a wider vision and agenda, for he saw an underlying need to achieve a scientific understanding of the threatened marine environment.[10]

Baird was soon able to compile a convincing report finding that fully nine-tenths of the fish population available in 1800 had already disappeared, that the remaining numbers were constantly declining, and that the evident cause was unbridled overfishing.[11] Two possible quick solutions leaped to mind.

One was to place limits on the methods, catches, or seasons of the fisheries. But any such broad regulations seemed to Baird and many others at the time impractical both economically and politically, and also questionable legally. Prophesying the virtual extinction of some species of inshore food fish if fixed traps and nets were not somehow restricted, however, Baird proposed a cleverly engineered compromise whereby they would not be used two days each week during the prime spawning season. But even this modest proposal failed to gain legislative approval amid the political warfare between the trappers and their commercial and recreational fishing opponents.[12]

The other quick fix was to make lots more fish, and this was the one chosen by the Fish Commission and by the federal government, which immediately began financing extensive hatchery programs designed, somewhat like factories, to produce fish. The immediate goal was to try to produce salmon even faster than the cannery factories could consume them. Thus to solve a problem created by industry and technology, Americans characteristically turned to industry and technology for a solution: Let's manufacture more fish.

Trying to improve on nature—and to win political support from states that had no salmon—the Fish Commission strewed millions of eggs and fry around the country. Spencer Baird was quite frank about the political purposes of disseminating salmon eggs promiscuously: "The object is to introduce them into as many states as possible and have credit with Congress accordingly."[13] Within four years of the 1869 completion of the transcontinental railroad, fish fry in open milk cans were steaming back and forth across the nation. A few years later, Pacific salmon eggs were zooming to the East Coast in specially equipped railcars that returned with eggs and fry of Atlantic salmon, shad, and striped bass. Salmon eggs from the Sacramento River went to other rivers likewise exposed to blistering heat, from the mid-Atlantic to the Potomac and the Mississippi. Half a million Atlantic salmon fry were stocked in six states in the Mississippi Valley. These epic efforts had some dramatic successes with other saltwater fish, such as shad and striped bass; never before found in the Pacific, striped bass are today one of California's major game fish. And the hatchery programs remain essential to maintaining a population of freshwater fish for recreational angling. But no species of salmon from either coast was able to survive in the wild anyplace else.[14]

The failure of the trap compromise and the salmon program, however, actually furthered Spencer Baird's hidden agenda. Baird realized that human understanding of the marine environment was exceedingly primitive and that without a true marine science it would be impossible to comprehend the problems of America's fisheries or arrive at practical solutions. In 1872, Baird met and soon recruited as his assistant George Brown Goode, a young man who had just done graduate work under Louis Agassiz at Harvard and who was destined to change marine science and how America related to that science. The relation between Baird and Goode would be the matrix for the most comprehensive and influential publications to date on American fish and fisheries, most especially menhaden and their past, present, and future roles in American history.

Brown Goode (as he was generally known) died in 1896 at the age of forty-five. His record of accomplishments in that brief life is awe-inspiring. Eminent as a scientist, historian, administrator, and writer, he was able to combine these roles in a dazzling synergy. Sometimes referred to as "the father of the modern American museum," Goode developed systems of classification, helped make the U.S. National Museum of the Smithsonian a leading institution, and pioneered in making museums accessible venues of education for ordinary people. His book on deep-sea fish, published months before his death, virtually opened the ocean's abysses for modern study. Goode was a cutting-edge historian of science, with innovative works such as "The Beginnings of Natural History in America" (1886), "The Beginnings of American Science" (1886), and "The Origins of the National Scientific and Educational Institutions of the United States" (1890). He cofounded the American Historical Association (still the nation's leading organization of historians), and his profound interest and fine skills as a historian were essential to what he achieved in his major works on American fish and fisheries, the most important of which would be his study of menhaden.

Spencer Baird was certainly not an ecologist or environmentalist. After all, he was a prime sponsor of the gill net for the cod fishery and an adaptation of the beam trawl for dragging the bottom for flounder, two inventions with dreadful consequences. Baird's passion for the study of marine science was consistently motivated by a desire to modernize and increase the productivity of American fisheries. Thus he chose the most technologically advanced, most modern, and most thoroughly industrialized American fishery — the menhaden fishery — to be the subject of the commission's first full-scale study.[15] Goode was the man he chose for this task. The result was the book indispensable for anyone seriously interested in the past, present, and future of menhaden: *A History of the Menhaden by G. Brown Goode with an Account of the Agricultural Uses of Fish by W. O. Atwater And an Introduction, Bringing the Subject Down to Date*, a volume of almost six hundred pages with thirty plates, published commercially in 1880.[16]

It is not by chance that this monumental study of menhaden was the first major publication to come from the U.S. Fish Commission, because understanding both this spectacularly abundant species and its explosive fishery seemed crucial to understanding the crisis of the marine environment and all other American fisheries. This book is not just the first significant study of menhaden. It is also the first major study of any American fish or fishery.

While that book was in press, Baird enlisted Goode to carry out an unprecedented mission: as part of the Tenth Census of the United States, and on behalf of the U.S. Fish Commission, he was to compile a definitive history and analysis of the nation's fisheries and fishery industries. In a radical break from nineteenth-century reliance on the amateur gentleman scientist, Goode organized a modern research team of more than two dozen people who were to investigate all commercially useful marine animals and the history, current practices, and economic roles of each of their fisheries. The results were seven massive volumes published between 1884 and 1887 under the imprimatur of the U.S. Commission of Fish and Fisheries as *The Fisheries and Fishery Industries of the United States* by "George Goode Brown and a Staff of Associates." This encyclopedic work is a landmark in marine science and history that remains a treasure chest for all subsequent research on U.S. fisheries.[17] Two volumes are atlases of wonderful plates, including thirty-two illustrations of the menhaden industry. One of the 1887 volumes contains Goode's second major contribution on menhaden, titled "The Menhaden Fishery by G. Brown Goode and A. Howard Clark."[18]

Goode's 1880 *A History of the Menhaden*, on which he worked for six years, is by itself a groundbreaking work of scholarship and scientific inquiry. Unlike both the gentlemen scholars of the nineteenth century and the highly specialized marine scientists of the twenty-first century, Goode cast his net widely and boldly to capture as much as he could of the workaday experience of people who had the most direct contact with menhaden. He sent questionnaires (he called them "circulars") containing fifty-eight key questions to hundreds of people, including fishermen, factory owners, other scientists, and every lighthouse keeper and customs inspector on the Atlantic and Gulf coasts. Then he followed up with two hundred personal letters soliciting more information. He personally observed and dissected menhaden, and he collected about a thousand varied specimens for the U.S. National Museum. While gathering observations and information from as many people as he could, Goode was aware of fishermen's "superstitions" and "fancies," the shortcomings of anecdotal evidence, and how vested interests can, even unintentionally, alter one's perception of reality.

This volume was not being written in an historical vacuum. America was transforming pell-mell from a rural, agricultural society into an urban, industrial society. A smaller and smaller population was growing food and a larger and larger population needed to be fed, placing more and more demands on what had once seemed God's boundless gift to America, an inexhaustible supply of fish in its seas. But just as the nation was demanding that its commercial fisheries provide more and more fish to eat, the food fisheries seemed increasingly imperiled by the booming menhaden reduction industry. Commercial fishermen charged that the menhaden fleets were wiping out their bait and depriving valuable fish of their food. With the menhaden industry at the center of a brewing maelstrom, the crucial question was, in

Goode's words, what is "the place of the menhaden in nature"? After analyzing systematically all of the various evidence he had amassed, Goode came to a startling conclusion: "It is not hard to surmise the menhaden's place in nature; swarming our waters in countless myriads, swimming in closely-packed, unwieldy masses, helpless as flocks of sheep, close to the surface and at the mercy of any enemy, destitute of means of defense or offense, their mission is unmistakably to be eaten." [19]

This conclusion had far-reaching implications and would prove to be profoundly influential. As Goode went on to explain this "mission," he described what we now call a food chain:

> In the economy of nature certain orders of terrestrial animals, feeding entirely upon vegetable substances, seem intended for one purpose—to elaborate simpler materials into the nitrogenous substances necessary for the food of other animals which are wholly or in part carnivorous in their diet. So the menhaden, deriving its own subsistence from otherwise unutilized organic matter, is pre-eminently a meat-producing machine.

Looking closely at these statements, one can see that Goode was also a man of his particular time and place and that his consciousness was shaped by his culture, in this case a dynamically changing culture bubbling with contradictions between a past religious overview and an emerging industrial utilitarianism. Menhaden have a "mission," animals are "intended" for a "purpose," but that mission or purpose is to become a "machine," a machine that produces something useful.

Goode concludes by spelling out the particular usefulness of menhaden in that post–Civil War America with its increasing demands for food from the sea:

> Man takes from the water annually six or seven hundred millions of these fish, weighing from two hundred and fifty to three hundred thousand tons, but his indebtedness to the menhaden does not end here. When he brings upon his table bluefish, bonitos, weakfish, swordfish, bass, codfish, what is he eating? Usually nothing but menhaden!

It would be hard to overstate the importance of Goode's insights. Looking backward, they go a long way toward explaining why and how America's seas were filled with those unbelievable swarms of fish that inspired such awe in Europeans. Looking forward, they prefigure an emerging ecological consciousness. Yet Goode was seeing only half of menhaden's "mission" or "purpose," or, as we might say, "role" or "function." The existence of unimaginable quantities of menhaden might explain where all those other fish came from, but what explains where the menhaden came from? What is this "otherwise unutilized organic matter" that the menhaden eat in order to be eaten? Nobody then knew. Only within the last few decades have we begun to understand that menhaden's other great "mission" in North American ecology is to eat unimaginable quantities of phytoplankton, thus maintaining the health of our inshore waters.

Goode was producing this book amid rapidly intensifying storms of controversy about menhaden and the menhaden fishery, and his own position was not quite as value-free as he thought. Both he and Spencer Baird—as well as the U.S. Fish Commission itself—were closely tied to commercial interests, and their outlook was fundamentally utilitarian, not environmental or ecological. It's not by chance that the Fish Commission's successor, the National Marine Fisheries Service, still functions as part of the Department of Commerce, not the Department of the Interior, and that government regulation of fisheries is still determined by commercial, not environmental, interests and consciousness.

In an addendum to the book hastily added in December 1879, Goode revealed his own partisanship in battles that were just beginning then and are still unfolding today. Responding to angry protests from other commercial fishermen, Maine had just passed a law banning the menhaden reduction industry from state waters. Goode immediately expressed his support for the industry's legal appeal:

> The attempt of the Maine Legislature to regulate the fishery in that State has been of little moment, owing to the unexpected absence of the

menhaden from that region. This movement has met with much opposition on the part of the oil and guano manufacturers. It is to be hoped
that the constitutionality of the law will be tested in the courts.[20]

The manufacturers dropped their legal challenge for a simple reason: Maine's law was rendered moot because there were no more
schools of menhaden there to be caught. In 1879, Goode could not yet
know that the disappearance that year of the fish from Maine—where
about twenty factories had sprung up to exploit the annual run of the
Atlantic's largest and most oil-laden menhaden—was just the beginning of their absence for many years and that this marked the beginning of the collapse of the northern fishery. Nor could he possibly have
guessed that 127 years later a similar battle would be swirling around
Omega Protein, the monopolistic successor to the "oil and guano
manufacturers" of 1879.

Goode's vision of menhaden's place in nature would be interpreted
and used in contradictory ways by the forces clashing over fish and the
sea they inhabit. Nobody seriously disputed that menhaden's natural
"mission" was to be eaten, to be the "meat-producing machine" for all
those marine carnivores. But Goode's formulation demanded a larger
conception of the marine environment and human relations to that
environment. For hanging over his work was the big question: Where
do we fit into this picture?

Funded by a government agency created to deal with what seemed
a commercial crisis and viewing the fish in the sea as a utilitarian
"resource," Goode was perceiving the issues from a perspective we
would call "environmental" or "ecological." These concepts, in fact,
were just barely beginning to emerge, thanks, as we will shortly see, to
the battles over menhaden. Moreover, Goode had a profound sense of
the vastness of the ocean, the immensity of the life within it, and the
relative puniness of the human population of the time. Hence he, like
Spencer Baird, tended to believe that our catches of menhaden, no
matter how huge they seemed to us, were insignificant compared with
the continual slaughter by those countless hordes of natural predators.

In England, Thomas Henry Huxley, who also had close ties with commercial fisheries, had already made the same argument in relation to herring.[21]

Goode cites Baird's estimate that adult bluefish alone consume, just on the coast of New England, "ten thousand millions" (ten billion) every day, making their annual consumption in just this one area and in a mere four-month season "twelve hundred million millions of fish." This is more modest than the outlandish calculation Goode had made the previous year, when he claimed that the annual menhaden kill "by predacious animals may be estimated as 1,000,000,000,000,-000,000."[22] Arguing that such calculations, even if they are "nothing more than vague approximations," make us "appreciate more clearly the luxuriance of marine life," Goode goes on to extrapolate from Baird the total annual kill by all the menhaden's predators, including "squeteague, bonito, sharks, horse-mackerel, cod" and "schools of porpoises and whales" along the entire Atlantic seaboard. He arrives at the figure "three thousand millions of millions," "in comparison with which the number annually taken by man is perfectly insignificant." Too careful a scientist to offer this as any kind of proof, Goode does caution, "Whether there is any likelihood that the myriads which now swarm our waters will ever be perceptibly diminished by the loss of six or seven hundred millions of their number annually I will not presume to say."[23] But his inclination was clearly to see menhaden as inexhaustible, just as Thomas Henry Huxley saw herring as "inexhaustible." Dazzled by both the overwhelming dimensions of the sea and the awe-inspiring abundance of ocean fish, neither of these nineteenth-century scientists could conceptualize the devastation that puny little "Man" might be able to inflict on ocean life.

Goode's logic, however, nevertheless seems somewhat puzzling. He was part of a generation that was witnessing the destruction of two terrestrial American species that had once seemed absolutely inexhaustible: the bison and the passenger pigeon. When the nineteenth century opened, thirty million bison roamed America. As that century closed, there were about a thousand left. The story of the passenger pigeon is even more shocking and also more relevant to the story of menhaden.

The passenger pigeon, with its distinctive blue back and pink breast, may have been the most abundant bird in the planet's history. Even after unending slaughter throughout the seventeenth and eighteenth centuries, flocks would still darken the skies for many hours or even several days at a time. As late as 1813, John Audubon observed a flock continually passing for three days at the rate of more than a billion every three hours. Even in the early 1870s, flocks could fill the skies like dense clouds all day long. In 1878, two years before Goode's *A History of the Menhaden*, one single nesting was discovered in Michigan that was forty miles long and perhaps ten miles wide. But these were the days of their doom. The commodification of the birds for their meat and feathers had been industrialized after the Civil War by the railroad, the telegraph, and the factory system. By 1880, the large flocks had already disappeared from the eastern states, and by 1890, the passenger pigeon was extinct as a viable species. The last wild passenger pigeon was discovered in 1900. The last member of the species, a bird named Martha, died in the Cincinnati Zoo in 1914 at the age of twenty-five.[24]

Neither bison nor passenger pigeons were subject to significant nonhuman predation. So why would the existence of tremendous natural predation appear to guarantee the inexhaustibility of a species? Wouldn't that, on the contrary, make the viability of the species more, rather than less, precarious? That is, if menhaden were continually subject to awesome predation, couldn't an additional potent predator, the one that had almost wiped out the bison and was visibly annihilating the passenger pigeon, upset the natural balance and also throw this species into jeopardy?

From the perspective of the early twenty-first century, it's easy to see that Goode was underestimating the explosive power of our technology. Few observers of the ocean today can seriously entertain the notion of inexhaustibility (although the menhaden reduction industry is still arguing, as it was then, that there should be no limit whatsoever on its catch). But to be fair to Goode and his contemporaries, that conception of the ocean as a self-regenerating repository of inexhaustible human resources persisted well into the second half of the twentieth century. The vision of inexhaustibility lingers even in Rachel Carson's otherwise marvelous 1950 *The Sea Around Us*, which ignores the growing contradiction between the limits of marine biology and the insatiable demands of marine commerce.[25]

Goode's formulation of menhaden's place in nature drew heavily on the practical experience of commercial fishermen. But it was commercial fishermen—aided by recreational anglers—who were to challenge the dominant scientific consensus that ocean fish were "inexhaustible" and then give Goode's concept of menhaden's place in nature a far more radically ecological interpretation. This may seem a surprising statement in our era of continual struggle between commercial fisheries on one side and environmentalists and recreational anglers on the other. But in the final three decades of the nineteenth century, it was the struggle by those who fished for the predators—the valuable food fish—against those who fished for the prey—menhaden—that generated a fundamental ecological concept, one that helped form the turn-of-the-century conservationist movement. These commercial fishermen, as we will next see, were developing out of their own workaday experience and in their own fight for survival a vision, ultimately radical, of the interdependence of species.

FOOD FISH VS. FACTORY FISH

The menhaden steamers were expensive to build and costly to operate. Unlike sail ships, they burned coal, lots of it (as I can attest, having worked as a deckhand and mate on the last steam tugboats in New York Harbor), requiring stokers and crewmen to haul and dump the ashes. Steam power also powered the apparatus for hoisting the fish onto the ship. At the height of the nineteenth-century menhaden boom, the size of the ships bloated to accommodate "double-ganging," that is, having two purse seines and a double crew of about forty men on each vessel. The cost of all this, plus the money needed to build, maintain, and run multiple factories, placed the menhaden fishery, as the *New York Times* put it in 1884, "in the hands of capitalists."[26]

Compared with the increasingly industrialized and heavily capitalized menhaden fishery, the typical commercial fishing operation of the nineteenth century was just a small business. The owner—often an individual or family—did not also own a factory; did not hire workers on land to process, transport, or distribute the catch; and certainly did not have capital to build even one steamship, let alone a fleet of them. A commercial fishery business—before that too became a corporate enterprise—often consisted of a single vessel that went out, caught fish, brought them back, and sold them to a fish market or merchant (or even directly to customers on the dock). So it's not surprising that many commercial fishermen seethed with resentment against the ultramodern steamships of the menhaden corporations.

The deadly purse seine of the menhaden vessels was an immediate object of this resentment. Since a school of bunkers was usually under attack by predators, especially bluefish, striped bass, mackerel, drum, and weakfish, it was inevitable that the purse seine would snare in its escape-proof enclosure some of these valued food fish feeding on the school. Angry firsthand reports of this "by-catch" and equally vociferous denials were frequent items in nineteenth-century newspapers. Even *United Service: A Quarterly Review of Military and Naval Affairs* asserted that the menhaden steamships "destroy, by myriads, not only the shoals of fish which are worthless as food for man, but the fish which are good to eat, and which follow the shoals for food. All are taken together, and all together go to make fish-oil and compost for manure."[27] Occasionally a menhaden captain would acknowledge such an unintended catch, as when one admitted that in a single set "he caught 50,000 mackerel and a number of fine river shad" and, "not being near a market, he threw them in with the menhaden to be tried out for oil."[28] Whether such "by-catch" was large enough to diminish any fish populations was in dispute then and remains so today.

More directly threatening to the livelihood of commercial fishermen were menhaden hunters using their purse seines intentionally to catch enormous numbers of food fish, either to be sold to the fish market or, more outrageously, to be reduced to oil and guano in the menhaden factories. For example, the *New York Times* reported the following as evidence that all fears about declining fish populations were "groundless":

> As an example of the general good luck that attends the fishermen, it may be stated that one day last week Capt. Clinton Clark, of East Marion, while in pursuit of menhaden, discovered a school of drum-fish covering about an acre of surface, and by putting out a little more than half of his seine he made a haul equal in measurement to 80,000 menhaden, the average weight of the fish being sixty pounds. In the haul were also found seventy-six striped bass, averaging forty pounds each, total 3,040 pounds; the largest weighing seventy pounds. The value of the catch may be estimated when it is stated that drum-fish yield a very rich lubricating oil, in the preparation [*sic*] of three gallons to the weight of 1,000 menhaden, and bass sell readily in the New-York market at a good price.

The same article noted that a menhaden vessel out of Greenport "caught sixteen bass weighing 800 pounds, or an average of fifty pounds each."[29]

New Jersey and New York's Raritan Bay, a major spawning ground for menhaden, weakfish, fluke, and striped bass, was a constant battle-ground throughout the 1880s between commercial fishermen and the menhaden vessels that would sneak into the bay to scoop up the prized food fish illegally "by thousands in their immense seines."[30] Thirty train-car loads of weakfish were actually discovered at a dump belonging to a menhaden factory, and it was proved that the seines were also tearing up the bay's precious oyster beds.[31]

But nobody had any objections when a menhaden seine came up with "five good-sized porpoises, and no other fish," since porpoises had no market value as food and these fifteen hundred pounds of mammal would yield blubber to "make about 10 gallons of oil."[32] There was considerable outrage, however, when a Long Island newspaper reported that several men "employed for years on the menhaden steamers" acknowledged

> that the catch of edible fish in the purse-nets is often enormous; that frequently weakfish, bluefish, and sea bass are taken by the ton, and that not one-tenth of these fish so taken can possibly be marketed, and when it is possible to reach a market the fish are in such poor condition as to be almost worthless; that not one "catch" in ten is ever reported; and that generally it pays better to let them go in with oil and manure stock and say nothing about it.[33]

The menhaden companies were even brazen enough to unload big catches of food fish at America's biggest fish market, the Fulton Market in lower Manhattan.

During what would be a climactic struggle in 1882 between commercial fishermen and the menhaden industry, a special committee of the U.S. Senate came to the New York area to hear testimony about the intentional taking of food fish by the menhaden fleet. Eugene Blackford, a leading wholesale dealer at the Fulton Market and a member of the New York State Fish Commission, testified that

> he knew of several instances where the menhaden fishermen had caught schools of food fishes and brought them to market. In the early fall of 1881 there was an unusually large catch, and four or five vessels came to Fulton Market with about 200,000 pounds, nearly all of which was weak-fish. Owing to the warm weather at that time only about a quarter of this large catch was placed on the market. The remainder was taken to the menhaden factories and made into oil and fertilizers.[34]

By 1882, "a hundred steamers," "an absolute cordon of vessels," was "following the moss-bunkers day and night."[35] This unremitting slaughter could not, G. Brown Goode notwithstanding, go on forever. Sure enough, the steamers were already running into intermittent periods of real scarcity of their prey. But because the fleets of menhaden steamers and their associated factories were so expensive to build and costly to run, it was imperative that they keep continually catching huge amounts of fish. What could they do as they ran short of menhaden? One answer was to turn to mackerel, another densely schooling fish almost equally vulnerable to the purse seine, and quite oily as well.

In July 1882, a menhaden steamer was refitted for mackerel, provoking anger among the fishermen in the principal mackerel port of Gloucester, Massachusetts, as well as this editorial comment: "The fact that menhaden are scarce and the oil works are in danger of standing idle is nothing to us. The oil men, having killed the menhaden goose, must not be allowed to begin upon another species to extract golden eggs."[36] But by September the refitted vessel, with its great speed and ultramodern equipment, was easily outfishing the old mackerel boats. In reporting this, the *New York Times* noted that the ship "had no appliances of refrigeration, nor had she a crew who were acquainted with the methods of preparing fish," and then editorialized:

> Here, then, was the case of a valuable edible fish which was used like menhaden. Of course, any one may do what he pleases with his own, and if mackerel are more valuable for the factory than for the market, no one has the right to make objection. Still, it must be remembered that the use of mackerel for oil is depriving us of much more valuable food and tending to enhance its price.

The editorial noted the absurdity of catching "edible fish for manufacturing purposes" while "the United States is spending a great deal of money for the purpose of propagating edible sea fish."[37]

The following month, the *Times* discovered that there had actually been at least three, probably five, and possibly more menhaden steamers "engaged in catching mackerel all along the coast from the Bay of Fundy to Cape Cod." The *Times* denounced the conversion of mackerel into oil or fertilizer as "wicked," implying that such usages were proper only for junk fish such as menhaden:

> [S]ince the menhaden has grown scarce there will be every inducement for more of the menhaden steamers to enter into mackerel catching. If there is no restriction to taking mackerel it is quite probable that in time the mackerel would become very scarce—as difficult to find as the menhaden. Again, it is to be repeated, that to the wholesale catching of mackerel there can be no objection, providing they be used for food; but to convert the fish into oil or guano is a wicked waste of good material.[38]

The prophecies of doom were accurate. The year before menhaden steamers began fishing for mackerel, the old mackerel vessels sailing out of Gloucester alone caught 116,793 barrels of fish. By 1887, the entire New England fleet was able to catch only 56,919 barrels, and by 1889, a mere 10,342. By 1890, the seemingly inexhaustible schools of mackerel that had greeted the European colonists were almost all gone, and the United States was having to import the bulk of its mackerel from Canada and Europe.[39]

What Took the Fish Away?

There are those who argue today that global warming is just part of a natural cycle, uninfluenced by human activities. As menhaden became scarcer in the late nineteenth century, there were those who argued that this was just part of a natural cycle, not the result of overfishing. Although this would seem to be a blatantly more dubious argument than the one offered to protect the producers of greenhouse gases, it is one still offered today by the reduction industry and its protectors. The first formulation of this argument, and its first great test, came in a surprising time and place.

It was on the coast of Maine where the post–Civil War menhaden boom exploded in full Gold Rush frenzy. Between 1866 and 1876, more than twenty large-scale oil and guano factories suddenly materialized on these rocky shores, and steamships were being mass-produced to keep supplying the factories' insatiable appetite for fish. By 1875, thirty-six modern steamers were part of a flotilla of about three hundred vessels hunting the massive schools of "pogies."[40] Although the Maine season for these highly migratory fish was short, by the time they reached this northern coast in June they were already the largest, fattest, and most oil-filled of any found on the Atlantic or Gulf coasts, and they kept getting bigger, fatter, and richer in oil.

At the time, nobody had any clear idea why the menhaden were there or why they were getting so corpulent, because nobody knew they were planktivores and so had come to feast in these plankton-rich northern waters. These waters were also filled with the most valued food fish, especially cod, there to devour the menhaden and other swarming planktivores, such as herring and capelin. Then there were the deadliest predators, those people who had come originally from Europe to hunt these hunters of the planktivores (as well as some of the planktivores themselves, including baleen whales). From the earliest arrival of these fishermen, they had discovered that menhaden were their best bait for cod and the other predators they sought. Hence one of Maine's most significant industries had long been a fishery targeting pogies for bait.[41]

As the menhaden steamers of the Maine Oil and Guano Association spread their huge purse seines and hauled millions of menhaden back to their factories for industrial processing, both the fishermen whose livelihood was catching menhaden to be sold as bait and the commercial fishermen who used that bait revolted. They rioted in the towns of Bristol and Bremen, and burned down at least one menhaden factory. Later, in their desperation, they turned to the Maine legislature to demand restrictions on the reduction industry, arguing that it was destroying both the bait fishery and the food fisheries.[42]

The manufacturers responded that menhaden are "practically

inexhaustible." In the main text of his 1880 *A History of Menhaden*, G. Brown Goode discussed this conflict and predicted, "It seems very unlikely that any legislature will at present interfere with so extensive an interest as that of the menhaden manufacturers."[43] But then came two unanticipated events. The legislature did act. And, simultaneously, the menhaden disappeared. So while the book was in press, Goode had to write that December 1879 addendum noting "the unexpected absence of the menhaden" and expressing his hope "that the constitutionality of the law will be tested in the courts."

Goode's ties to the menhaden industry became quite clear a few weeks later, on January 14, when he was the main speaker at the seventh annual meeting of the United States Menhaden Oil and Guano Association. After dinner, Goode read an exhaustive paper on the natural and economic history of menhaden. "One of the most interesting portions of the discourse," according to the *New York Times*, "consisted of an endeavor to explain the failure of the fish to appear this season off the coast of Maine, where the great head-quarters of the trade is situated":

> This has happened but twice in the history of man. After reciting numerous theories on the subject, and showing their improbability, the speaker gave it as his opinion that they were kept away by the decrease in the temperature of the water, caused probably by a deflection of the polar currents.[44]

The manufacturers enthusiastically applauded and gave Dr. Goode a unanimous vote of thanks.

One of the manufacturers present at the meeting, however, had a quite contradictory explanation for the menhaden's disappearance, offered in a letter to Spencer Baird as head of the U.S. Fish Commission and printed later that year in *Forest and Stream*. Captain W. J. Terry, a former ship captain who had been in the menhaden business for sixteen years, currently as the owner of Long Island's South Bay Oil Works, argued that the customary migrations of the fish had been disrupted by the unrelenting hammering of the menhaden fleet, including its eighty-one new steamships. "For the last few years the entire coast line, from end to end, has been run over almost every day by the fishing vessels," he wrote, and the fish are "continually harassed from morning to night every day." Though the problem was especially acute in Maine, it was being felt throughout the northern waters, he pointed out, so that in midsummer, usually the season of "our best fishing," "the factories have had to be closed up" the entire hundred-mile length of Long Island "from Barren Island to and including Gardner's Bay." He concluded by asking whether "we have not killed the goose that lays the golden egg," a metaphor that would be repeated with increasing frequency throughout the rest of the century in reference to the menhaden fishery.[45]

Who was right? Was the disappearance in 1879 just that rare third time when the fish would vanish for one season from Maine, probably because of cold water? Or was the range of the species shrinking from overfishing?

Five years later, the *New York Times* cogently summed up the spectacular rise and collapse of the Maine menhaden fishery:

> Ten or twelve years ago the waters off the coast of that rugged State were fairly alive with the bunkers. . . . The Eastern fever broke out among the local fishermen, steamers were built to conduct the fishing on that rocky coast, the Maine harbors were studded with oil-works, and millions of barrels of fish were taken. Colossal fortunes were made by the speculators. The steamers which, the first year, were an initial experiment, were enlarged, "double-gang" boats were built, dozens of these powerful craft were hurried into those waters, and year after year the golden harvest continued. And then suddenly, about five years ago, menhaden became as scarce on the Maine coast as they had before been plenty. And they have been scarce ever since.[46]

Yet in the very same year as the *Times* account of this tragic history, the United States Menhaden Oil and Guano Association adopted the following resolution: "The plentitude or scarcity of sea fish is wholly independent of the operations of man, but is determined by the forces of nature."[47]

By the time Goode published his next and last major work on menhaden in 1887, the answer to the question *Overfishing or Cycles?* was written in glowing capital letters on the wall, and it didn't take a Daniel to interpret the message. The mysterious disappearance of 1879, Goode was now forced to recognize, had spread from Maine and become part of an ongoing scarcity throughout the northern fishery: "Since 1879 these fish have not appeared north of Cape Cod, except in very limited quantities, though they were formerly very abundant along the Massachusetts coast."[48] What a vastly different world from 1879, when the popular *Harper's Weekly* could enthuse about the "myriads" of "moss-bunkers," sometimes in "one vast school" forty miles long, and note confidently that "every bay and river mouth along our coast is filled with them every summer."[49]

What had happened to these myriads, especially in Maine, where they had been so wonderfully fat, oily, and abundant? Even in 1888 some people still couldn't figure it out: "Neither have the fishermen been able to discover why the masses of fish which once lined the rugged shores of Maine with each succeeding Summer no longer go there, but now the factories there are rotting down."[50]

What took the fish away? For more than another hundred years, the question kept recurring as fish would sometimes return, get caught in huge numbers, and then disappear. After no significant school of adult menhaden were seen north of Cape Cod from 1993 through 2004, some people still had not figured out why and others were arguing that this latest mysterious disappearance is just part of a natural cycle, not a product of industrial overfishing.

POLITICAL CONFLICT AND ECOLOGICAL CONSCIOUSNESS

With few fish in Maine and the other waters north of Cape Cod, in the waning years of the nineteenth century the full force of the mighty northern menhaden fleet was unleashed on the bunkers as they migrated into the northern limits of their ever-contracting range. And in addition to operating these "monster" vessels, as their opponents called them, the menhaden manufacturers were spreading deadly pound nets in bays and estuaries, trapping whole schools that entered these waterways to spawn, thus wiping out subsequent generations. That 1879 battle in the Maine legislature became just the leading edge of similar conflicts rapidly spreading down the coast.

The pound nets that enveloped schools of fish entering Buzzards Bay incited outrage in Massachusetts, which also passed one of the first state laws banning the purse seine in its waters all the way out to the three-mile limit. New York prohibited purse seining in its waters of Raritan Bay, and both Connecticut and New York legislated against pound nets in their respective waters of Long Island Sound. The fiercest and most far-reaching struggle broke out in New Jersey, soon spread to Congress, and raged well into the twenty-first century.

One reason for New Jersey's crucial position is geographical.

As menhaden and many of their valued predators migrate from southern waters north along the coast each spring, they run smack into a major barrier, the 110-mile east-west length of Long Island, which, together with the shore of northern New Jersey, forms the New York Bight. This great right-angle area, rich with nutrients flowing from the Hudson and Raritan rivers, induces hordes of those north-south migrators to hang around well into late fall. Meanwhile, multitudes of east-west migratory predators are moving from their offshore winter hideouts into these inshore waters, which are soon teeming with juvenile mehanden. Thus that spectacle, so amazing to those seventeenth-century Dutch travelers, of New York Harbor—which sits right at the apex of the Bight—swarming with whales, porpoises, moss-bunkers, and legions of other fish. Long before any Europeans arrived, many species of fish had evidently also decided to make the estuaries at this corner one of their main spawning sites. Every spring, the largest weakfish, known as tiderunners, run through Raritan Bay to spawn in the lower Raritan River, passing through and chomping on the masses of bunkers that are there for the same reason. Right on the tails of the bunkers come female striped bass, just after they have spawned in the Chesapeake, followed soon by some North Carolina females waiting to spawn until they get to the Raritan or Hudson rivers. Another major population of striped bass has set up permanent residence in the Hudson River and its estuary, making these waters second only to the Chesapeake for stripers. The waters used to be thick with northern kingfish, whiting (silver hake), and ling (red hake). Before their alarming decline, weakfish used to abound throughout the Bight, which is still one of the areas of greatest abundance for fluke (summer flounder), scup (porgies), tautog, tunnies, sea bass, and many other species of fish and shellfish. By May, the area is mobbed with bluefish, mainly attacking the bunkers but devouring whatever else they can find (including lots of their own juveniles).

This marine cornucopia made commercial fishing a prominent New Jersey industry in the nineteenth century, one threatened by the flotillas of menhaden steamers, sometimes fifty in number, plowing back and forth with their purse seines. Belching black smoke and sometimes leaving vast slicks of oily, smelly gurry or offal to wash up on the beaches, the menhaden ships also endangered another New Jersey industry, one growing swiftly and with an obviously important future — tourism.

Combined with the state's splendid beaches, the abundance of fish had long made the New Jersey shore a prime summer retreat, but only for mansions of the rich and for presidential vacations. In the post–Civil War period, however, railroads opened the shore of New Jersey, along with that of other northeastern states, as a summer resort area for middle-class people and a day-trip oasis for many urban workers.[51] Until the plundering by the menhaden industry, claimed the *New Jersey Coast Pilot*:

> [O]ur bays and sounds along the New Jersey coast were stored with bluefish, weakfish, and other food fishes, affording excellent sport to the amateur fishermen. Many a toil and desk-worn disciple of Izaak

FIGURE 5.1   Mammoth fleet of steamers close to shore. From Goode, 1887.

Walton was thus allured from the city to spend an occasional day on our health-giving coast, greatly to his own benefit, mentally and physically, as well as to the advantage of hotel-keepers, boat-hirers, and many others. But our marine inlets are becoming completely depleted of their finny tenants, and our city sportsmen are beginning to weary of fishing in tenantless waters, and are disappearing accordingly. Thus a good round sum of money threatens to be lost annually to our coast.[52]

U.S. Senator W. J. Sewell of New Jersey, in a passionate 1882 letter, urged New Jersey's commissioner of fisheries to take any necessary means against this "evil":

The evil is a crying one and must be suppressed by the best means at hand. The growing popular interest in the shore line of our State and its magnificent summer resorts has really brought the question up as one of the principal industries of New Jersey, from which we receive revenue equal, if not in excess, of that from our manufacturing interests. The protection of fish for the use and amusement of a population of 250,000 during the summer months and still increasing is of so much importance that it behooves the State to give it the consideration it deserves.[53]

The governor opened the first session of the state legislature in 1882 by railing against "the wholesale destruction of fish along the New-Jersey coast by the use of purse-nets in the catching of menhaden or moss-bunkers for manufacturing purposes" and declaring that "every means should be resorted to [*sic*] prevent this injury."[54] But three months later, the governor vetoed a bill that would have barred the menhaden purse seiners from New Jersey waters, declaring that the state did not have the power to extend its jurisdiction three miles from the shore, as provided in the bill.[55]

All along the Jersey shore, the battle raged for well over another hundred years, sometimes verging on literal warfare. In 1877, fishermen and recreational anglers threatened to procure cannons and "fire on the marauding steamers."[56] In 1922, residents of Cape May and Wildwood announced that unless the government took immediate action against "the advent of more than forty menhaden steamers within a stone's throw of the beach"—perhaps by having the nearby "prohibition navy" force them away—"they will mount a cannon on the end of the fishing pier and take a shot at the fish pirates who are ruining the fishing along the New Jersey coast."[57]

The fight to get the menhaden reduction vessels out of Jersey waters would go on intermittently until 2001, when the legislature passed and the governor signed a bill very similar to the one vetoed in 1882, much to the consternation of Omega Protein and the delight of anglers. In the few years since that 2001 law took effect, there has been a remarkable resurgence of menhaden along the northern New Jersey shore, along with a spectacular abundance of striped bass and bluefish feeding on them.

After the New Jersey governor's veto in 1882, the scene of legislative action shifted to the U.S. Senate, where Senator Sewell introduced a similar bill to curb the menhaden fishery along the whole coast. The bill was referred to a subcommittee of the Committee on Foreign Relations, which held important hearings but also decided the United States could not act without violating fishing reciprocity agreements with Canada and Britain under the 1871 Treaty of Washington.[58] This in turn led the United States to abrogate this important treaty in 1885, ostensibly, among other reasons, to give the government a free hand to restrict the menhaden fishery. No such federal restriction has yet been enacted.

So amid all the political furor of the 1870s and 1880s, no real restraints were placed on the menhaden purse seiners except in the waters north of Cape Cod, where few bunkers remained. Did nothing then emerge from these struggles?

One interesting outgrowth was an alliance between commercial fishermen and the ever-growing legions of recreational anglers. As late as the last decade of the nineteenth century, when food market fishing was still predominantly hook and line, the people who fished for pleasure were welcomed as a key ally by commercial fishermen in their struggle for survival against the menhaden fishery, as described in an 1895 *New York Times* article: "For years the two chief branches of the fishing industry have been in conflict, the hook-and-line market fishermen, with their powerful allies, the salt-water anglers, being the aggressors, the menhaden purse-seiners their opponents."[59] However, as nonmenhaden commercial fishing continued to industrialize and capture increasing percentages of the continually declining stocks of fish, this alliance disintegrated and eventually was replaced by the ongoing conflict between commercial and recreational fisheries so familiar today.

A far more important and durable by-product of the struggle was an emerging environmental consciousness, maybe even a potentially holistic vision of human relations to the life of the sea. And this was all because of a deepening comprehension of menhaden's "mission."

This new consciousness was arising from the view that the purse seiners were destroying the fisheries. How? Not simply by hauling in tons of valued food and game fish as bycatch, or even as intended quarry—these ongoing complaints were peripheral and relatively trivial. Far more important was the growing recognition that food fish were being destroyed or driven away because they were being deprived of their essential food. If G. Brown Goode was right and menhaden's mission was to be eaten by all the other fish, then the menhaden had to be protected. This conclusion demanded an extremely radical shift in cultural consciousness.

From a twenty-first-century perspective, this may not sound very radical. But that's because we are used to thinking along similar lines. Food chain, web of life, ecology—these are everyday ideas for many millions of people. But the concept of protecting prey in order to conserve predators demanded a revolution in thinking, especially in American cultural thought up to that time. To think like this was to begin to comprehend the interdependence of species.

From the colonists on, Americans' attitude toward terrestrial predators that might threaten people or livestock had been simple: Shoot them on sight! Trap them! Poison them! Make the world safe for our sheep and chickens and cattle and horses. The colonists had a massive —and fairly successful—program aimed at exterminating wolves.[60] Protecting prey in order to preserve predators seemed like protecting sheep in order to preserve wolves.

Some of this cultural thought was an expression of eating habits. Although other humans have eaten almost every kind of terrestrial animal and insect, the land animals generally eaten in Europe and America are not predators. So we raise sheep, cattle, pigs, chickens, ducks, geese, and turkeys for us to eat, and we protect them against the other animals that want to eat them, such as wolves, foxes, mountain lions, coyotes, raccoons, and possums.

Although the animals at the meat counter are mostly terrestrial prey species, the animals at the fish counter are mostly marine predators. When it comes to fish from the sea, we Americans generally eat the eaters of other animals, whether they are, like herring and shad, placid filterers of microscopic zooplankton or, like most of our other favorite food fish, devourers of flesh and savage predators of other fish.[61] So protecting menhaden to guarantee a good supply of their predators at the fish market wasn't *really* like protecting chickens to guarantee a good supply of foxes at the meat market—because we don't eat menhaden and we do eat bluefish. But if predators depend on prey and we value the predators—well, you see where that leads: to that radical notion of the interdependence of species.

So the battle cries of those accusing the menhaden steamers of *indirectly* destroying the food and game fish came straight from G. Brown Goode's declaration that the mission of menhaden was to be eaten. What Goode wrote about the place of menhaden in what he called "the economy of nature" now became tied in complicated knots with human economy. When in 1885 a bystander witnessed a scene in which hundreds of thousands of menhaden were "destroyed or turned from their natural purpose of feeding others of their kind to making oil and debasing themselves into fertilizer," he penned an angry article titled "Murder Most Foul" that displayed the radical implications of the new way of seeing relations among humans and the animals in the marine environment:

> Here were . . . two enormous marine monsters prowling up and down our coast with maws of infinite capaciousness, taking the food of the bluefish by the millions, and incidentally every other species that may be found with them, and converting the whole into a comparatively worthless article of commerce. . . . It almost makes a person an anti-monopolist when he thinks that in spite of this impending ruin hanging over the fisheries, the poor people of our bays who follow moderate fishing for a living cannot get the invasions and murderous operations of these foreign marauders stopped, and will not be able to do so till there is nothing left for them to catch.[62]

Were the purse seiners indeed taking away the fish that the other fish needed to eat? Was this a major cause of the obvious decline of America's food fish? Were the menhaden "monopolists" and "capitalists" menacing the livelihood of fishermen? Or was the menhaden fishery a great beneficiary of American industry and agriculture, a boon

for employment, and—in a new argument advanced by the manufacturers—actually a great blessing for the marine environment? Arguments and counterarguments reverberated for decades in the only
public media of the period, newspapers and magazines. This fierce
fight for public opinion succeeded in making environmental questions
part of popular discourse and consciousness.

In the early stages of the debate, the *New York Times* scoffed at the
"great deal of undigested stuff" that "has been presented to the public
in regard to that relationship which one creature is supposed to bear to
another." This 1882 article in the *Times* ridiculed "the charge brought
against the menhaden fishermen . . . that by the enormous takes of the
Brevoortia tyrannus they deprive edible fish of their food, for the menhaden is supposed to be the main support of several fish on our coast,
notably the striped-bass and the blue-fish." The article attempted to
refute such a silly popular notion by using the inexhaustibility argument advanced by Goode in 1880, which it parroted as established
science: "It has been shown over and over again that man's take of the
sea fishes is utterly insignificant when the whole bulk of the fish is considered. Predaceous fish and birds, all the natural enemies of the fish,
destroy more perhaps in a single hour than man captures in the
year."[63]

Not yet having witnessed the full destructive potential of human
technology, even some of the opponents of the menhaden reduction
industry agreed: "We believe it to be a fact that nothing that man
can do to the immense shoals of menhaden will equal their natural
destruction from their aquatic enemies." But the article making this
concession then went on to develop an argument that expressed the
evolving environmental consciousness:

> The menhaden have withstood their enemies for centuries, a proof
> of which is their presence in such numbers to-day; but man has stepped
> in and disturbed the balance of life, and his efforts, added to those of
> the enemies referred to, have operated disastrously upon what were
> supposed to be the inexhaustible schools of the ocean. Forty years

ago no one would have believed that the buffalo, which roamed our prairies in herds of millions, would to-day be reduced to a few hundred individuals. [64]

The United States Menhaden and Guano Association responded to their foes by firing salvos of new arguments, particularly in a widely reprinted 1882 public statement. Appealing to the residual cultural hatred of predators, they ballyhooed their destruction of sharks: "We destroy the most destructive enemy of food fish—the shark. It is a matter of record that this season the fishing menhaden fleet have killed off the coast of New Jersey these past four months over 6,000 sharks, varying from 20 pounds to 300 pounds each." After playing on readers' fears, they next played on the ignorance of those not intimately familiar with the marine environment: "Fish which are used for table food, such as salmon, cod, herring, porgies, shad, eels, weakfish, blackfish and flounders, do not require menhaden for bait or food." Weakfish, in fact, are highly dependent on juvenile menhaden, which are also a favorite dish of summer flounder (fluke), and cod are voracious consumers of adult menhaden; this is why menhaden are a prime bait for all three species. Even the two planktivores on this selective list— herring and shad—slurp up lots of larval menhaden. Does the industry's slippery statement mean that these listed food fish do not consume menhaden or that they don't absolutely require them to exist? In either case, the implication is that the industry can destroy as many menhaden as it wishes without affecting these desirable species. But what about those food fish that habitually and normally prey on menhaden? Well, "the menhaden, following the first law of nature— self-preservation—give their enemies a wide berth." [65] Imagine all the schools of menhaden steering clear of those bad neighborhoods where gangs of predators hang out just waiting for innocent fish to swim along.

Attentive readers might have noticed that nowhere in the association's statement was there a mention of striped bass, the species whose decline was causing the most concern. A few months later, one of the menhaden manufacturers issued a fourteen-page pamphlet to prove that striped bass don't eat menhaden at all! Attacking an article in the *New York Herald* of November 13 for "boldly advocating the theory" that striped bass do eat menhaden, this 1883 pamphlet included sworn and notarized testimony from a bass fisherman, who also worked on the menhaden vessels, that he had never found a single menhaden in the "tens of thousands of bass" he had prepared for market over a thirty-year period and that he had "never observed or heard of bass feeding on or troubling menhaden."[66] Quite a contrary defense of the menhaden reduction industry was offered in the twenty-first century by Barney White, corporate vice president of Omega Protein and chairman of the National Fish Meal and Oil Association, who claimed that it wasn't his industry that was depleting the menhaden: "We think the problem is the striped bass eating all the juveniles."[67]

Besides the mind-boggling claim that striped bass never eat menhaden, the 1883 pamphlet also maintained that all allegations against the steamers were "wholly baseless and unreasonable," for "what effect on the habits of fishes can the floating around on illimitable space of water of some three or four hundred small steamers and sail vessels have?" On the contrary, "it is well known to all intelligent men that a free and full catch of fish, especially those hugging the shore, tends rather to their increase than extermination."

Five years later, such bizarre arguments were still being advanced by the manufacturers. J. W. Hawkins, who had used the wealth amassed from his menhaden business to get elected as a New York state senator, maintained that he "never found a menhaden in the stomach of a striped bass. As a matter of fact very few of the food fishes were known to eat menhaden. Those who lived upon menhaden were principally sharks, porpoises, and whales."[68] *Forest and Stream* magazine pointed to an inconvenient problem for the manufacturers' argument: "The claim that our food fishes do not feed upon the menhaden is as false as it is absurd, for if they did not feed upon them, then they would not be desirable bait." So when Hawkins and other manufacturers tried to convince a committee of recreational anglers that not even bluefish and weakfish feed on menhaden, "it was apparent to all that their opinions were formed in their pockets."[69]

Once the debate plunged into the environmental waters, it became increasingly difficult for the industry. Wherever the arguments swirled, they kept tending to flow toward some kind of awareness of the interdependence of species. Hence the argument with the greatest popular, and perhaps even political, appeal was all about that dreaded and hated predator, the shark. In 1886, Oscar Friedlender, the secretary of the United States Menhaden Oil and Guano Association, made this bold assertion:

> The greatest enemy of all fish is evidently the shark, and their destruction by the menhaden fleet should not be underrated, as it destroys at a low estimate 50,000 during the fishing season. . . . Take it for granted that half of the 50,000 sharks caught would give birth to two young ones every year, and these young ones would again thus multiply, there would be today an addition of 102,850,000 sharks to the present stock if the menhaden steamers had not destroyed that number every year for the last ten years. I need hardly say that the above-mentioned contents of a shark's stomach indicate that in such case there would probably be a scarcity of food fish now; so the menhaden steamers should, if anything, be considered protectors of food fish, and not their antagonists.

Having made such a powerful environmental case, Mr. Friedlender argued that Congress should subsidize the fleet.[70] It would not be until the twentieth and twenty-first centuries, however, that Congress would subsidize the menhaden reduction industry.

In the meantime, between the publication of Goode's 1880 volume and the beginning of the 1890s, there had been a dramatic change in consciousness, indeed a surprisingly radical shift in such a brief period. In 1893, just eleven years after pooh-poohing the concept of the interdependence of species and menhaden's role as fundamental forage for America's most-valued food and game fish, the *New York Times* published a major article with headlines spelling out its new position:

FOOD FOR PREDATORY FISH: MENHADEN, THE OCEAN'S VAST
ANIMAL PASTURAGE. THE COMMON FODDER THAT AFFORDS
SUBSISTENCE TO ALL THE GAME SPECIES OF THE SEA
GRADUALLY DECREASING — NECESSITY OF PROTECTING
MOSSBUNKERS IN ORDER TO PRESERVE THE FOOD FISH —
DESTRUCTIVE RESULTS OF THE USE OF PURSE NETS

Here appeared a true ecological vision of menhaden and the sea:
"Like the grasses of the far-rolling prairie are they in number, and like
them they transmute the raw material of the soil into fit and assimil-
able substance for a multitude of other forms of life."

Although ecological, this vision of menhaden was only partial and
certainly not holistic. Repeating Goode's 1880 formulation, it still saw
only half of the whole: "The menhaden is to be considered as mere
fodder; his mission is to be eaten; he exists only for others." A touch of
wonder comes from sensing the scale of this mission: "The need therefore of its existence in swarming myriads is readily appreciated, and
renders creditable statements that otherwise would seem too marvelous for belief. In the opinion of competent authorities the number
of menhaden annually destroyed by other fish along our coast exceeds
in weight that of the entire human population of the globe, and yet the
surviving multitude is impressive in its vastness." The *Times* now
stated as fact, not mere assertion about what it had called ten years earlier this "mongrel fish" (January 5, 1883), that the menhaden "renders
subsistence to every predatory fish that inhabits its waters," including
"bonitos, pollock, dogfish, whiting, cod, bass, and weakfish" as well as
sharks, halibut, porpoises, swordfish, and "the tunny, or albacore, a fish
sometimes attaining a length of twelve or fifteen feet, [that] rush with
incredible swiftness through the swarms of hapless menhaden, raging
about like demons, scattering them in every direction, and flinging
hundreds in the air with their powerful tails."

This early ecological vision, too, is a bit myopic even within the
half that it does see. A fine description of the ravages of bluefish, for

example, gets carried away with its metaphor of the wolf, with all its associated cultural baggage of dread and hate, and thus misses the larger picture:

> But of all these dire enemies no single species works the havoc of the bluefish, the wolf of the sea. Dashing into a terrified school he snaps right and left, rending and tearing, sometimes chopping in half and sometimes snipping off a mere chip, but always destroying far more than he eats. His path is a stream of blood and fragmentary fish, and the consequent smoothening of the sea by the exuding oil form the familiar "slicks" so often observed upon the Summer seas. Such smooth areas remain often for weeks, ghastly reminders of the carnage of this relentless sea butcher, who is credited with frequently disgorging what he eats that he may the better continue his devastation.[71]

Missing from this picture are all the other animals—fish, birds, crabs, lobsters—that get to participate in this feast on menhaden flesh precisely because of what the bluefish are actually doing. Thinking about the second metaphor in this passage would reveal that this "sea butcher" is doing just what human butchers do: preparing convenient pieces of meat for others.

Clearly, by the 1890s many people had begun to grasp one of menhaden's stupendous environmental roles—being eaten—and how this role incarnated the interdependence of animal species, including our own. It would take another century before we began to see that menhaden had another, equally astonishing ecological role: eating.

At War with Menhaden

chapter 6

UNCLE SAM TO THE RESCUE

By the end of the nineteenth century, the oft-repeated prophecy that the menhaden industry might be killing the goose that laid the golden eggs seemed to be coming true. When some of the northern states during the 1870s, 1880s, and 1890s restricted the menhaden steamers and pound nets or banished them outright from state waters, one result seemed to be intermittent signs that menhaden might be making a comeback. Some years, huge schools poured into Long Island Sound, the bays of eastern Long Island, and the coastal waters of New Jersey. Occasionally there were moderate catches even in Maine.

But it was too little and too late to rescue most of the northern industry. In a pattern that would be repeated in the mid-twentieth century, a collapse of the menhaden population plunged the industry into bankruptcies, consolidation, a tendency toward monopolization, and a movement into less fished-out waters. "A Menhaden Trust" was the headline of a December 1897 front-page story in the *New York Times* that reported "a combination of the menhaden interests of the country": "It was learned to-day that menhaden factories' steamers from Delaware to Maine have been bought by a syndicate of English and United States capitalists." In this era, when the railroad trust, the meat trust, and the oil trust were busy divvying up much of the nation's economy, "syndicate" and "trust" were alarming words. When the *Times* two weeks later front-paged the news that this new company, the American Fisheries Company, had "purchased all the independent factories, as well as the ships of the Long Island fishermen," it also revealed the identity of another investment partner besides the English capitalists: the Standard Oil Company, which intended to make "a fine illuminating oil" by mixing menhaden oil with "Standard Oil refuse now thrown away." Amid the decline of the menhaden population, even these new deep-pocketed owners could not save the northern fishery. In late July 1899, at the very peak of the season in these waters, the *Times* reported that "the American Fisheries Company has decided to lay off a number of its menhaden steamers, as the run of fish has played out and but few are being caught." Most of the vessels "will be put out of commission," while the rest "have been sent to Southern waters in the hope that they may have better luck there."[1] So in the final fishing season of the nineteenth century, these steamers joined the southern exodus that had begun in 1865, the year the Civil War ended.

By 1912, two-thirds of the menhaden factories and vessels were operating in the South, mainly in Virginia. By the mid-1920s, only 7 of the 38 factories and 27 of the 114 vessels were operating north of Virginia. And the entire industry was in serious decline.[2] Looking backward from 1920, Ralph Gabriel wrote wistfully of the enormous shoals of menhaden that had once made Long Island the industry's booming center:

Many an older resident still lives along the shores of Peconic Bay or Great South Bay who well remembers the time when the menhaden came frequently to those sheltered arms of the sea. He can recall the sudden appearance of vast schools of these fish, sometimes hundreds of thousands of them, rushing into the shallow waters, pursued, perhaps, by their voracious enemies, the sharks or the bluefish. . . . There were times when the bays seemed full.[3]

The theory that the population of menhaden might be cyclical was originally advanced in 1879 to explain the sudden disappearance of the fish from Maine as a natural phenomenon. Looking backward from the early twenty-first century at the history of menhaden, it is indeed easy to see cycles. These cycles come not from acts of nature, however, but from actions of men.[4] These men are the menhaden fishermen who have exploited the species, the commercial and recreational fishermen who have tried to limit the slaughter, and the politicians and members of regulatory agencies who have sometimes restricted but more often fostered the industry. And these cycles form a distinct pattern: abundance, overfishing, crash, regulation, and partial resurgence in one region, and then a repetition of the same story in another region. We will see how the New England story was repeated in the Middle Atlantic states, was repeated again in the south Atlantic region from Virginia to Florida, and is now repeating in the Gulf of Mexico.

The boom-and-bust cycle has also kept repeating within areas as well. For example, the southern fishery had an exceptionally large catch in 1911, which led to the frenzied construction of twelve new factories and twenty-seven new steamers from then into 1913. The newly expanded fleet then of course had to race to fill the newly expanded production facilities with millions more bunkers. This in turn led to a calamitous failure of the fishery in 1913, which, needless to say, was attributed to a natural cycle. By 1913, some of the brand-new factories were in receivership.[5]

Overfishing was not the only human activity menacing menhaden, as well as almost every other marine species that had once thronged America's north Atlantic coast. The area was already an ecological nightmare by the beginning of the twentieth century. Factories were spewing pollutants into the rivers, dams blocked fish from spawning, the great harbors were awash in sewage from the cities built around them, and black globs of tar and oil drifted up and down the coast, covering swimmers and suffocating fish. Menhaden were especially vulnerable to the pollution. Not only were masses of menhaden exterminated by poisoning and suffocation, but the toxic chemicals and sludge also destroyed much of the inshore phytoplankton they needed to eat. As the fish became fewer and fewer, the percentage taken by the fisheries inevitably became larger and larger.[6]

But the biggest threat to the very survival of the menhaden reduction industry in the early twentieth century was not the crashing fish population but its growing irrelevance to modern industrial society. Who really needed either menhaden oil or menhaden "guano"?

Although Standard Oil may have toyed for a while with menhaden oil as a component of a minor product, by the end of the nineteenth century petroleum and natural gas had certainly marginalized it as a significant source of either industrial lubrication or illumination. The remaining market for the oil was merely as an additive to paints and varnishes.[7] Catching millions of bunkers might be a lot cheaper than catching the equivalent weight in whales, but profiting from their oil in a world increasingly dominated by oil and gas corporations was almost as anachronistic as whaling.

Meanwhile, modern industry was also undermining the value of menhaden's first use by humans, as fertilizer. One major competitor was the huge meatpacking industry headquartered in Chicago, which was sending out trainloads of cattle manure and by-products of the slaughterhouses, such as phosphorus-rich bone meal, to fertilize America's family farms and the agribusinesses that were replacing them. Then there was the booming chemical industry, whose awesome powers would soon be manifest in the high explosives and poison gases devastating Europe and the Middle East in the War to End All Wars. Already not far behind its world-leading German counterpart even before the war, the American chemical industry was mass-producing chemical fertilizers, including petrochemical-based sources of highly concentrated nitrogen. Indeed, with each decade of the twentieth century, more and more of these chemical fertilizers would flood huge quantities of nitrogen, phosphorus, and potassium onto America's farmlands, golf courses, and suburban lawns until they succeeded in stimulating disastrous growths of phytoplankton in the nation's bays and estuaries.

Finally, and ironically, scientists studying the late twentieth-century dead zones caused by these nutrient overloads in the Chesapeake Bay and Gulf of Mexico would discover menhaden's other great ecological mission. And so at last, in the dawn of the twenty-first century, some people would ask, Where are the menhaden now that we need them? When we need them, that is, to help fix the environment that we have been ruining.

From at least the middle of the nineteenth century on, the country has in fact never really needed those enormous quantities of dead menhaden to fulfill any human need. We have just been using them as cheap industrial commodities. Their oil was cheaper to obtain and hence more profitable than whale oil. Their bodies could be made into fertilizer more profitably than the authentic guano we were importing from Peru. In other words, the sole purpose of the menhaden reduction industry has always been simply to make money. So in the first decades of the twentieth century, at the point when menhaden oil and "fish guano" could no longer be produced at a profit, the industry seemed ready for consignment to the junkyard of history.

But at precisely this point, the United States government rode to the rescue—not of the fish but of the reduction industry. Whereas the menhaden entrepreneurs of the nineteenth century continually designed new technology and found new markets for their products, twentieth-century menhaden corporations had much of their research and development done at taxpayer expense. In 1918, the Bureau of Fisheries of the U.S. Department of Commerce got together with the

Bureau of Chemistry and the Bureau of Animal Industry of the U.S. Department of Agriculture. They all put on their thinking caps and began reasoning like this: If the menhaden schools could no longer be profitably caught, cooked, and pressed into oil and fertilizer, what could they possibly be used for that would convert them into profits for the manufacturers? What about feeding them to pigs and cattle and chickens?

Displaying the memory span of a distracted kindergartener, the *New York Times* and other publications forgot all about the discovery of that great ecological mission of the menhaden—to be eaten by other fish—and began cheerleading for the government's plan to feed them instead to terrestrial animals never known to crave fish in their diet. Enthusiastic articles ballyhooed the innovative thinking and technology developed by government scientists and engineers. "The Federal Bureau of Fisheries has begun a movement to interest the menhaden fishermen in converting their fish waste into fish meal, rather than into scrap," immediately reported the *Times* under the headline "Wants More Fish Meal: Federal Bureau Plans Greater Use of It as Food for Hogs": "In the Chesapeake region, where driers are employed, the only additional equipment required will be a satisfactory grinder."[8] "Fish Meal for Pigs: A Valuable Food Product Added to Animals' Diet" was the headline of a jaunty story beginning cutely: "The common domestic pig, though not ultra-modern in the matter of etiquette, knows how to order a meal, declares the Bureau of Chemistry of the United States Department of Agriculture. As an addition to his salad and vegetable diet, he is in a fair way to demand a fish course. He will take his fish in the form of fish meal." The farmer as well as the pig will be happy, because "by diverting the fish meal to his animals instead of supplying it directly to his land as fertilizer, the farmer loses but a trifle of its fertilizer value and gains its entire feeding value—thus making the material yield two profits in the place of one."[9]

This cheerleading for the gleamingly modern twentieth-century makeover of the menhaden fishery reached new levels of enthusiasm in a 1924 article by Orville M. Kile in the popular *McClure's Magazine*. *"Half a Million Fish in a Single Catch!"* proclaimed the article's italicized banner. "Only within the last decade," according to Kile, had the menhaden fishery "been developed into an organized industry with modern equipment and extensive output": "And now, since the war, this industry is entering upon a new phase which promises to change this product from a fertilizer to a food for cattle, hogs and poultry. Already, hundreds of tons of ham and thousands of dozens of eggs are coming indirectly from the sea."

Like many similar nineteenth-century articles touting the reduction industry, this twentieth-century piece takes its comfortable readers on a thrilling tour of the entire process, emphasizing its efficiency, its excitement, and, in this case, its happy workers:

> The colored crew make up a happy-go-lucky crowd. They work hard for short periods when a "set" is being made, but they usually have long hours with nothing to do but chatter and shoot "craps." And this scheme of life suits them perfectly.

And those readers are led to appreciate the almost idyllic lives they themselves enjoy in the sparkling twentieth century, thanks in many ways to menhaden:

> The chances are that some of the paint on your house, some of the soap in your bathroom and some of the artificial lard in your pantry trace their origin to the sea via the menhaden route. If you boast an especially fine string of near-pearls it is possible that these, too, stole their iridescence and lustre from the lowly menhaden. . . .
>
> Thus it is that this non-edible fish, this denizen of the seas that seems to live on nothing—it sifts out the microscopic plants called diatoms from the water—is made to contribute not only to the nation's breakfast table, but to the beauty, health and satisfactions of our homes and persons.[10]

The U.S. government's assistance in developing a profitable new use for menhaden—as animal feed—did indeed solve the industry's problem of demand for its products, at least until near the close of the twentieth century. Government scientists and engineers continued to labor to help design the processes needed for turning the fish—profitably—into cattle feed, hog feed, chicken feed, and even pet food.[11] Later, when soybean meal began to threaten these profits, the government would help the industry try to develop new uses, including feeding the commodified remains of menhaden to farmed fish, which of course was far more desirable—at least for the industry—than letting wild fish eat the bunkers.

Federal help was crucial in solving the problem of demand. But then what about the problem of supply? The profitability of the menhaden reduction industry has always depended upon a tremendous supply that was readily and easily available. But because of overfishing as well as the pollution of the coastal waters, especially on the mid-Atlantic and New England shores, huge schools of menhaden no longer abounded close to land. Even in the Chesapeake region, where the bay itself still often teemed with bunkers, the fatter fish with richer oil could be caught only offshore.[12] To solve this problem, at least temporarily, the U.S. Navy sailed to the rescue.

During the First World War, Navy seaplanes patrolling for German U-boats off the coast of Massachusetts spotted huge bunker schools and routinely sent coded radio messages of their locations to the commercial fishing vessels. This wartime secret and its postwar sequel were revealed dramatically in "The Seaplane Turns from War to Fish-Scouting," a 1920 article in the *New York Times Sunday Magazine* by "Earl N. Finprey," a nom de plume for Earl N. Findlay, the editor of the semi-official *U.S. Air Services* magazine. These Massachusetts fish "will never know the combinations which were carried out for their undoing," Findlay crowed. He saw this "war baby" maturing into a major enterprise, thanks to the close cooperation among the Bureau of Fisheries, its parent the Commerce Department, the Navy Department, and commercial fisheries, particularly those hunting menhaden on the Atlantic coast and sardines on the Pacific. After initial experiments off the Virginia capes in February 1920, June 14 was chosen as the "historic date" when "regular patrols left the Naval Air Station at Hampton Roads" to launch a public display of flights directing the menhaden vessels to offshore schools, many fifteen and even twenty miles from land. With the Navy planes guiding the hunt, the catch was increased "from one thousand to three thousand per cent." Thus these "denizens of the deep," previously beyond the effective range of the fleet, would now, just like the inshore schools, be made into many "substances useful to the harried human race."[13]

While the Bureau of Fisheries and the Commerce Department enthusiastically supported the seaplane patrols, the Navy had ulterior motives for hurling its might against small fish, specifically in 1920. The Navy's campaign against the "denizens of the deep" was actually a grab for media attention. It was designed to display the peacetime value of a Navy to a public whose traditional American opposition to a large standing army or navy during peacetime had been intensified by revulsion against the horrors of the War to End All Wars.

The Navy was also up against a formidable foe of another sort, Army general Billy Mitchell, a media maven who all during the year 1920 was waging his own brilliant public relations campaign to prove that the Navy had no significant function in the epoch of the land-based heavy bombers of the Army Air Corps. Mitchell's influence in Congress forced the Navy that year to agree to allow him to test his bombers against the most invulnerable ships under their command. Within months of Findlay's article, a far more dramatic scene than a menhaden chase took place in precisely the same waters off the Virginia coast: it was there that Mitchell's heavy bombers sank the unsinkable German dreadnought, the *Ostfriesland*, a scene that his movie crews would deliver overnight to movie theaters across the nation.[14]

Of course the Navy could not afford to offer its aerial services indefinitely. Having proved, according to its unofficial spokesman Earl Findlay, that "seaplane spotting is a positive necessity," the Navy discontinued its fish patrols on both coasts. It was now up to "those large interests having in their grasp the fish and canning business of the nation" to buy their own fleet of seaplanes—and thus give a boost to the public image of the Navy and naval aviation.[15] The technology of war had played a major role in the creation of the menhaden reduction industry in the years after the Civil War and would play another decisive role in the years after the Second World War. In the years after the First World War, however, the industry evidently did not have the capital to build fleets of oceangoing vessels capable of operating consistently fifteen to twenty miles from land, along with squadrons of airplanes to guide them. There were not enough large schools up north to make this pay off, and in the south most of the fishing was done in Chesapeake Bay, from which fully 75 percent of the entire annual catch was being taken.[16] The peaceful use of the airplane against menhaden would have to wait until after military technology could show its full powers in the Second World War and help create the postwar national technofrenzy.

The flurry of media attention to the menhaden reduction industry in the early 1920s proved fleeting. Unlike its nineteenth-century glory days, the industry in the years between the two world wars received little national attention, possibly because it was now fundamentally a southern fishery and the national media were mainly based in the north. Yet it was still the largest American fishery. Although the menhaden's range, their schools, and the average fish were now all smaller, the annual catch consistently surpassed, in both numbers and tons, that of any other Atlantic species. From 1912 through 1923, the factories were still processing more than a billion bunkers a.year. Unrestrained fishing continued to decimate the menhaden population. Between 1924 and 1929 the factories were able to get "only" an average 600 million fish a year, but that was hardly a trivial slice of the schools.[17] In 1931, the Bureau of Fisheries assigned Roger Harrison to draw up a full investigational report "because the industry in recent years has encountered difficulties which must be solved if the menhaden factories are to regain the full measure of prosperity formerly associated with them." Harrison reported, "Within the last decade the apparent supply of raw material has suffered a decline." He also noted that the "effect of this decline upon the industry is aggravated because of the huge size of the present plants."[18] Nevertheless, even in this very low year of 1931, more than 230 million pounds of menhaden were caught, far exceeding in weight, not to mention numbers, the catch of any other Atlantic fish.[19] The Department of Commerce continued to provide considerable research and development aimed at improving the industry's equipment and developing new uses for menhaden, especially in various synthetic products. The manufacturers continued to modernize their fleets, which gradually converted from coal steamers to gasoline- and diesel-powered vessels. In 1939, the year the Second World War began in Europe, 575 million pounds of menhaden were caught, approximately equal to the combined weight of that year's catch of cod, haddock, mackerel, and tuna on both coasts. Within twenty years this would double, then triple, and then almost quadruple—this time thanks to the Navy and the airplane.

WAR!

A joyous delirium of victory swept across America in 1945. The Second World War had ended in what seemed a triumph of American technological might, and the nation looked forward to an epoch when the genie of technology would continue to grant the country invincibility and boundless prosperity. America seemingly had no limits.

And indeed there were no limits for the menhaden reduction industry. Military "surplus" from the war was essentially being given away. While not getting quite the bargain given to the Greek entrepreneurs who bought the entire fleet of "victory ships" anchored in New York Harbor for a dollar apiece, numerous menhaden corporations scooped up almost brand-new minesweepers and submarine chasers at negligible cost. These rugged vessels had been designed for rough ocean seas and were already equipped with state-of-the-art communications equipment. Once retrofitted for bunker fishing, the weapons of war could be hurled at the huge offshore schools that had so far withstood three-quarters of a century of assaults from the industry.

Now all that was needed was a modern method to locate these schools. The obvious solution was what had been tried and abandoned after the First World War: the airplane.

Brunswick Navigation Company of Southport, North Carolina, embodied much of the twentieth-century history of the industry. Originating in 1916 as part of the migration to the South, it had gone through bankruptcy in the bunker-starved year of 1933, but after the end of the war had managed to buy almost cost-free from the Navy a fleet of five modern minesweepers.[20] Brunswick decided in 1946 to try using an airplane to spot offshore bunker schools for its new ships. All they needed was someone to fly the plane and identify the schools. They found Hall Watters, who would revolutionize the menhaden industry as its first spotter pilot.

Watters had been a youthful fighter pilot during the Second World War and was working as an instructor pilot in his hometown of Wilmington, not far from Southport. Brunswick hired him because, he said, "I was the only pilot around who knew what menhaden looked like."[21]

Watters, who logged fifty thousand hours spotting bunkers for thirty-four years, pioneered many of the techniques still used in the fishery. He would tell the ship's captains where the fish were, how to deploy the boats, when to open the nets, and when to close them. "I flew high, especially in the fall season. From ten thousand feet I could see ten miles on either side." The effects on the fishing were dramatic —and fateful.

Locating the schools no longer depended upon the sharp vision of a lookout in the crow's nest of a ship wallowing amid the ocean's waves. A spotter plane, canvassing huge areas at relatively high speeds, could quickly spy schools that ships would not have encountered. For the first time, menhaden's oceanic spawning was seriously endangered. Menhaden in southern waters usually spawn far out at sea, and the eggs and larvae must be carried by currents and winds to the inshore waterways where they mature. Guided by Watters, Brunswick's ships, designed for transatlantic patrols, were able to net schools as far out as fifty miles, some with so many egg-filled females that the nets, he said, "would be all slimy from the roe."

Watters remembered that in the early postwar years menhaden filled the seas. In 1947, he spotted one school about fifteen miles off Cape Hatteras so large that from an altitude of ten thousand feet, it looked like an island. Although a hundred boats circled the school, many fish escaped because their sheer weight "blew the nets." But as the industry's technology kept getting more and more lethal, no school was too big to be caught.

The ships soon carried gigantic fish pumps that could suck the entire catch from the purse seine quickly instead of waiting for an elevator-like mechanism to laboriously empty the net. Before the fish could be pumped aboard, they had to be "hardened up"; that is, the men in the two purse boats had to use all their strength to slowly tighten the net to pull the fish into a tight mass next to the ship. But beginning in 1956, the "power-block" drastically reduced the number of men needed and the time required to tighten the net. In 1954, nylon replaced cotton and linen, so even the heaviest school could no longer blow the net. In 1957, wooden purse boats were replaced by aluminum boats, and encircling a school was now much faster and easier.[22]

Hall Watters believed that "1960 was really the turning point" in the one-sided war against the fish. He vividly remembered a telling example from that year, when he spotted a school about "five city blocks in diameter" and "dragging mud in 125 feet of water," that is, solid all the way from the surface down to the seabed 125 feet below. "I couldn't believe they could destroy a school that size," he said, but boats managed to surround and annihilate the entire school. After 1960, he observed that the schools kept getting smaller.

The popular media expressed boundless—and patriotic—enthusiasm for the unrestrained slaughter. "Menhaden—Uncle Sam's Top Commercial Fish," proclaimed the headline of a 1949 article in *National Geographic*, which reported, quite accurately, that "more menhaden have been taken from American waters than any other species." Echoing Orville Kile's 1924 puff piece for the industry, the article told the readers how "Uncle Sam's largest commercial fishery" made their lives so pleasant:

> The soap in your kitchen and bathroom is apt to contain menhaden oil. The linoleum on your kitchen or office floor, the varnish and paint that decorate the furniture and walls in your home, and your waterproof garments may have been made with the oil. Steel manufacturers use the oil in tempering their product.
>
> Since animal protein is important to the health of cattle, hogs, and poultry, menhaden meal, mixed with their food, often brings this fish indirectly to your table.[23]

Readers of *National Geographic* then got the first-person grand tour, like that in many similar nineteenth-century articles, first of the exciting hunt for the fish and then of the factory machinery and processes that cooked the oil from their flesh for industrial uses and turned the "scrap" into mountains of animal feed.

LIFE magazine's 1951 treatment, titled "Biggest Ocean Harvest: The lowly menhaden, top U.S. commercial fish, is hunted by scientifically equipped task force," expressed the true ethos of the period by focusing on the electrifying wonders of science and technology. To reap the "rich marine harvest" of this "most-caught fish in American waters," the "menhaden men" use the very latest in technology: airplanes, "the radio telephone," and "their most important scientific acquisition," the Bendix "electronic fish finder," adapted directly from wartime sonar.[24]

The victories over the menhaden, while of course not as spectacular or devastating as the thousand-plane bomber raids that thrilled the nation during the actual war, were in their own quiet way certainly formidable—and ominous for the environment. In 1948, more than a billion pounds of menhaden were cooked and ground into industrial products, almost double the 1939 catch. In 1956, this doubled again to two billion pounds, exceeding by far in weight the total catch of all other fish. Of course it dwarfed in numbers the combined catch of other species, because by this time modern fishing methods had already destroyed the main competition, the Pacific sardine fishery, which had fallen from 1.2 billion pounds in 1939 to 9 million pounds in 1953. In 1959, the menhaden catch was 2.2 billion pounds and still expanding.[25] By the mid-1980s, the average annual catch would be 2.7 billion pounds. And menhaden would continue to exceed in both weight and numbers the combined catch of all other species through 1985.[26]

Looking just at the total menhaden catch, however, conceals what was really happening. Around 1940, a significant fishery had begun to develop in the Gulf of Mexico for Gulf menhaden, the species closely related to Atlantic menhaden. In the postwar years, as the increasing catch of the Gulf fish continued to be added to the overall total, it tended to mask the impending collapse of Atlantic menhaden, which Hall Watters was clearly detecting in 1960. In 1963, for the first time the catch of Gulf menhaden surpassed that of Atlantic menhaden. Even though the Atlantic fish weigh more, they would never again catch up with the Gulf haul.

The peak year for Atlantic menhaden was actually 1956, when 712 thousand metric tons were caught.[27] By 1967, this had shrunk to 193 thousand tons, a decline of 73 percent in eleven years. Given the vastly increased range, electronic aids, and efficiency of the fleet, the drastic fall in the number actually caught is a clear indicator of the collapse of the menhaden population.

The crash looks even more ominous when viewed by area. The peak year in the North Atlantic was also 1956, when 98,500 tons were caught. By 1966, the catch for the entire North Atlantic—the region of the greatest nineteenth-century boom—had plummeted to 1,800

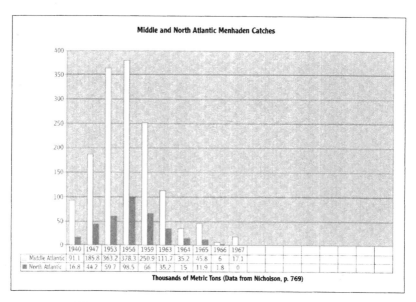

GRAPH 6.1 Middle and North Atlantic Menhaden Catch.

tons. This is what a single primitive sailing vessel might reasonably have expected to catch in a week or two back in the 1870s. In 1967, there was no significant catch at all in the North Atlantic. In the Middle Atlantic, the peak year was also 1956, when 378,000 tons were caught. By 1966 to 1967, the average annual catch had plunged to a mere 11,600 tons. The Chesapeake Bay, South Atlantic, and North Carolina inshore fisheries, areas where Hall Watters was flying, didn't peak until 1958, and the collapse was not as dramatic there. Yet by 1967, the catch was already just half what it had been merely nine years earlier.

The decline in the landings, moreover, does not reveal the full decline in the fish population, because more effective means of finding and catching the fish can more than compensate for fewer fish. One of the main fallacies of fishery management is the belief that the catch is proportional to the population and the fishing "effort" (a calculation based on the number of vessels and the time they spend fishing). This is especially misleading for a species like menhaden that always schools, no matter how few fish are left. "The stock gets smaller but still tends to school," says Jim Uphoff of the Maryland Department of Natural Resources. "The fishery gets more efficient at finding the schools. Thus they take a larger fraction of the population as the stock is going down."[28]

Hall Watters's personal experience illustrates how catch statistics blur the vast difference between the early postwar years, when the sea was full of menhaden, and the mid-1960s, when the fish had become scarce. When he first began, "you would start at daybreak, and you could usually load a boat and be back in at the dock by 8:30 a.m. A boat would do two sets, load up, and be in. We used to get solid blowouts." By the mid-1960s, he was having to fly fifteen hours to find enough fish to fill the boat. In the early years, "we only fished the big schools. We used to stop when the schools broke up into small pods. We'd call it a day then." But by the time he quit in 1980, "we caught everything we saw," because the companies wanted "to fish on both ends of the organism," catching both the mature spawning fish and the "peanuts so small that you could put six of them on a matchstick."

After he quit, Watters was appointed to the Marine Fisheries Board of the state of North Carolina, where he found nobody willing to confront the industry. Twenty years later, at the age of seventy-five and still living in his native North Carolina town of Wilmington, Hall Watters (who died in 2004 at age seventy-nine) summed up cogently what had happened to Atlantic menhaden and what he saw in the future for Gulf menhaden: "The industry overfished their own fishery and they destroyed it themselves. And they're still at it." Referring to himself and the other spotter pilots, he said, "We're the worst culprits," because the airplane meant that "the menhaden had no place to hide." "If you took the airplanes away from the fleet," he said, "the fish would come back, but the company would go out of business because they couldn't find the fish."

When Hall Watters used the word "company" in the year 2000, he

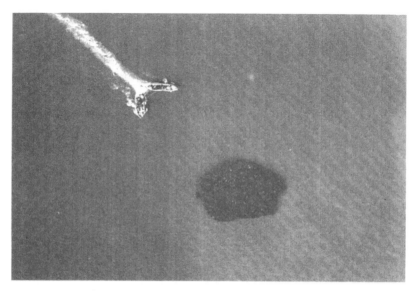

FIGURE 6.1 Boats deploy toward menhaden school seen from spotter plane as dark patch. Photo by Hall Watters. Copyright 2001 by Hall Watters. Reprinted by permission of Rosa Lee R. Watters. All rights reserved.

meant just one company, because by then that's about all that was left. The familiar pattern of overfishing, population collapse, and industry consolidation, seen first in Maine in 1879, later in the rest of New England, and then in the Middle Atlantic states at the end of the nineteenth century and intermittently throughout the first four decades of the twentieth century, had repeated itself with a vengeance along the entire Atlantic seaboard and already had begun to extend into the Gulf.

As the menhaden population crashed, numerous small and medium-sized companies went bankrupt or were bought out by bigger companies. In 1964, the Brunswick Navigation Company was sold to what was then the largest menhaden corporation, the Standard Products Company, one of the only two survivors of fifty companies that had once operated out of Reedville, Virginia.[29] According to

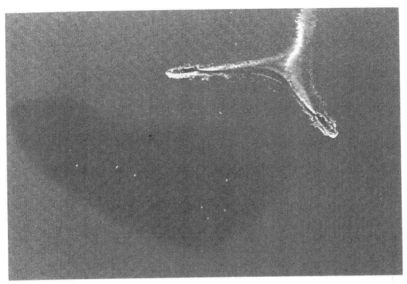

FIGURE 6.2 Boats approaching the school. Photo by Hall Watters. Copyright 2001 by Hall Watters. Reprinted by permission of Rosa Lee R. Watters. All rights reserved.

Watters, his aggressive new employer "wanted to catch everything but the wiggle." The corporate consolidation continued relentlessly. One by one, all but local companies that fished exclusively for bait were gobbled up by a new force in the Atlantic: the Zapata Corporation.

In 1953, George H. W. Bush cofounded Zapata Corporation, a wildcatting oil and gas exploration company headquartered in Houston. After Bush sold his stake in Zapata in 1966, the company began to branch out into commercial fishing in the Gulf of Mexico, "wringing oil out of fish," as one business journal snidely put it. In 1973, Zapata took over one of the two remaining companies in Reedville, the almost-century-old Haynie Products, then renamed Zapata-Haynie. In the early 1990s, reclusive real estate mogul Malcolm Glazer took control of Zapata, installed his son Avram as president and CEO, sold off the company's oil and gas interests, used the proceeds to

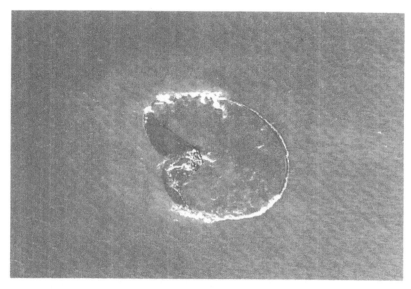

FIGURE 6.3 Frenzied menhaden foam the pursed net. Photo by Hall Watters.
Copyright 2001 by Hall Watters. Reprinted by permission of Rosa Lee R. Watters. All
rights reserved.

buy some miscellaneous businesses owned by the Glazer family, purchased the Tampa Bay Buccaneers (forcing the city to impose a sales
tax, still in effect, to build a grandiose new stadium), and turned Zapata
into a mere shell for a subsidiary with a jazzy new name more fit for a
health-food company—Omega Protein.

The Glazers started snapping up what was left of the competition
like so many menhaden. Most of the eastern companies had already
gone bankrupt or frantically merged with each other. But under a program of the National Marine Fisheries Service (the old U.S. Fish
Commission set up by Spencer Baird in 1871), Zapata obtained U.S.
guaranteed loans to finance an aggressive expansion. In 1997, Zapata
completed its monopolization of the industry by taking over its
remaining large competitor on the Atlantic seaboard, Reedville's
American Protein (successor to Standard Products), and its main Gulf
competitor, Gulf Protein of Louisiana. To avoid being classified as a

monopoly and thus falling under certain regulatory requirements, Zapata left one small independent on each coast.[30] The nation's entire menhaden reduction industry was now virtually one company: Zapata's subsidiary, Omega Protein. A few months later, Omega was spun off as a public company, with the Glazers maintaining majority ownership. One man and his family now had a monopoly on the industry that annually sweeps up billions of the nation's most important fish, grinds them up, and turns them into animal feed, paints, linoleum, cosmetics, soap, lubricants, and other industrial commodities.

It may not have been mere coincidence that in a 1997 episode of *The Simpsons*, evil tycoon C. Montgomery Burns claims that, under the tutelage of relentless environmentalist Lisa Simpson, he's become a benefactor of society because he sweeps hundreds of millions of fish from the sea, grinds them up, and turns them into "Li'l Lisa's Patented Animal Slurry"—"a high-protein feed for farm animals, insulation for low-income housing, a powerful explosive, and a top-notch engine coolant." "Best of all," he boasts, "it's made from 100 percent recycled animals." When Lisa tells Mr. Burns that what he's doing is "evil," he responds, "I don't understand. Pigs need food, engines need coolant, dynamiters need dynamite. . . . and not a single sea creature was wasted."[31]

Ecological Catastrophes

THE RUINS OF AN INDUSTRY

Disintegrating fish factories and rotting bunker vessels are scattered along the East Coast of the United States, grim remains today of the industry that wiped out most of the Atlantic menhaden. These are not tourist attractions like the Monterey Bay Aquarium and the restaurants in the old factories of what used to be Cannery Row in Monterey, memorials to the industry that destroyed itself along with most of California's sardines. Some, though, are still used as local landmarks. Fishing maps of New Jersey's Little Egg Harbor and Great Bay, for example, mark the site of a crumbling menhaden factory—prominently labeled "Stink House." An occasional glimmer of interest flickers, such as a prestigious Manhattan photo gallery's 2006 exhibit called *Industrial Ruins*, featuring the striking images of Ruth

FIGURE 7.1 Ruins of a menhaden factory, Gardiner's Bay, Long Island. Photo by Ruth Formanek. Copyright 2006 by Ruth Formanek. All rights reserved.

Formanek's "A Fish Factory in the Hamptons." And there is the Reedville Fishermen's Museum, located on Main Street in Reedville, Virginia, on Cockrell's Creek.

Down Cockrell's Creek from the museum is all that is left of the once vast industry that hunted Atlantic menhaden from Maine to Florida: Omega Protein's East Coast factory complex, airfield, and eleven-ship fleet. Across the creek from Omega's plant are rusting hulks of various vintages and the smokestack of an abandoned factory, leftovers from competitors bought out by Omega. Farther up the creek are more crumbling menhaden factories, trees pushing up through their vine-covered ruins. In the heyday of the industry, more than sixty steamers brought their daily menhaden hauls to eight factories clustered along this remote little tributary of the mighty Chesapeake.[1]

After the slaughter of Atlantic menhaden during the boom following the Second World War, the fishing ships had to be modernized once again to hunt their increasingly scarce prey. In the 1970s, the ships were almost all equipped with refrigeration, which allowed them to make much longer voyages while preserving their catch. Modern communication systems, computers, and global positioning system

FIGURE 7.2 Rusting hulks of decommissioned menhaden ships, Cockrell's Creek. Photo by the author.

technology have now made these vessels even more efficient hunters than their predecessors. Until recently, the Omega fleet would cruise up the coast about twice annually, zeroing in on the schools and strip-mining them along the way to the bunker-rich waters along the New Jersey shore. But one by one, all the states north of Virginia banned the reduction fleet from their state waters—all except New Jersey. Outrage ignited by the conspicuous impact on that state's population of valued food and game fish evoked a protest movement eerily similar to that of the 1870s, 1880s, and 1890s. So at last, in 2001, New Jersey enacted a law—virtually identical to the one vetoed by the New Jersey governor well over a century earlier, in 1882—banning the reduction industry from fishing within the three-mile limit of its jurisdiction. This leaves Virginia and North Carolina as the only eastern states that allow menhaden to be fished for conversion into industrial products.

Omega was already having problems finding enough fish to fill its

FIGURE 7:3 A menhaden factory acquired by Omega Protein now overgrown by weeds. Photo by Ruth Formanek, Cockrell's Creek, 2006. Copyright 2006 by Ruth Formanek. All rights reserved.

expensive modern fleet of ships to their large capacity. Although it owns sixty-six ships, it mothballed thirteen in 1991 and ever since has used only about forty for fishing. A mere eleven remain active on the Atlantic seaboard, down from twenty as recently as 1997.[2] Despite their long-range capabilities, these eleven vessels fish mainly within the Chesapeake Bay, mostly within an hour or two's sail from the Reedville factory. Why? Because the once-great oceanic schools beyond the states' three-mile jurisdiction are now too scarce for profitable exploitation, and it's easy and cheap to locate and snare bunkers once they enter the relatively narrow confines of the bay to filter-feed in its waters.

Geography combines with politics to put these menhaden in perilous straits. Although about half the waters of the Chesapeake lie

Map 7.1 Chesapeake Bay

within Maryland, which banned the reduction industry from its juris-diction in 1950, the mouth of the bay and its lower half are entirely within Virginia, where the legislature has routinely complied with all of Omega's wishes. To reach Maryland waters, the fish would have to swim about seventy miles through Virginia waters, heavily patrolled by Omega's fleet. Needless to say, very few survive their attempted journey, although hundreds of millions try. Those fish that do get through the gauntlet heading north are the tiny larvae, which in early summer head into the historic prime nursery for juvenile menhaden, the Maryland tributaries of the Chesapeake. In the fall, having quad-rupled to about finger size (about one and a half to seven inches), the juveniles head south on their migration to the ocean, only to fall by the hundreds of millions into Omega's purse seines.

Thus Omega Protein now gets about three-fourths of its Atlantic catch, measured by weight, from the Chesapeake. This is more than a quarter of a billion pounds a year, enough to make Reedville the second-biggest fishing port in the United States by weight.[3] Measured by numbers of fish, the Chesapeake catch must be well over 80 per-cent, since these fish are much smaller than those caught at sea. A closer look at the statistics reveals their profoundly disturbing significance.

Atlantic menhaden do not reach maturity until they are three years old, when they become capable of spawning. Only 6 percent of Omega's catch in the Chesapeake are three or more years old. The rest are babies and juveniles, with an average weight of only about six ounces.[4] Thus Omega every year on average is removing well over half a billion menhaden from the waters of the bay.[5] So it's no surprise that there are hardly any adult fish left, because Omega is massacring the juvenile fish before they can reach maturity and spawn to make more fish.

As early as 1971 it became apparent to marine biologists that "the decline in fish older than age 2 was much greater than the decline in numbers of fish younger than age 3" and "with present levels of fishing effort, the spawning stock of Atlantic menhaden is inadequate for the recovery of the population."[6] By the opening of the twenty-first century, it was beginning to seem that the menhaden population was close to a catastrophic crash. Bill Matuszeski, former executive director of the National Marine Fisheries Service and then director of the Environmental Protection Agency's Chesapeake Bay Program, said in 2001, "We need to start managing menhaden for their role in the overall ecological system." He advocated immediately placing estuaries like the Chesapeake Bay off limits to menhaden fishing, adding, "That would be inconvenient for the industry, but it would be inconvenient for the species to be extinct."[7]

As for the Chesapeake Bay itself, it may have already begun to crash.

Extracting the Liver of the Chesapeake

Chesapeake Bay is the largest and most spectacular tidal estuary in the United States. Here the waters of the Atlantic Ocean meet and mingle with the outflow of 150 rivers, creeks, and streams, concocting a fabulously rich stew of marine life. Before European colonization, gray whales, dolphins, alligators, sea turtles, giant sturgeon, and manatees all flourished in the bay. Hundreds of species of fish still inhabit or range into the Chesapeake, once the world's capital of striped bass, bluefish, weakfish, croakers, blue crabs, oysters, and, of course, menhaden. The bay once produced more seafood per acre than any body of water on Earth. That is not "once" as in "once upon a time"; it was true until 1975.[8] But today this tremendous ecological wonderland is fast becoming an ecological nightmare.

Two marine species, both filter feeders, combined to keep the Chesapeake's waters healthy and crystal clear, thus also nurturing the lush seabed garden that hosted the bay's profusion of animal life. Pouring through all its waters were billions of menhaden. And on the bottom were the oysters.

When the Europeans arrived, the oyster population was so large that it was capable of filtering a volume of water equal to the bay in three days.[9] The oyster reefs were once so thick that they constituted a hazard to navigation. As late as 1912, special express trains full of oysters from the Chesapeake left Baltimore every night headed for St. Louis and Chicago, while canned Chesapeake oysters were sold around the world.[10] They seemed inexhaustible. But by the 1930s, the oyster population was crashing from overfishing. Only after oysters crashed did hypoxia—a state of severe oxygen depletion—become noticeable in the bay. The lack of oxygen helped wipe out much of the remaining oyster population, either by suffocating them outright or by debilitating them until they became vulnerable to disease and parasites.[11] By the 1990s, the bay's oyster population was less than 1 percent of what it had been in the 1890s. Today, after repeated failed attempts to bring back the native oyster population to help restore the bay's health, an effort is under way to introduce and encourage the growth of an Asian oyster, an experiment with quite unpredictable outcomes.[12]

Virtually eliminating the oysters and drastically reducing the population of menhaden, on the other hand, has had one set of quite predictable outcomes: overall degradation of water quality, turbidity that keeps sunlight from nourishing the seabed's plant life, and dangerous overgrowth of various forms of algae, some toxic, causing frequent devastating algal blooms. That could be predicted even if we were doing nothing else to harm the bay's ecology. But of course we have been doing lots of other damage as well. Sewage and industrial pollutants have poured into the bay for decades, although here progress has been made in remediation, at least at the sources.[13] (Omega Protein has been doing its own little bit to help pollute the bay, for years illegally discharging cyanide, ammonia, and PCBs into Cockrell's Creek.[14]) More intractable and ever increasing is the flow of excess nutrients, especially nitrogen and phosphorus, from the bay's colossal sixty-four-thousand-square-mile watershed, which spans the states of Delaware, Maryland, Virginia, West Virginia, Pennsylvania, and New York.[15] Into the east side of the bay alone flow enormous quantities of chemicals from the vast industrialized poultry and hog farms of the Maryland peninsula.

Nitrogen is the main culprit because it stimulates fast and copious plant growth—and algae are plants. The entire watershed has long been deluged with the nitrogen used to fertilize farms along the Chesapeake's many tributaries. When golf courses and urban/suburban sprawl displace farms, the problem is actually worsened. At least the farms use soybeans, alfalfa, and other nitrogen-fixing crops to retain nitrogen in the soil. But the golf courses use nitrogen promiscuously, and excessive amounts are splattered all over suburbia to produce the fashionable but environmentally destructive fetish of the perfect grass lawn. (Overstimulating these grass lawns with nitrogen is one of the main occupations of suburban landscaping companies, which then profit by cutting the grass as often as possible, while also spraying insecticides and herbicides to protect this overly lush vegetation, thus eliminating natural predators and poisoning aquifers.) As population and development have boomed all around the bay, more and more land has been paved over, and more and more runoff filled with nitrogen, phosphorus, and other chemicals flows directly and indirectly into the Chesapeake. And the rain washing this diabolical concoction into the bay is acid rain, brimming with nitrogen oxides and other pollutants from the burning of fossil fuels.

So juiced-up algae run amok until their population explodes into unprecedented huge blooms that menace the environment. Some of these blooms are toxic, and these often directly poison huge numbers of fish. But the main damage done by algal blooms, whether or not toxic, is more pervasive. When the blooms die, they sink in dense carpets to the seabed, where they smother vegetation. Their decomposition then robs the water of the dissolved oxygen needed by fish, shellfish, and most other animal life. As these carpets accumulate, they create dead zones that expand year by year, making larger and larger portions of the bay uninhabitable by any life forms that require significant amounts of oxygen.

Relatively few people around the bay have lived in the region long enough to remember what it used to be like. If some think that algal blooms and dead zones are just part of the bay's natural history, they are mistaken. Extensive scientific research has now demonstrated that the current environmental nightmare is a new phenomenon, a product of human activities in the decades since the Second World War—including the onslaught on the menhaden population.

A truly alarming study published in 2004 by James Hagy and other scientists of the University of Maryland's Center for Environmental Science traces with precision the timeline of the phytoplankton over-growths that are literally choking the Chesapeake and creating its ever-expanding oxygen-depleted dead zones. Using bolder language than one usually hears in scientific studies, the authors state outright, "Suggestions that current levels of hypoxia and anoxia are a natural feature of Chesapeake Bay are demonstrably false." Anoxia—the total absence of dissolved oxygen—is associated with eutrophication, the process by which a bay, lake, or estuary eventually becomes a bog or swamp. The geological record does show that there has been some ecological change ever since Europeans first arrived, but "eutrophication and increased hypoxia" have been "largely limited to the 20th century." Hypoxia did increase somewhat between 1934 and 1948, but the rate of change did not begin to soar until 1950 and continued to accelerate "dramatically" through 2001, the end date of the study. A disturbing new phenomenon appeared first in 1968: persistent anoxia —that is, no oxygen at all—in portions of the bay. Because anoxia has terrible consequences, this "marked an important shift in the ecologi-cal history of Chesapeake Bay." The second ominous feature of the 1950–2001 trend is "the massive expansion, largely since 1980, of the volume and area of the bay affected by moderate hypoxia." The study notes that this expansion has been especially pronounced in "Virginia waters," and "this pattern of expansion to the south corre-sponds directly to the long-term increase in phytoplankton biomass, in which the largest increases have occurred in the southern bay."[16] This disaster is taking place precisely where and when Omega Protein has been slaughtering by the billions the main consumers of phytoplankton.

The Hagy study expressed a glimmer of hope that the degradation of the bay might be reversed or at least stabilized in the post-2001 period. However, Benjamin Cuker, professor of marine and environmental studies at Hampton University, has discovered that these dead zones have continued to enlarge every year since 2000: "All the way from south of the Potomac to the Bay Bridge the water below eight meters [26 feet] is now anaerobic, uninhabitable by any organism that demands any significant amount of oxygen."[17] At one point in the summer of 2005, 41 percent of the bay's main stem had too little oxygen for most fish and crabs to survive.[18]

Eutrophication would require an awfully long time or a geological shift to reach endgame—actually becoming a swamp—for the Chesapeake, thanks to the bay's sheer size, its multitude of tributary rivers, and its enormous influx of ocean tides. Some changes in the bay's marine animal life display characteristic parts of the process, however. For example, the bay is increasingly infiltrated by shoals of comb jellies (ctenophores), planktivores that feed on zooplankton rather than phytoplankton. As Hagy has pointed out, "blooms of ctenophores have been identified around the world as a possible consequence of eutrophication."[19] These comb jellies then accelerate the process by feeding on the main herbivore other than menhaden left in the bay, copepods, a form of zooplankton that consumes considerable quantities of phytoplankton.[20]

The butchering of menhaden is not the primary cause of the bay's eutrophication. Ending the slaughter would not miraculously restore the bay to its state before we started wantonly abusing it. But menhaden are arguably the most important force we have to help save the bay. As Bill Matuszeski says, "With the oyster population gone and little hope of its return, menhaden are absolutely critical to restoring the health of the bay." Matuszeski dismisses the argument that the decline of menhaden is merely cyclical, pointing out that "they make that argument about every fishery." The problem is that "one company has a monopoly" and they have "undue influence over the fishery management."[21]

David Festa, director of the oceans program for the nonprofit Environmental Defense, calls menhaden "the card in the bottom of a house of cards in an ecosystem."[22] According to Jim Uphoff, the stock assessment coordinator for the Fisheries Service of the Maryland Department of Natural Resources, "There's nothing in Chesapeake Bay that can take menhaden's place—menhaden are king." Uphoff points out the multiple ironies of our "choosing to use our menhaden as forage for chickens rather than forage for fish," since the runoff from many large poultry farms then pours "right into the bay," stimulating the phytoplankton overgrowth that the menhaden might have been able to prevent.[23]

Bill Goldsborough, senior scientist of the Chesapeake Bay Foundation, sees an even darker irony in the fate of menhaden, "the main filter feeders that keep the bay's food web in balance." These guardians of the bay become victims of a deadly "perfect circle": "Menhaden are big targets of Pfiesteria, the toxic phytoplankton known as 'the cell from hell.' The menhaden are ground up and fed to the big chicken farms on Maryland's Eastern Shore. Chicken manure from these chicken farms is the dominant source of the nitrogen entering the Chesapeake from the Eastern Shore. The nitrogen triggers the Pfiesteria, which then infects the menhaden."[24]

What could a restored menhaden population contribute toward reversing eutrophication and saving the Chesapeake? A single adult menhaden is able to filter at least four gallons a minute, 240 gallons an hour, 5,760 gallons a day. A landmark study back in 1967 calculated "that if all of the menhaden landed in Chesapeake Bay in one season were present in the bay at one time, they could filter all of the water in the Virginia portion of the bay and its tributaries twice in 24 hours."[25] More recently, Sara Gottlieb estimated that before their decimation, the menhaden population of the Chesapeake had the ability to filter a volume of water equal to the entire bay in two days.[26]

This filter feeding, however, is only one of menhaden's great ecological missions. What are the consequences of interfering with their other one—being eaten?

THE CASE OF THE SICK STRIPERS

The signature fish of the Chesapeake Bay is the rockfish, better known up north as the striped bass. The watershed of the bay is, in fact, the world's principal spawning area as well as nursery for this magnificent fish. Perhaps as many as 80 percent of the stripers ranging up and down the Atlantic coast were actually spawned in the tributaries of the Chesapeake. It is not mere coincidence that this main spawning area and nursery for striped bass also happens to be the Atlantic Ocean's main nursery for their most essential food: menhaden.

Back in the early 1980s, Atlantic striped bass seemed to be a doomed species. The annual catch had fallen 90 percent in a decade, and the few survivors were menaced by pollution, wanton commercial overfishing, and a network of entrenched corporate and political interests that valued profits and power over any environmental concerns. Against all odds, a grassroots movement of anglers and environmentalists was able to bring the species back from near-extinction. The seeds of this movement were sown in the 1960s when a critical spawning area in the Hudson had been saved from Consolidated Edison. Along the way, this movement to save the stripers also helped achieve crucial victories for environmentalism in general. One was the first court decision recognizing "environmental standing"—that is, the right of citizens to sue a government agency to protect natural resources—a judicial principle that became U.S. law in the National Environmental Policy Act of 1969, which requires all federal agencies to consider the full environmental impact of all proposed projects. Because the movement persuaded states to impose moratoriums and compelled the U.S. government to halt all fishing for stripers in federal waters, which extend beyond state waters out two hundred miles from shore, these extraordinary fish are today once again abundant not just in the Chesapeake but along much of the Atlantic seaboard as well.[27]

The miracle of the striped bass is a wonderful success story and a thrilling lesson in what can be done when citizens take action to defend the environment. But at the same time it also highlights the dangers of failing to comprehend the holistic essence of ecology, specifically the interdependence of species. The dark side of the rockfish story has led to a deeper awareness of menhaden's complex role in the ecology of the bay and to a struggle whose outcome may determine the bay's future.

Jim Price is a fifth-generation commercial fisherman, or "waterman" as they are called around the Chesapeake. He was one of the leaders of the movement to save the stripers. In 1984, he also founded the Chesapeake Bay Acid Rain Foundation, now the Chesapeake Bay Ecological Foundation, a leading organization in the struggle to save the bay itself. Like the previous four generations of his family, Price has lived his entire life on the southern bank of eastern Maryland's historic Choptank River, near its four-mile-wide mouth as it merges with the bay. For ten years he captained a charter boat specializing in light-tackle fishing for rockfish. It was a terrific place to fish from, for the Choptank was one of the greatest nurseries for both striped bass and menhaden. Even today, more than two decades after Price gave up his fishing vocation, he can often be found around dawn casting lures into the river and catching a rockfish before breakfast.

One day in the fall of 1997, Price caught a rockfish covered with red sores eating deeply into its flesh. It was still visibly upsetting to him in 2000, when he talked to me about it. "I'd never seen anything like that in my entire life," he said, wringing his powerful, deeply tanned hands in distress. "It was so sickening it really took something out of me."

Price deposited several sick rockfish at the Cooperative Oxford

Laboratory in nearby Oxford, Maryland, and then began his own study. "I started writing down the numbers of these fish that I was catching, keeping track, weighing them, examining them," he said. When he scrutinized the contents of their stomachs, he was shocked. "I've been looking in the stomachs of rockfish for forty years," he said, "but I couldn't believe what I saw—nothing, nothing, absolutely nothing. Not only was there no food, but there was no fat. Everything was shrunk up and small."

An Oxford Lab pathologist speculated that the fish might have been "decoupled from their source of food," but Price was incredulous. "I thought to myself, with all the food here in the Chesapeake, that's a stupid idea. But then I got to thinking. In years past, at that time of year I would find their stomachs full of menhaden, sometimes a half dozen whole fish."[28]

Price began to hypothesize that malnutrition, caused by the decline in the menhaden population, was making the rockfish vulnerable to disease. Since then, his hypothesis has been confirmed by scientific research spurred by the deteriorating health of the fish. In 1997, Anthony Overton, now one of the leading scientists studying the diseased rockfish, began a doctoral study based on a systematic examination of Chesapeake striped bass, including the contents of their stomachs. Comparing his samples with those in a similar study completed just a few years earlier, Overton found a "dramatic drop" in menhaden consumption, to approximately one-seventh what it had been as recently as 1993. He told me in 2000 that many of the fish he sampled were "skinny" and infected with a mycobacterium causing a kind of "fish tuberculosis."[29] This was an ominous finding, because mycobacterial infections are notoriously difficult to treat and even to detect (many people infected with tuberculosis develop no symptoms).

Many scientists now believe that the rockfish are sick because they're malnourished and that they're malnourished because they're not getting enough menhaden to eat. The Virginia Institute of Marine Science estimated in 2005 that 76 percent of the rockfish in the bay are infected with wasting diseases caused by mycobacteria.[30] There may be ten or more different forms of these mycobacterial infections. The external symptoms are red lesions that ulcerate deep into the bodies of the fish. Some fish that outwardly appear healthy except for lack of body fat are in fact being eaten from inside by the infection in one or more organs. Fatal to fish that are severely stressed by malnutrition or low dissolved oxygen, these diseases can cause severe skin infections and possibly nerve damage in humans.[31]

The Choptank is also historically a major nursery for juvenile menhaden, which is no doubt why rockfish like to hang out in the river. Price began to put pieces of the grim puzzle together when ecological disaster struck in the Choptank right behind his home in May 1998. For almost three weeks, the river was red from a giant algal bloom that ran all the way from the mouth ten miles upstream. Although blooms had recently covered as much as thirty miles in the main part of the bay, for the Choptank "it was the largest bloom in anyone's memory," according to Professor Pat Glibert of the University of Maryland's Center for Environmental Science.[32] Price was in a perfect position, quite literally, to see the ecological consequences from the depletion of menhaden, including their interconnections. If there had been a normal amount of juvenile bunkers in the Choptank, their consumption of the algae would almost certainly have prevented the deadly bloom, and then there would have been plenty of algae-filled bunkers for the rockfish to eat.

In July 2005, Price was kind enough to take me fishing with him so I could get a firsthand look at the current conditions of the rockfish. It was very late on an almost windless afternoon as we left the dock at Oxford, near where the Choptank completes its meandering seventy-mile journey from Delaware through eastern Maryland to become part of the Chesapeake. Joining us were Joe Boone, an ex-paratrooper who had worked for twenty-seven years as an estuarine biologist in the Maryland Department of Natural Resources (DNR), and Jim Uphoff, currently the stock assessment coordinator for the Fisheries Service of the Maryland DNR. As soon as I had seen this river, I knew why Jim loved it. Sailing on it, as the low sun in the west lit its calm water in blues and golds while darkly silhouetting the wooded islands of its wide mouth, I began to feel hints of the same passion.

Up on his flying bridge, Jim steered the twenty-nine-foot Bertram in the same slow and deliberate way that he talked and walked. Used to the speedier style of the New Jersey friends with whom I usually fish, I was wondering why we weren't going a bit faster to the fishing grounds. But I soon realized why. Because we were making almost no wake, we could clearly see anything else that might be disturbing the water. And something was. About thirty yards off to our right, the surface was slightly ruffled, as though disturbed by a breeze, in a patch a bit smaller than the boat and moving in the same direction. Joe Boone, Jim Uphoff, and I all recognized it as a small pod of peanut bunkers, babies migrating out from their nursery in the river into the Chesapeake. Soon we saw another one, this time on our left. Then another, skittishly darting away from the boat. Then another and another, each small pod about the same size and widely separated from each other. Jim Uphoff and Joe were visibly excited by what we were seeing, and after they explained why, I began to share their excitement. The Choptank was once full of peanut bunkers, but in more recent years there had been extremely few. That was a symptom of the dangerously low level of "recruitment," the replenishing of the menhaden population with a new crop of babies. These small pods we were seeing were the first sign in years of at least some renewed recruitment, and they offered glimmers of hope that the menhaden were not irreversibly doomed.

As the other men talked about what the Choptank had been like in the past, I recalled an early-morning trip I had taken just three days earlier from a dock on Cheesequake Creek, a small, brackish tributary of New Jersey's Raritan Bay. New Jersey had banned the reduction industry from the state's waters three years before, and the resurgence of menhaden was startling. The morning was windless, and wisps of fog hung in the dawn light on the water's flat surface. On Brian Faust's twenty-three-foot Proline along with two other friends, I could hear a constant rustle, like a whisk broom on carpet. It came from peanut bunkers continually flipping and falling back into the creek, which they seemed to jam from shore to shore.

We were not the only ones enjoying their presence. All along the swampy banks, amid the reeds and cattails, snowy white egrets and an occasional great blue heron stood like statues until one would suddenly dart its beak into the water to pluck a baby menhaden. Tarry black double-crested cormorants—Brian calls them Exxon ducks—intermittently swam, dived, disappeared for a couple of minutes, and bobbed up gulping breakfast. Other cormorants decorated trees like ghoulish Christmas-tree ornaments, their four-foot black wings spread out to dry. At the mouth of the creek, we passed an active osprey nest on a metal tower. As I recalled the scene, I realized that as Jim Price's boat was slowly cruising down the Choptank late this afternoon, I was seeing surprisingly few birds.

When we finally arrived at Jim's chosen spot in the open waters of the bay, the sun was sinking below the horizon. After circling awhile to locate marks on the fishfinder, Jim had Joe toss out a buoy wound with a line tied to a weight that would anchor it to the bottom. For a few hours, we would now alternately drift with the tide and return to that buoy, with Joe, Jim Uphoff, and me fishing from the broad stern, using small metal jigs that could imitate wounded peanut bunkers or other bait fish.

The first few fish we caught were croakers. We noticed the snouts of a couple of cownose rays, forty- to sixty-pound monsters that we kept at a safe distance from our lures. Then as the dusk deepened slowly under a full moon, we saw a tell-tale swirl from the broom-like tail of a striped bass. Another appeared right behind the boat. No matter how long you've been fishing for them, this sight is always thrilling. The three of us began casting toward the swirls.

It was Joe Boone who hooked the first rockfish and brought it alongside, where Jim Price, in his customary unhurried style, scooped it on board with a long-handled net. I was a bit surprised at what happened next. Instead of the person who caught the fish unhooking it and then putting it in the cooler, Jim methodically deposited the fish from the net directly into the cooler, where it was unhooked with a tool. At no time during the hours we fished did anyone ever touch a rockfish, and no rockfish ever touched the deck of the boat. Was this just a way to keep the deck from getting slippery? Or was it because nobody wanted to be exposed to a dangerous mycobacterium? Well, at last I'd gotten my first look at a Chesapeake rockfish, but the precautions certainly killed any desire I had to handle one.

This first fish looked healthy and normal enough to me, though I wasn't used to seeing stripers this small being kept (the minimum Chesapeake size was eighteen inches, compared with the New Jersey minimum then of twenty-four inches, and now of twenty-eight inches). But Joe pointed out a small, rather unremarkable lesion near the anus, something I would have missed. This rockfish was the healthiest-looking we caught, however, except for one. The next fish, with bright red open sores gnawing deep into its side and belly, gave me a taste of that revulsion Jim must have felt back in 1997. One after the other, we caught diseased rockfish, each with horrifying symptoms.

When I had first interviewed Jim in Manhattan five years earlier, he had waxed enthusiastic about what he claimed was the greatest lure for catching rockfish and even convinced me to order a couple of these fairly expensive "Jackie Jigs" from California. So every year, after either catching my New Jersey striper limit or not finding anything else that worked, I would try one out. But no Jersey fish ever touched one. Finally, that night on Jim's boat, what felt like a big striper grabbed my Jackie Jig and ran straight out, peeling line off the reel. When Jim netted the fish, I was elated to see what looked like a truly healthy rockfish. Only after we measured it at thirty-four inches did I realize that even this fish, though it had no external lesions, was pathetically skinny.

As we fished, we talked. None of the three men, with their many combined years of studying the Chesapeake and catching its fish, had the slightest doubt about what was making its rockfish so malnourished and diseased: the loss of the bay's menhaden. "It's plain evidence of how critical menhaden are to the health of the striped bass," Boone said. "Menhaden are the keystone species." Jim Uphoff reiterated, "There's nothing in this bay that can take menhaden's place." Although I had interviewed both Jim and Joe years before and had read Jim's brilliant scientific analyses,[33] my long conversations with them that night made me understand far more clearly and deeply the crucial role of menhaden not only for rockfish but in the entire ecology of the Chesapeake.

THE CASE OF THE MURDERED CRABS

Along with rockfish and oysters, the third member of the Chesapeake's world-famous seafood triumvirate is the blue crab. Although not nearly as devastated as the oyster population and intermittently having a bountiful year (such as 2006), the crabs have been experiencing an ominous long-term decline despite being tough, resilient, and resourceful animals capable of thriving even in highly polluted environments. One threat comes from overfishing, which, as usual, produces some large harvests that give illusions of recovery when these big catches may be just depleting the stock more rapidly. Other, more complex menaces dramatically display how interdependent are the species of the bay.

Menhaden and crabs have very little direct interaction. Menhaden do not feed on crabs, although some crab eggs now and then may get slurped up in their filter feeding. Crabs do not feed on living menhaden, although a crab may occasionally be able to snatch an unwary passerby in its claws, and dead menhaden are perhaps their favorite dish (which is why crab traps are baited with bunker chunks). Crabs, however, do need aquatic vegetation in which to spawn, hide from predators (especially as babies and when molting), and lurk for prey and dead animals to scavenge. Because the menhaden population has been severely depleted, the bunker schools have not been able to carry out part of their ecological mission of clearing the water of detritus and plankton. Thus clouds of algae and detritus prevent the sunlight necessary for the growth of this protective vegetation from penetrating to the bottom. What is reaching the bottom are carpets of dead algal blooms, which smother what vegetation does exist. Hence underwater grasses and other aquatic plants today flourish in only 12 percent or less of the bay's bottom they once covered, severely limiting the environment congenial to crabs. Furthermore, those carpets of dead algal blooms also suck precious dissolved oxygen from the water, and crabs cannot survive without adequate oxygen.

The bay's crab watermen blame much of the crabs' decline on the resurgence of rockfish. The familiar complaint is that the rockfish are eating all the baby crabs, as reported in a *New York Times* story that told of one rockfish with "87 baby crabs in its gut." The *Washington Post* ran an article titled "For Resurgent Rockfish, the Special Is Bay Crab," which reported a rockfish with 113 tiny crabs in its stomach and noted that crabs stay intact in a striper's stomach for only one day.[34] There is indeed some validity in the watermen's concerns. But one historic feature of the Chesapeake is its superabundance of both rockfish and blue crabs, which obviously coexisted with no problem. So what has changed their relationship?

One part of the answer is simple. The rockfish are consuming prodigious numbers of young blue crabs because they are being deprived of their normal diet: menhaden. The Maryland DNR has an extensive collection of the stomach contents of hundreds of striped bass caught in the 1950s. When scientists analyzed these contents, they discovered that 99 percent of what the rockfish had been eating were fish, predominantly menhaden. Menhaden led the list of prey items with a total of 777. The total number of crabs was 2.[35]

The Maryland DNR also has an archive of rockfish scales taken from 1982 through 1997. Bryan Taplin, an environmental scientist in the Atlantic Ecology Division of the Environmental Protection Agency, has been analyzing the carbon isotope signature of these scales to determine whether there have been changes in the diet of the bay's rockfish. What he has discovered is a steady shift away from the oily menhaden, loaded with vital high-energy lipids, to crabs and other invertebrates that provide considerably lower nutritional value. This shift has correlated closely with a loss of muscle and a decrease in the weight-to-length ratios of striped bass. The Chesapeake bass, he told me, now tend to be "long skinny stripers" that have been forced to shift their diet because the "menhaden population has crashed to an all-time low."[36]

So although rockfish may indeed be guilty of the murder of baby crabs, they can legitimately plead extenuating circumstances. After all, they too are victims of the real culprits in this case. And what clearer lesson could one want about the interdependence of species? As Gene Mueller, outdoors columnist for the *Washington Times*, put it, "Take away the menhaden and you soon have hungry fish swimming about, eating whatever they can wrap their gums around, or going without and pretty soon showing signs of malnutrition."[37]

None of this is just a Chesapeake Bay concern. When Joe Boone later sent me some pictures of our fishing, he included a note saying that in writing my book about menhaden, "You can't overemphasize the importance of this fish to the ecology of the entire East Coast."

THE CASE OF THE MISSING FISH: SHAD AND RIVER HERRING

The spectacular resurgence of striped bass after they seemed doomed to extinction has taught us two great lessons. First, with enough dedication and consciousness, ordinary people can change political reality enough to recover some of the most precious parts of our lost environment. But second, as Dick Russell has written, "If we want to preserve species, we can't do so one by one; rather, we must look at the entire ecosystem of which they—and we—are a part."[38] A grassroots movement brought back the stripers, huge hordes of them. But now they need food, enormous quantities of food. What will they eat?

Unlike fish such as flounders, fluke (summer flounder), tautogs (blackfish), cod, and ling (red hake), which spend much of their existence lurking on the bottom, stripers require large quantities of high-fat food to give them the necessary energy to chase their prey, often during frantic protracted pursuits. They evolved to chase fish such as menhaden and this is also why they are so dependent on menhaden, their most lipid-rich prey. The females need even more such prey, and not just for procreation. Most Chesapeake male rockfish spend their entire lives in the bay. Most of the females, however, migrate up the coast, swimming great distances often at high speeds. (When fluke get ready for their fall ocean migration out of the bays and estuaries where they have been lurking in the mud all summer, they too begin voraciously feeding on juvenile menhaden.) Stripers burn so much energy that they often feed day and night. If they don't have enough menhaden to eat as they range up the Atlantic coast, what will they have for breakfast, lunch, dinner, and midnight snacks?

Bluefish have the same dietary needs, only more so, which is probably why they too feed day and night and why their attacks on menhaden schools are so frenzied. Like stripers, bluefish didn't choose to be so dependent on bunkers. The dark, oily flesh of bluefish, pulsing with copious hemoglobin-loaded blood, is the kind of muscle tissue needed for—and sustained by—their powerful long-distance swimming and relentless predation. The white flesh of those bottom-dwelling fish, in contrast, is a different kind of muscle tissue, designed for long periods of effortless suspension punctuated by sporadic quick attacks on their prey. These bottom dwellers store most of their lipids in their liver, whereas oily fish—such as bluefish and menhaden—are oily because they store their lipids in their muscle tissue.[39] Even more than stripers, bluefish need to eat menhaden, or something very similar. So if bunkers aren't available, what will *they* ravage?

Well, what are the closest relatives of menhaden available in quantity in some of the same waters? Answer that question, and you may solve the mystery of the disappearing shad and river herring.

"Shad and river herring" is a category of related species defined by the Atlantic States Marine Fisheries Commission to include the American shad, hickory shad, alewife, and blueback herring. These are all clupeids, such close cousins of menhaden in the herring family that they caused all that confusion about species from the seventeenth century well into the nineteenth. Unlike menhaden, they are also all anadromous; that is, they spend most of their adult life at sea and return to freshwater to spawn in the spring. American shad evidently once spawned in every accessible Atlantic coast river from Canada to Florida, and they have played significant roles in American history and life.[40] The populations of all these anadromous fish (as well as Atlantic salmon) were devastated by industrialism's dams and pollution.

For many decades, by means of strict regulation, habitat restoration, and hatcheries, we had been gradually restoring their population river by river.[41] Considerable progress was made. Bob Sampson, who worked in the EPA's Anadromous Fisheries Program in the 1970s, recalls that back then, "alewives and blueback herring were so thick" in some of Connecticut's rivers that at places "you couldn't see the bottom," and runs of American shad were fluctuating between 800,000 and 1.5 million fish each spring. In the last few years, however, there has been "a complete reversal": "shad runs in the Connecticut River are down by about 90 percent . . . alewife totals were so small they weren't even counted, and blueback herring counts dropped from a few hundred thousand per year to only about 534 during the 2005 spring runs."[42] Christopher Powell of the Department of Environmental Management of Rhode Island's Division of Fish and Wildlife and John Torgan of Narragansett Bay Keepers report the same collapse in the Narragansett region. According to Torgan, by 2005 there had been a "95 percent reduction of river herrings since 2000."[43] So in 2006, Connecticut, Rhode Island, and Massachusetts all took the drastic action of banning all fishing for river herring in an attempt to preserve their dwindling spawning stock.

"Why are there such tremendous declines in herring and shad populations throughout most of the Northeast?" asks Bob Sampson. While he admits that there may be multiple possible causes, he notes that many suspect that "heavy predation from the tremendous increase in the striped bass (and bluefish) populations up and down the coast is the primary reason." He himself has "long believed that when the commercial seiners essentially wiped out the bunker (menhaden) populations in Long Island Sound, and stripers were restored, they turned to other species," such as the shad and herring, "as prey because the once abundant menhaden were not present anymore."[44] Without large schools of menhaden to occupy the predators, they have every inducement to ambush these vulnerable anadromous fish as they bunch up to enter their freshwater birthplaces.

The Case of the Dead Shellfish

Narragansett Bay dramatizes the fundamental ecological problems of the Chesapeake on a scale that is much smaller but therefore also more easily observable. A striking example occurred in the summer of 2001.

Like the Chesapeake, the Narragansett is subject to nutrient overloads that stimulate devastating algal blooms, which create hypoxic dead zones. The Narragansett also has lost most of the filter feeders that might be able to keep these algal overgrowths under control: not just menhaden but also the bivalves—oysters, clams, and mussels—that live on the bottom, suck in algae, and spew out clean water. Menhaden were missing for decades until 2005, oysters were virtually wiped out by the 1930s, and so clams and mussels are almost all that are left to deal with the algae. But because these shellfish dwell on the bottom, they are especially vulnerable to the oxygen depletion caused by the algae blooms.

In 2001, mussels seemed to be making a sudden and spectacular comeback. Two researchers from Brown University, Andrew Altieri and Jon Witman, snorkeled repeatedly throughout the summer to study nine reefs of mussels covering an area equivalent to 229 football fields. Because of the mussels' filtration, which theoretically could process the bay's entire water volume in twenty days, the waters for a while were remarkably clear, and the two researchers observed the gleaming blue-black acres of shellfish as they fed and were fed upon by starfish, crabs, and fish. But one day in late August, after the summer's heat had stimulated the algal growths, the mussels' predators began climbing away from their prey, evidently searching for oxygen, just as Altieri and Witman recorded an alarming drop in available oxygen. Within days, an entire reef of mussels was dead. Within a year, 4.5 billion mussels had been killed by hypoxia, which also caused a number of clam die-offs and fish kills around the bay.[45]

Without either the vast schools of menhaden that once swarmed through the upper waters or the great beds of oysters on the bottom, the mussels and clams fell victim to the algal blooms and hypoxia that they could not remedy by themselves. The more filter feeders that are lost, the more dire the future for Narragansett Bay. As in the Chesapeake, oysters cannot make a comeback until the waters become much healthier. So the only immediate help the Narragansett can get from nature's armies of filter feeders is probably a return of menhaden.

STRIPERS, CRABS, river herring, oysters, mussels, clams—these are just a few of the life forms whose fate is interwoven with that of menhaden. This is what Joe Boone meant by "the importance of this fish to the ecology of the entire East Coast." Menhaden are evidently essential not just for the fish that prey upon them, but also for other fish and shellfish that these same predators may seek as a substitute, as well as the fish and shellfish that rely on filter feeders to keep the water habitable. The web of ecological interdependence is even wider and more complex than that extending above and beyond the sea.

THE BIRDS

After the menhaden Gold Rush of the 1870s annihilated most of the bunkers north of Cape Cod, the center of the industry shifted, as we've seen, to the Middle Atlantic states, especially Long Island, where vast schools still purpled the waters. A spectacular fishery boomed in Gardiner's Bay, a body of water formed by the fishtail eastern end of Long Island. Sixty-nine sailing vessels and four steamships hunted menhaden in this small bay, which was ringed by eleven factories converting hundreds of millions of fish into oil and fertilizer.[46] The great abundance of bunkers back then also appealed to another kind of hunter: the osprey, or fish hawk.

Fish hawks indeed, ospreys live on fish and are admirably designed for this life. Even while scouting at great heights, their keen vision allows them to focus on an individual fish beneath the waves. They fold their wings, power-dive at great speeds, somersault 180 degrees an instant before hitting the water, extend their powerful fish-catching legs, and pursue their prey underwater like a homing torpedo. The pads of their feet bristle with hundreds of sharp spines and inch-long opposable talons, all perfectly designed for clutching the slipperiest fish, even slimy menhaden. Whereas most hawks and falcons that hunt birds in flight kill their prey as they hit, the osprey often bursts from the water with a living, squirming fish, always held headfirst for aerodynamic efficiency.

Ages before the spotter plane, these marine raptors had used aerial searches for menhaden to help establish on Gardiner's Island, in the middle of the bay, an immense, world-famous rookery. During the nesting season, the female osprey would guard the nest while the male would each day deposit several menhaden for the voracious chicks. In 1812, Alexander Wilson's monumental *American Ornithology* reported "at least three hundred nests of Fish-Hawks" on this small island, and the same number of active nests was still there as late as the mid-1940s.[47]

But following the Second World War, the same enthusiasm for technology that had introduced the menhaden spotter plane led to the promiscuous spraying of insecticides, especially DDT, discovered in 1939 and used widely during the war. The ospreys on Gardiner's Island fell victim to the unrestrained spraying of the mosquito-breeding wetlands around the bay, and the number of active nests steadily plummeted to twenty-six.

Then in 1962 came Rachel Carson's *Silent Spring*, a book that awakened much of the nation to the environmental catastrophe our pesticides, especially DDT, were initiating. One of the people who joined the environmental movement inspired in part by Carson was Paul Spitzer, then a youthful field biologist who came to Gardiner's Island in 1969 to study the surviving ospreys, an experience that has continued to be central to his life. The following year, DDT was banned by New York state, and then in 1972 also by the federal government. As Spitzer witnessed the near-extinction of the ospreys during the heyday of DDT, their thrilling resurgence as the effects of DDT faded, and then an unanticipated new decline, he began to suspect that something in addition to the chemical was threatening the survival of the birds. His research in the years since then has convinced him that "the DDT era masked the impact on Gardiner's ospreys of a coinciding collapse of the menhaden population."[48]

"I saw the brood-size reductions, and the nestling starvation from DDT back then," Spitzer recalls, and he says he is seeing precisely the same thing today. In 2000, he told me that since 1994, "there has been an absolute steep decline from seventy-six active nests to forty-one." Then, in a 2005 article, he reported that "the Gardiner's Island colony remains in rapid decline, down to twenty-seven nests," almost equal to their DDT-related nadir of twenty-six.[49] Moreover, the mortality of the starving chicks has now reached the same level as the worst of the DDT era, with a survival rate of only one chick per two nests. Now spanning almost four decades, Spitzer's studies lead him to conclude that the osprey chicks' starvation seems directly associated "with human overharvest of the migratory menhaden schools which formerly arrived in May, in time to feed nestlings." "The collapse of the menhaden," according to Spitzer, "means endgame for Gardiner's Island ospreys." He sees the same pattern of decline in other famous osprey colonies, including those at nearby Plum Island, Delaware's Cape Henlopen, Virginia's Smith Point, and New Jersey's Cape May. Gardiner's Island, says Spitzer, is just "the smoking gun."

Another bird dependent on menhaden for part of its life cycle is the migrating common loon, which makes an autumn stopover in the Chesapeake Bay. Loons are water birds that usually spend warmer months in northern lakes and then frequently winter in coastal regions. Just as migrating adult menhaden used to arrive every May, right in time for the nesting of Gardiner's Island ospreys, vast schools containing hundreds of thousands of "peanuts"—the juvenile menhaden—used to pour out of the tributaries of the Chesapeake every fall, right in time to provide essential forage for large flocks of migrating loons.

Spitzer, who has also spent years studying these birds, has described how the loons flock-feed on the peanuts, diving from the surface, getting under the fish, pushing them up, greedily devouring them, and, between bouts of these dramatic "menhaden banquets," emitting *yip* calls that can be heard for miles, attracting more and more flocks. Since 1988, Spitzer has done statistical counts of the flocks passing through a 150-square-kilometer prime habitat on the Choptank River tributary of the Chesapeake, near where Jim Price first made his alarming discovery of starving and diseased striped bass. Between 1989 and 1999, his count of loons dropped from 750–900 per three-hour observation period to 150–200. Even more disturbing, the maximum size of the flocks fell from 750 birds to 50. Although here there may be other factors at work, Spitzer strongly suspects that the declining loon population is another marker of the menhaden crash.[50]

Although starving fish and degraded waters may be more obvious symptoms of an ecological problem, Spitzer believes that the bird populations he studies also offer a warning "barometer for all of us who love the health of the ocean." That barometer is now displaying ominous signs of an impending ecological tempest caused by the depletion of menhaden, which Spitzer calls "the absolute keystone species for the health of the entire Atlantic ecosystem."

THE GULF

While continuing to fish Atlantic menhaden to catastrophic levels in Chesapeake Bay, the reduction industry has now become essentially a Gulf of Mexico enterprise. The industry didn't really get going in the Gulf until almost a century after it began in the Atlantic, but then it swiftly outstripped its rapidly declining Atlantic predecessor. Bursting on the scene during the boom of the 1940s, by 1963 the industrial harvest of Gulf menhaden had not only surpassed the Atlantic but had become by itself the nation's largest commercial fishery. By the end of the 1980s, however, it was already beginning to show signs of decline, and in the 1990s it went through the same collapse into monopolization as the Atlantic fishery.

There are some records of small catches of menhaden in the Gulf, probably for bait, as early as 1880 off west Florida. A small factory in Texas processed menhaden until it went out of business in 1923, and there were also two or three small plants prior to 1940 in Mississippi and Florida.[51] But as late as 1940, there were still only six vessels known to be hunting menhaden throughout the entire huge area of the Gulf of Mexico.[52] Then came that explosive growth of the entire menhaden reduction industry in the years after the Second World War. By 1948, 103,000 metric tons were being landed in ports in Florida, Mississippi, Louisiana, and Texas.[53]

In place of those six relatively primitive vessels of 1940, by 1956 there were eighty-one modern ships hunting the Gulf's menhaden schools, and in 1966 the fleet reached its peak of ninety-two. The number of reduction factories kept expanding until they reached their zenith in 1968, when fourteen plants stretched across the Gulf coast all the way from Apalachicola, Florida, to Sabine Pass, Texas. The Gulf fishery surpassed the Atlantic in 1963, and by the mid-1960s was catching an average of more than five billion fish a year.[54] As in the Atlantic, the Gulf fleet kept becoming more and more efficient—and thus deadlier. Between 1983 and 1987, close to a million metric tons— more than two billion pounds—of fish each year were slaughtered and turned into industrial commodities, mainly hog food and chicken feed.[55] Because Gulf menhaden *(Brevoortia patronus)* are generally smaller than their Atlantic cousins and because the Gulf fishery hauls in a disproportionate number of juveniles, these two billion pounds amount to more than 10 billion fish (and more than 11 billion in the peak years of 1984 and 1985).[56]

Then began the inevitable decline. At no point has there been, at least so far, a single event as dramatic as the various Atlantic crashes that began in Maine in 1879 and then worked their way down the coast. There are several possible explanations for why the Gulf industry's descent has been a more gradual slide. As Atlantic menhaden migrate north and south, they are moving up and down along the coast, thus making themselves vulnerable to heavily concentrated overfishing as the schools enter each area, especially toward the northern and southern reaches of their range. But as Gulf menhaden migrate north and south, they are moving toward and away from the coast, so that the schools arrive somewhat spread out all across the Mississippi Delta, thus avoiding that vulnerable concentration of fish passing through one area. Also, since it is not profitable to pursue the fish to their far offshore grounds, the industry has limited the fishing season to about half a year. The main reason for the more gradual decline, however, may have more to do with the life cycle of Gulf menhaden: they are able to spawn in their second year, whereas the Atlantic fish generally cannot spawn before their third year. This allows faster replenishment of the population.

Nevertheless, by 1998 the number of fishing vessels had been almost halved, from ninety-two to fifty; the number of plants had dropped from fourteen to five; and the landings had plunged almost 50 percent, from the peak of 982,874 metric tons to 497,461 metric tons.[57] The number of vessels since 1998 has remained fairly constant, and the five factories are still the four operated by Omega Protein (in Moss Point, Mississippi, and in Morgan City, Abbeville, and Cameron, Louisiana) plus the Daybrook Fisheries plant (in Empire, Louisiana). We are not allowed to know any landing figures after 1998, but the industry says they have been fairly flat.

Why isn't the public allowed to know any landing statistics after 1998? Because the Department of Commerce has ruled them confidential under "the rule of three." What is the rule of three? If a fishery consists of three or fewer companies, landing figures must be kept confidential, because otherwise each company could figure out what the other companies are landing.[58] Thus, in a classic catch-22, once Omega Protein monopolized the industry in 1998, while conveniently allowing one small independent to remain on the Gulf coast and another on the Atlantic coast, it thereby acquired the right to keep its landings confidential.

Furthermore, Omega and the industry dominate the Gulf States Marine Fisheries Commission (GSMFC), the organization of the five Gulf states that is in charge of policy for the Department of Commerce. Five of the eleven members of the GSMFC Menhaden Advisory Committee are industry representatives, including two of the most aggressive spokesmen for Omega. The GSMFC Web site actually advertises Omega's products and ridicules all arguments for placing any limit on menhaden catches as "myths." For example, in response to the "Myth" that "the Gulf menhaden is overfished," the GSMFC counters with this "Fact": "The Gulf menhaden population is *NOT* overfished. The menhaden reduction fishery removes (on average) only 20% of the total menhaden population each year." And to rebut the "Myth" that the "continual harvest of Gulf menhaden" threatens their population, the GSMFC offers the preposterous "Fact" that "only a few fish can completely replace the entire population."[59]

The 2002 GSMFC Fishery Management Plan (FMP) for menhaden is a terrific though unwitting revelation of precisely what is wrong with current menhaden management thinking and practice. While much of this 143-page document consists of useful summations of scientific research and industry statistics, the management plan itself is purely about proposed measures to protect and even augment the industry, which is still the Gulf's largest fishery. Nowhere in the 143 pages of the plan is there even a single hint of the role menhaden and their filter feeding play in the ecology of the Gulf.

Is this because the Gulf of Mexico, unlike the Chesapeake Bay, does not have any ecological problems—no deadly algal blooms, no expanding dead zone? Hardly. While cheerleading for the menhaden reduction industry on one section of its Web site, the GSMFC ironically has another entire section titled "Toxic Blooms," with links to the five Gulf states' sites on "Harmful Algal Blooms." Florida, Alabama, Mississippi, Louisiana, and Texas each have their own Web site devoted to information on (and the current status of) the various kinds of lethal algal blooms that have been periodically poisoning the waters of the Gulf coast and devastating its treasured populations of oysters, shrimps, crabs, and myriad finned fish. A Texas red tide (a bloom of toxic dinoflagellate algae), to cite just one rather typical incident, wiped out much of the state's oyster harvest and left millions of dead fish along its shores, including at least one line five miles long.[60]

In 1996, the New Orleans *Times-Picayune* won a Pulitzer Prize for "Oceans of Troubles," a series of articles about the grave menaces pushing the Gulf to the brink of catastrophe. Among these were the loss of vital wetlands, pollution, coastal overdevelopment, and overfishing. Citing the "menhaden fleet" as a "cause for worry" because it pulls billions of fish "from the Gulf each year to be used for oil and fish meal," the series noted, "the Atlantic menhaden fishery was wiped out by similar fishing fleets." The gravest threat discussed in the series was the seven-thousand-square-mile seasonal dead zone caused by algal blooms, which was already threatening permanent death to an area the size of Connecticut and Rhode Island.[61] For the last several years, that dead zone has expanded to average about eight thousand square miles, an "area as big as the entire Chesapeake and all its tributaries," according to James Hagy of the Gulf Ecology Division of the EPA. Hagy, author of the groundbreaking study of the ominous history of the Chesapeake's dead zone, sees similar escalating conditions in the Gulf, but on a far larger scale. Here the primary cause is nutrient overloading by "the outflow from the entire Mississippi basin."[62]

Draining all or parts of thirty states, the Mississippi pours vast quantities of nitrogen and phosphorus from America's agricultural heartland into the coastal waters of Louisiana and Mississippi. Predictably, this stimulates tremendous phytoplankton growth, always threatening as the water warms to burst into deadly algal blooms, the primary creator of dead zones. The phytoplankton also attracts vast schools of menhaden directly to these waters along the coast of Louisiana and Mississippi. That is why the menhaden fleet fishes almost exclusively in this area and why the five menhaden reduction factories are all located there. In other words, the menhaden come to eat the phytoplankton that are responsible for lethal algal blooms, but instead of being welcomed as a wonderful natural control mechanism, they are caught by the billions and turned into industrial commodities.

Although there is evidence that occasional episodic hypoxic events may be a natural feature of the Gulf, the first documented occurrence of a dead zone that recurred each year off the Louisiana coast was in 1972. Measurements began in 1985, and they have shown that the dead zone now does recur every summer and its tendency has been to keep expanding.[63] Perhaps it is not mere coincidence that this ecological catastrophe dates from the zenith of the menhaden reduction industry, from 1968 through the mid-1980s, when the annual slaughter reached 11 billion fish. It would be difficult to argue that annihilating many billions of menhaden has been a primary cause of algal blooms and the recurring dead zone. It would be more difficult to argue, however, that killing tens of billions of menhaden did not remove a significant check on those algal blooms and the growth of that dead zone.

As in the Atlantic, menhaden are also vital to the fish and bird populations of the Gulf. King mackerel, porpoises (dorado), jack crevalle, Spanish mackerel, bonito, and many other predators continually feast upon masses of menhaden. The sight of this feeding can be spectacular, as described by a *Houston Chronicle* reporter: "Acres of water churn with fleeing menhaden and attacking predators. Often, the predators go airborne as they strike."[64] But perhaps no Gulf animal is more dependent on menhaden than the brown pelican.

Back in 1917, commercial fishermen in Florida, Texas, and Louisiana began a systematic campaign to exterminate the brown pelican because they believed these voracious birds were eating too many food fish. The U.S. Department of Conservation dispatched an expedition to Louisiana, headed by ornithologist Stanley Clisby Arthur, to determine what the pelicans were actually eating. Arthur reported that the expedition "absolutely ascertained that the pelican's food was over 97% menhaden" and that the "hundreds of stomachs" they examined contained not "a single food fish." Arthur described the breeding colonies on islands all along the Louisiana coast, including one containing more than fifty thousand breeding birds, with the average nest containing four eggs. During its nine-week life in the nest, the typical baby pelican is now known to consume about 150 pounds of fish. Arthur wrote that "the racket 200,000 baby pelicans can make when they clamor for their fish food can be best described as deafening" and they are "hungry *all* the time."[65] Thanks to Stanley Clisby Arthur and his expedition, the brown pelican—the state bird of Louisiana—was saved from extinction.

But that was before the menhaden reduction industry was established in the Gulf. By 1970—right at the peak of the industry—the brown pelican of Louisiana was indeed extinct, and the bird was placed on the national endangered species list. The primary cause of the pelican's demise was almost certainly the effect of DDT and other insecticides and pollutants. But with the population already under stress from our chemical warfare, its mortality was certainly also driven by loss of its readily available food and incursions into its prime nesting areas by the menhaden industrial fishing fleet.

Depletion of Gulf menhaden may also be contributing to an ominous proliferation of jellies, both a native species and a gigantic Pacific species. Researchers believe the swollen jelly population could have a devastating effect on Gulf fishing because jellies consume the eggs and larvae of many species of fish. As Monty Graham, senior marine scientist at Alabama's Dauphin Island Sea Lab, explains, "aggressive menhaden fishing" seems to have allowed the jellies—"opportunistic planktivores"—to fill in. An expanding population of jellies also worsens algal blooms by consuming tiny copepods that feed on algae. Studies have demonstrated that this has been a main cause of late-summer algal blooms in Narragansett Bay, where jellies have competed with menhaden and caused the kind of ruinous chain reaction in the food web known as a "trophic cascade."[66] Whatever the cause, Graham sees the proliferation of both species of jelly in the Gulf as "symptoms of something gone wrong with the ecology."[67]

The environment, however, has never been of much concern to the Gulf States Marine Fisheries Commission. Or, rather, the GSMFC has been concerned only with the environment's possible impact on the industry, not the industry's impact on the environment. Thus it discusses how the loss of wetlands (now "approaching critical proportions in Louisiana which is the largest and most critical habitat area for menhaden"[68]), warming of the Gulf, pollution, algal blooms, and an expanding dead zone might reduce the menhaden population, but never how a reduced menhaden population might exacerbate the synergy of these dangerous forces.

Take one revealing example. In enumerating threats to menhaden, the commission's FMP notes that thirty species of the toxic algae dino-flagellates, the main cause of lethal red tides and other lethal algal blooms, occur in the Gulf of Mexico.[69] What they don't note is that menhaden, equipped with their amazing digestive system, are capable of happily consuming many (not all, it's true) of these dinoflagellates.

In fact, the Gulf States Marine Fisheries Commission is quite frank in stating that its FMP has one goal and one only. The entire section "2.2 Goal" reads as follows: "The goal of the Menhaden FMP is a management strategy for gulf menhaden that allows an annual maximum harvest while protecting the stock from overfishing on a continuing basis." The crucial question is obviously how "overfishing" is defined.

Operating on the assumptions that have dominated fisheries management ever since Congress established the United States Commission on Fish and Fisheries in 1871, overfishing would consist of reducing the population below the level needed to sustain the fishery at a profit-making level. So the FMP concludes there is no overfishing because "annual production, fishing effort, and fleet size appear reasonably balanced" and "the gulf menhaden stock appears reasonably stable."[70] This wording is taken directly from the concluding paragraph of a NOAA technical report, but it omits one key statement from that paragraph: "The Gulf menhaden fishery is currently fully exploited."[71]

It's probably true: if conditions stay about the same, the industry could go on for some time catching about the same number of menhaden each year, doing its bit to degrade the ecology of the Gulf. But wetlands are shrinking, the Gulf is warming, pollution is increasing, algal blooms are proliferating, hypoxia is intensifying, and the dead zone is expanding. As the FMP recognizes, any combination or even any one of these threats could have a serious impact on the menhaden population.[72] Then the industry would be rather quickly taking an increasing percentage of a shrinking population—a formula for disaster.

But what if the industry can go on forever fully exploiting a "reasonably stable" menhaden population at the current level. Is this a desirable outcome? And what is that current level?

Recall how the GSMFC defines that current level in the "Myth" and "Fact" game on its Web site. In response to the "Myth" that "the Gulf menhaden is overfished," the GSMFC counters with this "Fact": "The Gulf menhaden population is *NOT* overfished. The menhaden reduction fishery removes (on average) only 20% of the total menhaden population each year. The total population for Gulf menhaden at the beginning of 1995 was estimated to be around 19.2 billion fish, and the total number of fish removed from the Gulf of Mexico for reduction was estimated to be around 3.9 billion fish."[73] It's revealing that in 2006 the GSMFC would choose 1995 as the definitive year, since fewer fish were caught in 1995 than in any year in the published data, which date from 1964. In 1997, 5.95 billion fish were caught by the reduction industry.[74] Assuming that the population was still "relatively stable" and accepting that estimate of 19.2 billion fish (as though anyone can really estimate the number of fish out there), the industry's haul had climbed to 31 percent.

But let's not quibble over details such as whether the industry annually kills 20 percent or 31 percent of the population. Instead, let's compute a little differently. The current "relatively stable" population is evidently less than half what it was back in the peak years of the mid-1980s.[75] By then many tens of billions of menhaden had already been reduced to chickenfeed and other industrial commodities, so we have no way of estimating the size of the historic menhaden population that was an important feature of the natural ecosystem. If the present population is truly around 19 billion, an exceedingly conservative estimate of the population back then would be at least 50 to 60 billion menhaden out there happily slurping up billions of tons of algae, other phytoplankton, and detritus from the nutrient-rich outflow of the Mississippi. This was nature's main check on algal blooms and their deadly consequences, particularly a recurring dead zone. Now subtract 30 or 40 billion menhaden from the population. Add the greatly expanded nutrient flow from the growth of agribusiness in the Mississippi watershed and from urban/suburban development along the Gulf coast. Add the heat that Gulf waters have been gaining since the early 1960s. Subtract essential wetlands, which by 1987 were already being lost at the rate of thirty-five square miles annually. What do you get?

Or make a different computation. Take another "Fact" from the GSMFC Web site's Myth and Fact game: To rebut the "Myth" that the "continual harvest of Gulf menhaden" threatens their population, the GSMFC offers the "Fact" that "only a few fish can completely replace the entire population." This theme of menhaden's fecundity as a panacea for the industry's annual onslaught recurs throughout the FMP. It underlies the reasoning that legitimizes killing "only 20%" of the population each year. Without in any way questioning the assumption that such a level of "harvest" does succeed in maintaining a "stock" that is "relatively stable," consider what this actually means. Given the fabulous fecundity of the species, the industry is, according to its own analysis, acting as a major check on the *growth* of the population. The industry is thus maintaining the population at an unnaturally low level. By checking the growth of the menhaden population, the industry is thus preventing the fish from performing their natural ecological function of checking the growth of algae.

Left unchecked, could menhaden return to their immense historic population, and what would be the effects if they could? Could we have tens and tens of billions more menhaden to counter the effects of nutrient overloading and rising water temperatures? The usual natural check on the population of any species is some limit on its food source. But as we have seen throughout this book, what made for menhaden's unimaginably colossal population on both the Atlantic and Gulf coasts was their essentially unlimited food source. With the proliferation of phytoplankton in the Gulf, the fish have even more food to eat, not that they really need the surplus. The only significant natural check on the menhaden population is their innumerable predators. But since we would like to have more of our valued food and game fish back, we would hardly regret supplying them with many billions more delicious menhaden to eat. Anyhow, in the natural ecology, predation hardly seems to have made a dent in the masses of menhaden. So from an ecological point of view, there is simply no downside to limiting or even banning the industrial slaughter of menhaden.

So what is gained by allowing the industry — read Omega Protein — to continue to catch as many menhaden as it can or sees fit? When on the defensive, the industry has always presented itself as having great concern for providing jobs for working people — while doing whatever it can to eliminate as many jobs as possible, and quite successfully. According to the FMP, the entire reduction industry now has only "295 year-round or full-time employees" and "866 seasonal (April 19 through November 1) employees."[76] It lists as one of the industry's main problems "Inability to Secure a Qualified and Willing Labor Force": "Increased transiency and the increased availability of higher paying, less laborious jobs have reduced the quality and quantity of the labor force. Increased costs have resulted as the industry experiments with new equipment and methods to operate more efficiently with fewer people."[77]

Never, in the entire history of the reduction industry on either coast, has it provided any products that we could not get from other sources. Soybeans, which fix nitrogen in the soil and provide excellent nutrition for chickens and pigs (as well as people), are the main product that competes with menhaden fish meal. So the GSMFC whines, "Competition between the menhaden industry and the soybean industry for meal markets is also biased in favor of the soybean industry." Blithely ignoring all the government aid to financing for menhaden vessels and factories secured through the National Marine Fisheries Service under Title XI, the GSMFC complains, "The U.S. Department of Agriculture provides certain price supports for farmers while menhaden meal is produced with no assistance."[78]

Here's another "Fact" and "Myth" from the GSMFC Web site:

Myth: The Gulf menhaden fishery is unregulated.

Fact: The Gulf menhaden fishery is probably the most tightly monitored and managed fishery in the Gulf of Mexico. The menhaden industry has kept records of every single net set it has made since 1979 and provides these data directly to the National Marine Fisheries Service.

Since this Web site itself seems to be completely unregulated, it can thus craftily confuse reporting requirements with regulation or limitation of catch. The Securities and Exchange Commission, however, does not allow reporting corporations such latitude. Hence we can read the truth of this matter in Omega Protein's mandatory financial statement, Form 10-Q: "The Company's Gulf of Mexico operations also remain unrestricted."[79] Indeed, the only regulation or restriction of the industry's fishing in the Gulf comes from the fact that Florida, along with every other East Coast state except Virginia and North Carolina, has banned the reduction fishery in all its waters.

The Gulf States Marine Fisheries Commission offers a case study of everything that is wrong with the management of fisheries. The narrowly utilitarian thinking that rationalizes the industry's actions is tunnel vision that can focus only on the profits of a tiny group at the expense of almost everybody else. This vision misses what might be called "the big picture": the environment we inhabit. And without a glimpse of the catastrophic history of the Atlantic menhaden reduction industry, it invites a similar fate for the Gulf. Or worse.

Ten years after the *Times-Picayune*'s Pulitzer Prize–winning "Oceans of Troubles" series about the catastrophic menaces looming over the Gulf, the *Los Angeles Times* in 2006 ran "Altered Oceans," a far more terrifying five-part series about the world's oceans. It describes "the rise of slime," a ghastly nightmare emerging from the explosive growth of algae, overdosed with nutrients and no longer checked by filter-feeding fish and shellfish, that could hurl the seas backward in time "to the dawn of evolution a half-billion years ago when the oceans were ruled by jellyfish and bacteria," when there were "large areas with little or no oxygen—anoxic and hypoxic zones that could never have supported sea life as we know it." And among the 150 known dead zones in the world's seas, the second largest is that growing monster in the Gulf of Mexico.

Nancy Rabalais, executive director of the Louisiana Universities Marine Consortium, who has spent decades exploring this dead zone that resembles those of the primeval past, has peered into the layers of bacteria she describes as "white snot-looking stuff" that carpets the seabed: "The sulfurous smell of rotten eggs, from a gas produced by the microbes, has seeped into her mask. The bottom is littered with the ghostly silhouettes of dead crabs, sea stars and other animals. The cause of death is decaying algae."[80] This scene is off the Louisiana coast, right where the menhaden reduction industry annually captures billions of menhaden that would otherwise be slurping up the algae.

Collision Courses

R ECREATION OR INDUSTRY

The majority of the troops rushing to rescue the remaining menhaden schools from the cooking and grinding factories of the reduction industry are saltwater recreational anglers. Why? Answering this misleadingly simple question reveals layers and layers of meaning in the story of menhaden and America. Let's start back at the beginning.

When Captain John Smith observed the Indians leisurely fishing for the wondrously abundant fish of New England, he envisioned a future society in which colonists would be able "to recreate themselves before their owne doores, in their owne boats upon the Sea, where man woman and childe, with a small hooke and line, by angling, may take diverse sorts of excellent fish, at their pleasures." Almost four decades before the publication of the great bible of recreational fishing —Isaak Walton's *The Compleat Angler* (1653)—Smith was already expressing a similar ideal: "Now that Gardiner, Taylor, Smith, Sailer, Forgers, or what other, may they not make this a pretty recreation though they fish but an houre in a day, to take more then they eate in a weeke. . . . And what sporte doth yeeld a more pleasing content, and lesse hurt or charge then angling with a hooke, and crossing the sweet ayre from Ile to Ile, over the silent streames of a calme Sea?"[1] "To *recreate* themselves," as Smith put it, working people needed just such "*recreation*."

But the actual colonists who followed after Smith's voyage in New England were Puritans, who sternly frowned on idle pleasures. In fact, the Puritans turned the Indians' enjoyment of such leisurely labors as fishing into evidence of their "laziness" and unfitness to occupy the land. Because the Indians were "not industrious" and did not continually work to improve their land, it was actually "spacious and void," as one Calvinist ideologue put it, meaning free to be taken by the English. The Puritans' greatest scorn was for the "lazy" Indian males, who spent so much of their time fishing and hunting. As William Cronon has written, "the Puritan objections to these 'leisure' activities" were loaded with ideological content during a period when "Isaak Walton would soon proclaim the virtues of angling and hunting as pastimes." This Calvinist ideology would continue to play a major role in destroying the ecology the Europeans found.[2]

Ironically, the Pilgrims, whose charter was to set up a fishing colony, didn't even bring any fishing tackle with them, so they starved until "lazy Indians" such as Tisquantum taught them how to catch eels with bare feet and plant menhaden or some other herring-like fish with their corn. Throughout subsequent American history, there would be complex relations between the roles of "industrious" and "recreational" fishing, between fishing for profits and fishing for pleasure. And swimming around near the center of these relations would be menhaden.

The first people who tried to save the menhaden were those commercial bait and food fishermen in Maine who, after the Civil War, rioted and demanded legislation to ban the reduction industry from the state's waters. They won, but theirs was a pyrrhic victory, for by the time the law was enacted in 1879, Maine's fish had been virtually wiped out by the industry. In subsequent decades, other commercial fishermen fought against the industry's bycatch and intentional netting of food fish; its vast fixed nets, which trapped whole schools as they entered inshore waterways; and the annihilation of inshore menhaden, which drove their valued predators farther out to sea to seek their food. Groups of commercial fishermen even threatened, we've seen, to procure cannons and "fire on the marauding steamers."[3]

As the ranks of saltwater recreational anglers surged in the late nineteenth century, they joined forces with small-scale commercial fishermen in various battles to save the menhaden schools. In 1895, the *New York Times* described the two sides this way: "For years the two chief branches of the fishing industry have been in conflict, the hook-and-line market fishermen, with their powerful allies, the salt-water anglers, being the aggressors, the menhaden purse-seiners their opponents."[4] These struggles were successful in several states, which imposed significant restrictions on the reduction industry, though usually after much of the damage had already been done. But as the populations of desired food and game fish plummeted, almost all alliances between recreational and commercial fishers disintegrated. From around the middle of the twentieth century on, these two groups have collided more and more over the increasingly scarce fish prized by both.

ANGLERS AND ENVIROS, OR, A MARINE YELLOWSTONE?

Back in 1888, Congress was debating a bill that would have outlawed the taking of any menhaden within three miles of the U.S. coast. The explicit purpose was to prevent the reduction industry from massacring this species so vital to saltwater food and game fish. In denouncing the proposed law, outraged menhaden entrepreneur Captain Fitz Babson wrote, "Sumptuary legislation may be good in morals, but the life of the ocean is not amenable to the laws of man," for "the fish of the ocean appear or disappear for reasons over which man or his legislation has no control whatever." Alas, we know better than that now. As a leading outdoors journal replied, "The menhaden men, like most fishermen, want no restrictions on their business, they want the last fish and want it now, no matter what may be the future consequences."

There was more, however, to Captain Babson's vision of the ocean, which raised an issue that has actually become quite central to our current crisis. He declared that "the great highway of the nation should be ever open to the enterprise of its citizens, and not be made a marine Yellowstone park simply for the purpose of pleasure."[5]

The creation of Yellowstone Park as a national heritage was perhaps the first great achievement of the conservation movement. Although we tend to think of that movement as a very late nineteenth- and early twentieth-century phenomenon, associated with the iconic figure of Teddy Roosevelt, Yellowstone was actually created by Congress shortly after the Civil War. It was President Ulysses S. Grant who in 1872 signed the bill designating it as our first national park. This was just two years after Congress established the first federal conservation agency, the United States Commission on Fish and Fisheries, in response to the alarming decline of many of America's most valued fish. Both events occurred right in the middle of that first menhaden industrial boom, while dozens of steamers were depleting the schools to supply the mushrooming menhaden factories, thus displaying to conservationists that fundamental ecological concept of the interdependence of species (as we saw in chapter 5) and inciting them to more vigorous action.

As conservationism continued to develop as a powerful force in the ensuing decades and century, freshwater and saltwater anglers were always part of the vanguard of the movement.[6] Indeed, Captain

Babson's fury was aimed explicitly at those New Jersey "amateur fishermen" who were misleading Congress into believing that bluefish, striped bass, and other prized predators were becoming scarce because they could no longer find an abundance of menhaden. The passion and political engagement of anglers not only helped create our wonderful national park system, but also defined these parks as places where recreational fishing in a natural setting would be guaranteed for all future generations.[7] When Captain Babson thundered against turning parts of the ocean into "a marine Yellowstone park simply for the purpose of pleasure," he was expressing a nineteenth-century commercial version of the old Calvinist disdain for the idle recreation that the Puritans condemned in the Indians and that John Smith prophesied for the future New World. But the recreational anglers of the 1880s were certainly not lobbying for turning the seas into marine parks where commercial fishing would be banned, as it always has been in our national parks. Indeed, they were allies of commercial fishermen in opposition to the reduction industry, which was destroying the forage of the food and game fish sought by both groups.

A century later, the situation was quite different. The collapse of the marine environment had become alarming and ever more obviously caused not by nature but by people. The old alliance between anglers and commercial fishermen had been replaced by frequent conflicts. The traditional conservationism that emphasized preserving the environment for use was being challenged by those segments of the new environmentalism that seek to minimize human usages of the natural world.[8] Although many anglers were and still are activists within the environmentalist movement, parts of that movement have been formulating visions and agendas that do not include recreational fishing and are even hostile to it. At the beginning of the twenty-first century, contradictions between recreational fishers and some environmentalists were threatening to turn into open hostilities over the issue of Marine Protected Areas (MPAs), some of which might well be described as marine versions of Yellowstone Park.

The divisive issue is: What kind of version? Of course commercial fishermen as a body do not want any part of the sea set off as any kind of version of the national parks, where commercial fishing has always been forbidden. Of course recreational anglers as a body would love to see areas analogous to national parks, where they could fish, with appropriate limits and other regulations, but where commercial fishing would be prohibited not only from scooping up the fish but also from devastating their habitat with trawling machines. Some environmentalists, however, advocate quite a different version of MPAs: as areas where no fishing at all would be allowed.[9]

Feuding over Marine Protected Areas has led to some bitter spats between sportfishing and environmental organizations. The most pernicious problem has been the belief among many anglers that all MPAs would be no-fishing zones or that most environmentalists think they should be. Long before the term "Marine Protected Area" originated, anglers, acting for many decades as self-defined "conservationists" and later in alliance with "environmentalists," led the struggle to create what would now be called MPAs: for example, areas where certain equipment (such as purse seines or pound nets) is barred; or where dumping of certain kinds of material is not allowed; or where certain species cannot be caught; or where jet skis are banned (as in the Florida Keys National Marine Sanctuary, where commercial collection of coral is also banned); or where no commercial finfishing is permitted (as in the New York waters of Raritan Bay); or where, for that matter, reduction fishing for menhaden is not permitted (as in the coastal waters of all but two Atlantic states).[10] In response to the threat, real or perceived, of extensive "no-take" MPAs, a flurry of "right to fish" laws have been introduced in many states and the U.S. Congress.

Those environmentalists who do want to see many prime fishing areas turned into no-fishing MPAs include three overlapping constituencies. First, there are those who simply believe that the populations of innumerable species of fish are now so depleted and so close to virtual extinction that some fairly large areas, areas historically abundant with fish and therefore prime zones for both commercial and recreational fishing, should be turned into no-take MPAs that ban even catch-and-release fishing, so that these sites could serve as nurseries for large-scale restoration.[11] Second, there are those who seek to restore what some call marine "wilderness," where human activities are not permitted to interfere with nature in any significant way. Fights over the definition of "wilderness," and how or even whether wilderness should be open to use, have long been an integral part of American culture and history, so there's nothing fundamentally new in the current clashes between anglers who want to fish in waters they think of as wilderness and those who think of wilderness as waters where there are no anglers.[12] The third constituency pushing for extensive no-fishing zones comprises those animal rights activists, led by People for the Ethical Treatment of Animals, whose ultimate goal is to abolish fishing altogether, thus turning all the world's seas into a single no-take Marine Protected Area.

The disunity between anglers and environmentalists threatens to fracture an essential alliance that has worked effectively on issues such as industrial pollution, promiscuous dumping of potentially toxic dredge materials, and commercial overfishing. The largest political constituency in America that is vitally concerned about the ecological health of our coastal waters consists of the 12 million saltwater recreational anglers and their organizations. And the most powerful political infrastructure in America that is fundamentally committed to the ecological health of our coastal waters consists of environmental organizations, with their collective membership of 10 million.[13] An alliance between these two may be the only political force capable of protecting and restoring our marine environment.

Is there a realistic possibility of any working alliance that encompasses the entire spectrum of recreational anglers and environmentalists, from the most unabashed "meat fisherman" to the most uncompromising animal rights activist? Yes, there is at least one such possibility. Protecting menhaden from the reduction industry is one issue that every angler and every environmentalist can enthusiastically support and unite around. Even those environmentalists who want a pure wilderness ocean as uncontaminated as possible by all human activities, as well as uncompromising animal rights activists who adamantly oppose all fishing, can certainly back limiting, or maybe even abolishing, the reduction industry. Even anglers who want to be sure they get enough menhaden for bait, whether they snag the bunkers themselves or buy them at a bait shop that got them from a commercial bait fisherman, can certainly back limiting or even abolishing the reduction industry. After all, thirteen of the fifteen Atlantic states have already gone all the way and outlawed the industry in their waters.

ANGLERS TO THE RESCUE

There is no doubt whatsoever about the main cause of the depletion of saltwater fish. It is industrialized fishing—originally pioneered by the nineteenth-century menhaden fishery. A recent peer-reviewed study showed that "industrialized fisheries" typically reduce the biomass of each predator species they target "by 80% within 15 years of exploitation." This is a conservative calculation, according to the authors, whose analysis shows that in the past fifty years "the global ocean has lost more than 90% of large predatory fishes," including the bigger ocean species such as tuna, swordfish, and marlin as well as groundfish such as cod, halibut, and flounder.[14] Commenting on the study, lead author Ransom Myers, who holds the Killam Chair of Ocean Studies at Canada's Dalhousie University, said, "Since 1950, with the onset of industrialized fisheries, we have rapidly reduced the resource base to less than 10 percent—not just in some areas, not just for some stocks, but for entire communities of these large fish species from the tropics to the poles."[15]

Recreational anglers have been, for obvious reasons, among the very first to notice this collapse of fish stocks and to begin to take action. Recognizing that their own fishing can contribute to the decline of fish populations, most anglers now scrupulously obey the very strict limits placed on their catch. Many have switched to circle hooks or even barbless hooks to minimize mortality of released fish, and a growing number are committed to catch-and-release fishing only. Organizations of saltwater anglers such as the Coastal Conservation Association and the Recreational Fishing Alliance have mushroomed, linked up regionally, and focused increasingly on conservation. Whether meeting in their local fishing clubs, out with friends on a small boat, or chatting with strangers next to them on the rail of a party boat, saltwater anglers are almost as likely to be talking about what's necessary to save the fish as to be swapping stories about catching them. As part of the rapidly growing marine environmental movement, they have been in the vanguard in working to curtail the most destructive practices of the commercial fisheries: bottom-trawling machines that strip-mine and scrape the seabed flat, indiscriminately snaring all the fish in an area while transforming their habitat into a featureless, barren desert; long lines up to a hundred miles in length with thousands of baited hooks designed to catch swordfish, tuna, and marlin while incidentally killing innumerable other fish as well as countless animals including sea turtles, marine mammals, and sea birds; huge drift nets and gill nets, some forty miles long, that sometimes float loose, trapping and killing every form of marine life they encounter; wholesale slaughter and dumping of unwanted "bycatch"; and the deadly purse seine, the invention that revolutionized the menhaden industry, almost wiped out European herring in the 1960s, and is now used to scoop up schools of fish as large as tuna.[16]

Among all the contradictions between commercial and recreational fishing, none has generated more acrimony than the menhaden reduction industry. This is hardly a new phenomenon, as we saw in the history of the conflicts in the nineteenth century. For decades the industry—today incarnate in Omega Protein—has been wrapping itself in the mantle of the Puritan work ethic, portraying itself as a representative of the working class, and caricaturing recreational fishers as a wealthy elite that menaces the jobs of hardworking people.

Take, for example, a statement by Barney White, then corporate vice president of Omega Protein and chairman of one of its front organizations, the National Fish Meal and Oil Association, in a 1997 press release put out by Niels Moore, Omega's unofficial representative in many venues: "Political pressure groups like the ones attacking the menhaden industry in New Jersey are run by a wealthy, privileged elite who want the water for their personal enjoyment. . . . These radical recreational fishing advocates are unconcerned about the rights or the welfare of the people who make their living from the sea."[17] Expressing the same contempt for the pleasure-seeking recreational anglers that the Puritans expressed for the lazy, pleasure-seeking Indians, the menhaden industry asserts "rights" and legitimacy based on its industrious and profitable exploitation of natural resources—all, of course, in the interest of working people.

Just how concerned is Omega with the jobs and welfare of the workers in the industry? When Omega bought out American Protein in 1997, its only significant competitor on the Atlantic coast, it immediately closed the Ampro factory and decommissioned its fleet, even though the ships were right across Cockrell's Creek from its own facilities, thus throwing two hundred men and women out of work.[18] And when I interviewed Barney White in 2001, he waxed enthusiastic about the introduction of the power block because "the nets no longer had to be pulled by hand," which "enabled us to cut way down on our labor cost by employing far fewer men." And he explained Omega's financial problems this way: "When we paid men twenty-five cents an hour it was much easier to make a profit."[19] Of course, neither White nor any of the other Omega spokesmen ever mention the millions of dollars in cash, stock options, and other forms of profit drawn from the company by billionaire Malcolm Glazer, his son Avram, and the Malcolm Glazer Family Limited Partnership, who owned and controlled Omega until they sold it for $76 million at the end of 2006.[20]

The chorus of Omega voices only sang its familiar song about rich, selfish recreational anglers louder in 2005 and 2006 in response to the first challenge to the company's unrestricted right to all the menhaden in Chesapeake Bay. Toby Gascon, the official spokesman for the company, issued a press release that stated: "These fanatical big-game angler organizations appear willing to go to any lengths of deception and defamation in their attempts to expand the sport-fishing industry at the expense of the centuries-old, sustainable harvest of menhaden."[21] Omega's CEO, multimillionaire Joseph L. von Rosenberg III, wrote a letter to the *Washington Post* denouncing the recreational anglers who were calling for some limit on the company's Chesapeake catch as just a clique of "wealthy yacht owners."[22] When Menhaden Matter—a broad coalition of environmental and angler organizations as well as scientists and economists—released a report demonstrating that the anglers who target menhaden-eating fish support ten times more jobs in Virginia than the reduction industry does, Gascon responded, "Unfortunately, everybody doesn't have the ability to buy $50,000 sport boats and go fishing in their spare time. Most people have to go to work, and that's what we want to keep providing."[23]

Is it true that saltwater recreational anglers are "wealthy yacht owners," "a wealthy privileged elite" oblivious to the lives of working people? Based on my own experience fishing in the state of New Jersey, whose anglers and their organizations Barney White specifically portrayed as a rich, idle coterie, this caricature seems ludicrous. Up and down the Jersey coast, party boats are often crowded elbow to elbow with just the kind of workers Captain John Smith envisioned, four centuries ago, recreating themselves by fishing. They might look a little different from Smith's mental picture, since many are Latino, African American, and Asian American. But the typical saltwater angler is still the same kind of working person who was fishing the New Jersey shore more than a century ago, described this way back in 1882: "Many a toil and desk-worn disciple of Isaak Walton" is lured to "bays and sounds along the New Jersey coast" where "bluefish, weakfish, and other food fishes" provide "excellent sport," "greatly to his own benefit, mentally and physically."[24] Today some of these fishers, it is true, own a boat themselves—just as John Smith envisioned way back in

1616. But the great majority of these boats are not the yachts of the wealthy but the realized dreams of the working men who own them, the vessels in which they can literally, as Smith put it, "recreate" themselves.

Just as I was writing these words, I got a phone call from Brian Faust, whose twenty-three-foot Proline, the *Layla*, is the boat I usually fish on. I knew he would get a good belly laugh out of Omega's caricatures of the "wealthy, privileged elite" New Jersey anglers. Brian is a Navy veteran who spent many years working as a plumber for the New Jersey Transit railroad until he was disabled by his job. Another boat I fished on was owned by George Policastro. After retiring from his job sorting mail with the U.S. Postal Service, George bought a small boat and fished almost every single day, weather and health allowing, from spring through late fall until his death in 2006 at the age of seventy-two. Brian is an implacable foe of the menhaden reduction industry, and so was George. Why?

It's easy to understand contradictions between recreational anglers and those commercial fishermen who go after food and game fish. They are competing for the same fish. But when Omega Protein accuses recreational anglers of being selfish people "who want the water for their personal enjoyment," it's hard to understand what this is supposed to mean. Recreational anglers are not competing with the reduction industry over shares of the menhaden population. They aren't trying to fill their freezers with bunker fillets or barbecuing whole bunkers on their outdoor grills. So what's their motive?

Maybe it's easiest if I describe my own motive. This book has its origin in the early morning hours of a late summer day back in 1999. I was one of three men rendezvousing at 6:30 a.m. with George and his nineteen-foot Parker, docked at a marina in Keyport, New Jersey, on the south shore of Raritan Bay. George usually took three other men, who chipped in to pay expenses (it was $25 each back then) and also cleaned the boat at the end of the day. His dock was near the mouth of Matawan Creek, a two-and-a-half-mile-long tidal creek.

The Matawan was once infamous for multiple fatal attacks in 1916 by a lone ten-foot shark (one of the very rare shark attacks in New Jersey history), and the Keyport harbor at its mouth was once at least equally famous for its marvelous oysters, sold as "Keyports" throughout New York City.[25] At low tides, one can still see acres of old oyster shells, grim reminders of our folly in allowing overfishing and pollution to annihilate the great oyster beds of the Matawan and all of Raritan Bay. Today the Matawan's main role in marine ecology is as a major nursery for juvenile bunkers. Indeed, because of such tributaries, the Raritan Bay estuary is second only to the Chesapeake as a menhaden nursery. And because of the menhaden presence, the mouth of the creek sometimes abounds in their usual predators: striped bass in the spring and fall; bluefish, weakfish, and fluke in the summer.

We had hardly left the dock, and the sun was barely up, when we saw a tumultuous cloud of birds and heard their shrieks as they circled and plummeted just beyond the flotilla of small sailboats anchored in the creek's mouth. Of course we knew what this meant: bluefish were blitzing a school of bunkers. We were after weakfish this day, not bluefish. The only other boat already fishing belonged to George's friend Walter, almost always the first one out, who confirmed that there were indeed weakfish feeding under the bluefish on the bits and pieces left over from the carnage. George, who was about as expert an angler as I know, had us all rig our sinkers on eighteen-inch droppers, so that our baited hooks would float on their thirty-six-inch monofilament leaders just that distance from the bottom, right at the depth where weakfish like to hang in this kind of situation. We were using worms, a weakfish favorite, for bait, thus allowing our rigs to get down unmolested through the bluefish, which have exceedingly little interest in worms when they have an opportunity to devour menhaden. The fishing was spectacular, though occasionally the bluefish, known locally as choppers, left us just the bloody front half of a weakfish with a telltale dental signature identifying the killer.

Some time after we had caught our limit, a menhaden spotter plane appeared. With one set of its purse seine, the menhaden boat that soon followed hauled in the entire bunker school as well as some of the bluefish and weakfish that had been feeding on them. Although the industry has been denying ever since the middle of the nineteenth century that it has any significant "bycatch," the evidence here was unmistakable: the carrier vessel's hold was so full that the crew "deck loaded" part of the catch, giving onlookers an opportunity to take pictures of dozens of bluefish and weakfish writhing among the masses of bunkers. But bycatch was not the main concern. The following day and for days after, the mouth of the Matawan and the bay waters surrounding it were barren of menhaden, and because there were no menhaden, there were no bluefish and weakfish.

I had no prior interest in menhaden and almost no knowledge about their history or the issues surrounding them. But this incident of minor strip mining was disturbing enough to push me onto the long trail that eventually led to this book. On that trail, as I have learned more and more about the history of the reduction industry, I have also learned about the motives of other recreational anglers, who, like me, would simply like to halt the industry's century-and-a-half-long assault on the ecology of our marine environment—even right there, in Raritan Bay. The battle to keep the menhaden purse seiners out of Raritan Bay first raged more than a century earlier, throughout the 1880s. In 1888 recreational anglers gave eyewitness testimony that "these menhaden men insist on coming into the shallow waters of the bay and in destroying the oyster beds by dragging their nets over them and depleting the waters of blue and weak fish, which follow in the wake of menhaden, upon which they feed."[26]

The organizations of recreational anglers are formidable opponents of the most exploitative commercial fisheries because they are intensely motivated, broad-based, and, drawing upon the wide experience of their membership, very knowledgeable about fish and their environment. Despite well-funded public relations campaigns and intense lobbying by the menhaden industry, the recreational community seems to be gaining support in both the public and the political arenas.

As a result, regulatory management of the menhaden fishery, and therefore perhaps of fisheries in general, has arrived at an historic moment for the marine environment, with some exciting unity between anglers and enviros.

The ASMFC Thinks the Unthinkable

Fishery management for decades has been a battleground where recreational and commercial fishers contend over seasonal and area restrictions, catch limits and allocations, and habitat protection for the remaining fish. On the Atlantic seaboard, the ongoing site for many of the struggles has been the Atlantic States Marine Fisheries Commission (ASMFC). In 2005, the ASMFC became the center of what may prove to be the crucial contest that will decide the fate of both Atlantic menhaden and the Chesapeake Bay.

To understand this story, one needs to know something about the ASMFC and its role in the larger history of federal government interactions with American fish and American fishers. From the time that Congress and Spencer Baird created the U.S. Fish Commission in 1871, the U.S. government has always treated the coastal environment — including the Great Lakes as well as the three saltwater coasts — as essentially the province of industry and commerce. While giving assistance to freshwater recreational anglers, mainly through the hatchery programs that began in the nineteenth century, it has consistently aided and supported the commercial interests that control what are called the "fisheries" of the coasts. Ever since the end of the nineteenth century, in fact, Baird's original U.S. Fish Commission has been, except for one brief period, explicitly under the auspices of the Department of Commerce. "The National Marine Fisheries Service" and "NOAA Fisheries" are merely newer names for the old Bureau of Commercial Fisheries.[27]

Limitations on Atlantic coast commercial fisheries have come mainly from the individual states. In fact, toward the end of the nineteenth century, after individual states had legislated limitations or even bans on the menhaden reduction industry, the industry almost succeeded in getting Congress to take all control away from the states, an effort that failed only because it was deemed unconstitutional.[28]

In 1942, Congress created the Atlantic States Marine Fisheries Commission, which was to operate under the auspices of an interstate compact among the fifteen Atlantic coastal states. The stated purpose of the commission is "the prevention of the depletion and physical waste of the fisheries." Each state has three representatives on the commission: the head of the state agency in charge of "conservation of the fisheries resources"; a member of the state legislature; and "a citizen, who shall have knowledge of the interest in the marine fisheries problem, to be appointed by the governor."[29] Each state has one vote. Once management plans are voted by the commission, each state is obliged to implement its mandatory requirements. If a state does not comply, the U.S. Secretary of Commerce can impose a moratorium on that state's fishery.

The entire internal structure of the ASMFC is based on the concept that each species, or a related group of species, constitutes a distinct "fishery" that should be sustained. Therefore each species or species group has its own Management Board. The fundamental problem with this concept and resulting structure is that it denies the most elementary understanding of marine ecology. Charter boat captain and sportswriter Al Ristori, one of the most knowledgeable contemporary authorities on Atlantic fish, calls this "the fairyland of fisheries management, where each species is managed separately as if it existed all alone in the ocean and had unlimited quantities of food available with only predation from man to prevent the species from covering the bottom of the ocean." How can species be maintained, much less restored —which is now the stated goal of the ASMFC—"while the status of what they eat," asks Ristori, "is completely ignored?"[30]

There are twenty-two of these Management Boards, including one for Atlantic menhaden. Except for one, each board was constituted, like the ASMFC itself, of three commissioners from each state. The sole exception was the Atlantic Menhaden Management Board.

In 1990, the governor of New Jersey appointed Tom Fote as one of the state's three commissioners on the ASMFC, a position he continued to hold as either the governor's appointee or the representative of the New Jersey legislature until mid-2005. The son of a newspaper deliveryman, Tom grew up fishing the docks of Brooklyn and has been a dedicated saltwater fisher ever since. Permanently disabled from severe wounds he suffered in Vietnam, he has devoted most of his active life since 1970 to preserving, restoring, and cleaning the marine environment. Tom still remembers how shocked he was when he first became a commissioner and discovered the unique and bizarre structure of the Atlantic Menhaden Management Board.[31] No other board included a representative of the industry it was supposed to be regulating. But the menhaden board was explicitly established to have "an equal number of representatives of interested states and representatives of the menhaden industry," plus a representative from the National Fish Meal and Oil Association, the industry's trade organization. In practice, the board included five official representatives from the menhaden corporations and one representative from each of five states, which meant that the industry had a vote equal to that of all fifteen states on the Atlantic seaboard! Moreover, the menhaden board's official Atlantic Menhaden Advisory Committee (AMAC) contained four industry representatives, including the president of Beaufort Fisheries, who were all sitting on both the menhaden board and AMAC.[32] AMAC had the responsibility of assessing the menhaden population and making recommendations to the menhaden board.

For eleven years, Tom helped lead a struggle, joined by an increasing number of recreational fishing organizations, to remove the industry foxes from the job of guarding the menhaden chickens. Finally, in 2001, the Atlantic Menhaden Management Board was reconstituted to match the structure of the twenty-one other Management Boards, with three representatives from each of the fifteen states and no representative from the industry.[33] AMAC was abolished and replaced by an advisory panel that included representatives of both the industry and the recreational fishing community. Since that time, the menhaden board has begun to pay some attention to menhaden not just as raw material for the reduction industry but as a vital component of the marine ecosystem, both as food for predators and as filterers of the water.

Nevertheless, unlike every other species of finfish managed by the ASMFC, there has never been any catch limit for menhaden. Every year each of the fifteen states implements specific catch limits for all the other species, as determined by the ASMFC. Both recreational anglers and all other commercial fisheries must accept these restrictions as the law, with criminal penalties for violations, and the federal police of the National Marine Fisheries Service, as well as state police, are available for enforcement. Only the menhaden industry has always had the unrestricted freedom to kill as many of its targeted species as it could.

Although the ASMFC has never chosen to restrict the menhaden industry, all but two of the fifteen states in the Atlantic compact have recognized the disastrous consequences of the wholesale slaughter of menhaden and therefore have banished the reduction industry from their waters. This has left Virginia and North Carolina as the only states benighted enough, or still sufficiently under the control of the industry, to allow this assault on their environment. One result has been to turn the Virginia waters of the Chesapeake into a true omega, the last vortex swallowing great portions of the remaining schools of Atlantic menhaden. These waters have therefore become a battle zone where the fate of both the species and the bay may be decided.

The enormous harvest of juvenile menhaden from the Virginia waters of the Chesapeake Bay may even be taking its toll on the bunker population in nearby North Carolina. The small North Carolina town of Beaufort was once the home of eight thriving menhaden reduction factories and a fleet of vessels. When Omega Protein monopolized the industry in 1997, the company decided to leave one small independent on the Atlantic coast—Beaufort Fisheries, the last survivor of an industry that had operated out of the port since shortly after the Civil War. Until recently, Beaufort Fisheries could usually fill its two six-hundred-ton ships from North Carolina waters. But in 2005, Beaufort's ships evidently could not find enough schools to warrant profitable fishing. As a result, menhaden landings in North Carolina hit a record low of 13.3 million pounds, and this was all from bait boats rather than reduction vessels. This crash in the menhaden catch was the primary reason cited by the North Carolina Division of Marine Fisheries for 2005 also being the year of the state's smallest commercial harvest on record for all fish and shellfish. In 2004, even with Beaufort Fisheries in action, North Carolina's total menhaden catch had been a mere 50 million pounds in a state where annual catches had been averaging more than 300 million pounds. In 2006, Jule Wheatly, the owner of Beaufort Fisheries, finally closed his company, which had been in business under various names since the 1880s.[34]

This leaves Omega Protein as the sole survivor of the entire reduction industry on the Atlantic coast. Omega's point of view was expressed by company spokesman Toby Gascon, who protested against any attempt to limit the company's catch in the Chesapeake: "The bottom line is we have no other place to fish."[35] "This industry has been forced over the years to compromise itself into a box," Gascon lamented, making some observers wonder what compromises he was talking about. "We have compromised all that we can. We have nowhere else to go."[36]

Poor victimized Omega Protein! They have nowhere else to fish. What about the twelve-hundred-square-mile coastal waters of Virginia and North Carolina (not to mention the Gulf of Mexico)? Or were these waters, once teeming with schools of menhaden, now too barren to support even Beaufort's two vessels? And beyond those twelve hundred square miles lie all the boundless ocean waters outside the three-mile jurisdiction of any state, all wide open and free. Why not fish there? That's what Omega's Reedville fleet of spotter planes and eleven ultramodern refrigerated ships, all equipped with the latest electronic equipment, were specifically designed for. Could it possibly be that those astonishingly vast oceanic schools, the schools that Hall Watters remembered spotting as far as fifty miles off the coast of Virginia and North Carolina, have long since been annihilated by the reduction industry? It was fifteen miles off Cape Hatteras, while working for a company later gobbled up by Omega, that Watters spotted a school as large as an island with fish so dense that they kept escaping the nets of a hundred boats.[37]

If it's true that Omega has "nowhere else to go" besides the Chesapeake, it's because, as Watters put it in 2001, "The industry overfished their own fishery, and they destroyed it themselves. And they're still at it." So now the industry seeks to destroy what's left—the menhaden in the Chesapeake as well as the bay itself.

We have already seen the consequences for the Chesapeake Bay, particularly in Maryland. Operating without any limit in the Virginia waters of the bay, Omega's concentrated fleet sweeps up billions of menhaden before they can reach Maryland waters, as well as more billions of juveniles trying to get back to the ocean from Maryland's river nurseries. Since the Chesapeake estuarine system is by far the largest nursery for Atlantic menhaden, Omega's huge harvest in the bay also has severe consequences for the other Atlantic states. Because one of the telltale symptoms of a declining population is a contracting range, these effects have been most severe in the outer reaches of menhaden's historic range, especially Maine, the other New England states, and Florida. And because the vast majority of Omega's Chesapeake catch consists of juveniles that have not reached the spawning age of three years, the entire Atlantic stock has a very low population of spawners, thus providing a slim margin of protection for the species.

After years of surging protest and demands for action from recreational anglers and environmentalists, the ASMFC finally made the bold, unprecedented suggestion that it might, possibly, consider the unthinkable: placing a cap on the reduction industry, either in Chesapeake Bay or coastwide. This act took the form of drafting "Addendum II," then releasing it in the form of a May 2005 "Public Comment Draft" with an exciting title designed to attract public interest— "Addendum II to Amendment 1 to the Interstate Fishery Management Plan for Atlantic Menhaden"—and scheduling public hearings on this document before a final decision in the fall.

The response was startling. Overflow throngs packed the public hearings. The ASMFC staff was deluged by more than twenty-six thousand written messages, overwhelmingly calling for the commission to ban Omega's fishing in the Chesapeake altogether, to impose a moratorium on it, or, at the very least, to put some limit on it.[38] Never in the sixty-three-year history of the ASMFC had there been anything remotely approaching this intensity of public response on any issue. Menhaden might be an obscure fish for most Americans, but evidently many had come to realize its vital importance.

On to Cockrell's Creek

An extraordinary coalition now rallied to the cause of menhaden and the environment. Besides many recreational fishing, conservation, and environmental organizations—including the Chesapeake Bay Foundation, Coastal Conservation Association, Environmental Defense, Maryland Saltwater Sportfishermen's Association, Maryland Public Interest Research Group, National Coalition for Marine Conservation, and the Recreational Fishing Alliance—scientists from the Atlantic Ecology Division of the EPA and Maryland's Department of Natural Resources, as well as Howard King, director of its Fisheries Service, helped lead the struggle. Another crucial coalition member was the Maryland Watermen's Association, the state's most powerful lobbying group of commercial fishermen.[39] Their participation raised the specter for Omega Protein of a revival of the old alliance of recreational and commercial fishers that had fought the menhaden reduction industry for decades in the nineteenth century.

And then there was Greenpeace. "The minute they showed up," wrote *Baltimore Sun* outdoors columnist Candus Thomson, "it was clear Greenpeace members would change the tenor of the debate": "No offense to the gentle folks who have been fighting the good fight for years, but Greenpeace knows how to wage a robust, bare-knuckles public war against a bully."[40]

Primed by years of media caricatures of Greenpeace, many may have been relieved, and others disappointed, when no bands of fanatical agitators burst in prepared for hand-to-hand combat. Greenpeace members did join the throngs at all twelve ASMFC hearings in states along the coast, but they were there to deliver well-researched, carefully reasoned arguments in favor of a coastwide moratorium on the reduction fishery. They also proved to be adept in uniting with many of the anglers, watermen, scientists, and environmentalists at these meetings, disseminating potent press releases and embarrassing Omega spokesman Toby Gascon. Toward the end of some of the hearings, a Greenpeace member would ask for a show of hands on how many people would favor a moratorium rather than a cap or limit, the only option offered by the ASMFC (other than doing nothing at all). Typically, about 80 to 90 percent would raise their hands.[41] Unlike most other environmental organizations, Greenpeace focuses on organizing and direct action. By late July, it was ready to launch—on the Chesapeake, and on to Reedville.

Although Cockrell's Creek had been a hub of the reduction industry for a century and a quarter, it had never hosted a flotilla like the one that sailed in from the bay on July 23, 2005. Between Omega Protein's ten gray-hulled menhaden ships, docked in front of the company's factory and airfield on one side of the creek, and the battleship-gray rusting hulks of abandoned menhaden ships on the other, dozens of Zodiacs, sportfishing boats, and kayaks circled with a twenty-foot image of a fish skeleton and bright yellow banners proclaiming FACTORY FISHING IS OVERKILL. Virginia Marine Police had seven patrol boats bellowing stern warnings and an airplane circling overhead to protect Omega from this Greenpeace-led armada, but the mellow

FIGURE 8.1 Demonstration in Cockrell's Creek in front of Omega Protein's factory and fleet, July 2005. Photo courtesy of Greenpeace.

tone of the demonstrators soon had the police providing one of their boats as a site for Greenpeace representatives to meet with the press.

The demonstration garnered lots of media attention, but I believe a more interesting story, with more potential, was developing behind the scenes. The biggest boat that sailed with the demonstrators was the *Captain Jason*, a forty-eight-passenger ferry chartered by Jim Price on behalf of Greenpeace from the Maryland Eastern Shore town of Crisfield, once the nation's largest oyster-producing port. As a carload of us joined the early arrivals on the dock, we were met with sullen hostility from its captain, Larry, and a small group of good old boys hanging out on a couple of benches. Captain Larry said he hadn't realized he was going to be transporting Greenpeace radicals, and he wasn't about to allow any of them on his boat. "Besides," he said, "I'm not taking my boat out in this blow. . . . It's more than 30 knots out there," he claimed, probably close to double what it really was.

Long conversations were getting nowhere when Larry blurted out a more straightforward reason: "I've got to live with these people," meaning Omega Protein and the men who work its boats. As Charles

Hutchinson, who was there representing the Maryland Saltwater Sportfishermen's Association later explained, "The watermen believe that if you hurt one, you hurt them all. Get a waterman off to the side, and he'll tell you that what Omega is doing is bad, but he's not going to say that in public."[42] What it took to persuade Larry was a private conversation with Jim Price, that fifth-generation waterman who looks and talks just like one of those good old boys on the dock, plus Jim's raising the charter price for the day's outing from the agreed-upon $800 to $1,500. Another part of the new agreement was that there could be no banners or signs on board, including the T-shirts prominently worn by the Greenpeace people. The *Captain Jason* was to be officially a "press" and "observer" boat, not an actual part of the demonstration.

To enforce this, along came a paunchy Somerset County sheriff, another good old boy, in a Florida Gator T-shirt hanging over but not entirely concealing the nine-millimeter tucked into the back of his shorts. Sheriff Gator threatened to arrest anyone with a banner, a sign, or a Greenpeace T-shirt or anyone shouting slogans while at Reedville.

The real story, from my view, is how relations changed as the day wore on. Keith Walters—himself a longtime Eastern Shore resident, one of the founders of the Maryland Saltwater Sportfishermen's Association, a record-holder four decades ago for Maryland striped bass, now seventy-five and still writing an outdoors column for a local paper—recalls his own changes that day. "I was a little apprehensive," he said. "I expected a bunch of really radical, hostile kids. But they were nice kids, idealistic, well educated, all friendly. And some of the best-looking girls. I really liked them."[43] One could see the same changes taking place in the attitudes of Captain Larry and Sheriff Gator, who, like Keith and some of the other old-timers on board, seemed to expect the young Greenpeace people to be landlubbers who would get seasick or at least complain about the fact that the boat on which we were committed from morning to evening had no toilet.

Although the wind wasn't thirty knots, it was strong and coming from the north, thus rocking the boat violently from side to side on our three-hour east-west trip from Crisfield to Reedville. At times during the day's voyages, the waves did reach about four feet in height and the boat was battered by spray as it plunged from crest to bottom. "I was holding on for dear life," Keith remembers, "but the girl next to me was enjoying the spray." Maybe some of these "kids" were used to running around in Zodiacs chasing whale ships on the Pacific.

Evidence of common attitudes around the bay came into view as we made a brief stop at Smith's Island to drop off a couple who worked at the Chesapeake Bay Foundation's permanent station on the island. At the end of the crabbers' pier, stacked with hundreds of crab pots, was a big sign proclaiming DO NOT SUPPORT CHESAPEAKE BAY FOUNDATION.

Once we reached Cockrell's Creek, relations began to shift toward a feeling that we were all more than literally in the same boat. When one of the Greenpeace inflatables got swamped, Captain Larry cheerfully helped rescue the young man clinging to it, although Sheriff Gator still enforced the rule that he had to strip off his Greenpeace T-shirt before coming on board. Another crisis came when one of the main Greenpeace organizers was directing Larry to repeatedly maneuver the boat so many feet forward and backward, this way and that, to get the best angles for photographs. One such backward move left *Captain Jason*'s propeller hopelessly entangled in the line from a crab trap. Instead of being furious, Larry, who was wearing only shorts, calmly strapped a diving tank on his broad, muscular back, pulled on a diving mask, grabbed a big knife, strode to the stern, dropped on his back into the water, and emerged in a few minutes having cut the line free. Then, without any objection, he went back to maneuvering *Captain Jason* for more Greenpeace photo ops.

On the way back, there were lots more conversations among this medley of young greens and what some would call old rednecks, anglers, watermen, a few reporters, and even me and the sheriff. I guess Sheriff Gator was as surprised to find out that my main field of writing and teaching is the Vietnam War as I was to find out that he had been in charge of security for General William Westmoreland.

We arrived back at Crisfield after 9 p.m., having spent the whole day together. As we all said our good-byes, Captain Larry and the sheriff shook hands with each of us. Both men wished us all lots of success, telling us that we were fighting the good fight. I believe that these precious moments suggest the potential for an alliance that could change the course not just for menhaden but for the whole marine environment—and maybe even beyond.

CHALLENGES

Two weeks after leading the flotilla of menhaden champions into Cockrell's Creek and just before the ASMFC was due to meet, Greenpeace staged a quite different kind of demonstration. Turning the tables on the industry, Greenpeace got its own spotter plane (through Lighthawk, an environmental association of volunteer pilots) to locate Omega's vessels as they approached the bunkers. While their chartered helicopter photographed the scene, Greenpeace activists in three inflatables sped to the site and repeatedly scattered the schools. Although it took place for only a small part of one day, this was the first limit that anybody had ever placed on Omega's catch in Chesapeake Bay. The company tried to call in the Coast Guard, but the Guard stated that Greenpeace was not doing anything illegal. After all, as Greenpeace spokeswoman Nancy Hwa pointed out in a simple statement with profoundly radical implications, "The fish do not belong to Omega."[44]

The ASMFC was now in the glare of the media's spotlight, an unaccustomed and no doubt uncomfortable position. Eyes were now even turned to Addendum II, the fishery-management-lingo document that was supposed to guide public discussion. The cover of Addendum II proudly displays the "ASMFC Vision Statement": "Healthy, self-sustaining populations for all Atlantic coast fish species or successful restoration well in progress by the year 2015." Yet the document seems

FIGURE 8.2 Greenpeace Zodiac breaking up Omega's fishing on the Chesapeake, August 2005. Photo courtesy of Greenpeace.

to have a contrary vision and goal: maintaining an industry that severely threatens many of the coast's most-valued fish species. By claiming that "the stock is considered to be healthy coastwide," Addendum II demonstrates that the ASMFC definition of a "healthy" menhaden population simply means there are enough fish for the reduction industry to catch and remain profitable. Only by ignoring the history of the species is it possible to call the population "healthy," since menhaden now occupy only a fraction of their historical range, and a shrinking range is a key indicator of a collapsing species. Addendum II does concede that "the potential" exists for "localized depletion" in the Chesapeake Bay because of "concentrated harvest" and that "existing data suggest that predator-prey relationships could currently be compromised and recruitment of larval menhaden has chronically declined during the last two decades."[45]

When it turns to the data, Addendum II reveals truly alarming facts and statistics, but interprets them in ways friendly to the reduction industry. Although acknowledging that "recruitment" (the number of menhaden that survive to age one) not only has been declining for decades but is now at an all-time low, it suggests all kinds of possible causes except one: overfishing. A table almost inadvertently reveals that between 2000 and 2004 the percentage of age-three menhaden caught by Omega in the Chesapeake plummeted from about 25 percent to 6 percent, showing that among the hundreds of millions of fish netted each year there are hardly any mature fish capable of spawning. Tables show an erratic but remorseless decline of the coastwide catch. And yet the coastwide stock is defined as "healthy"—despite the fact, unmentioned, that no schools of adult menhaden had been seen north of Cape Cod since 1993.[46]

There is not a single word in this thirty-three-page document about the Chesapeake's ecological problems, including hypoxia, nutrient overload, the dead zone, loss of 90 percent of its sea grasses and 99 percent of its oysters, and diseased rockfish, much less the possible benefits from menhaden's filter feeding. Indeed, from this document a reader would never guess that menhaden are filter feeders or that they eat anything at all, much less the algae central to the bay's problems.

The most revealing—and disgraceful—feature of Addendum II is a solution it proposes to the Chesapeake's skyrocketing percentage of the total Atlantic catch. After implicitly blaming any problem on New Jersey's banishment of the industry from its waters in 2002, it suggests that the reduction industry would not be concentrating so heavily on the Chesapeake if it were given "renewed access to traditional fishing grounds, now closed to purse-seining north of Virginia."[47] This passage might as well have been written by Omega Protein, which has been complaining ever since 2002 that New Jersey is being unjust or even illegal by prohibiting the company from mining the state's waters, a crucial part of its "traditional" grounds. By officially proposing that New Jersey and other states repeal their restrictions, the ASMFC flaunts its ongoing complicity with the industry. It also violates a founding principle of this interstate compact, that the ASMFC will never attempt "to repeal or prevent the enactment of any legislation . . . by any signatory state imposing additional conditions and restrictions to conserve its fisheries."[48] The ASMFC is supposed to be in the business of developing only more stringent, never more lenient, regulations than its member states.

So the ASMFC seemed to be maintaining its traditional belief that its mission was to protect and foster the menhaden reduction industry, not the environment or the public. But given the extraordinary public support for a meaningful cap, if not a full moratorium, the commissioners evidently felt they had to do something. So they voted to cap the reduction industry's catch in the Chesapeake Bay at 105,783 metric tons a year for five years, while undertaking more scientific study. As the *Washington Post* editorialized:

> The cap of 105,783 metric tons a year is not exactly drastic; that's Omega's average catch of menhaden from the Chesapeake for the first five years of this decade. Moreover, the menhaden catch has been steadily declining for years. The cap, which is actually greater than Omega's catch in several recent years, would impose little hardship.[49]

Others put it more bluntly, calling this so-called cap or limit merely a license to allow Omega to keep doing what it was already doing — for at least another five years.

Omega, however, was not about to allow even this symbolic gesture to stand. It rejected the idea that the ASMFC or anybody else had the authority to impose any limit whatsoever on its leave-no-fish-behind "harvest" of menhaden. So it turned to the Virginia legislature.

As with all ASMFC decisions, the commission's limits, quotas, allocations, and other regulations must actually be implemented by the individual states. In this case, the only state that had to implement the cap was Virginia, because Omega's entire Chesapeake catch comes from Virginia's waters. While most of the media around the bay welcomed the limit as a promising first step, others cautioned that the Virginia legislature, "seduced by the contributions Omega spreads around," is accustomed "to do the bidding of Omega Protein," which is "fighting to preserved unfettered access to Virginia's bounty."[50]

For years Omega's lobbying and well-targeted campaign donations have been building an impregnable political fortress in Virginia. Whereas every other species of saltwater fish in Virginia is regulated by the Virginia Marine Resources Commission, menhaden are regulated by the state's General Assembly. And there Omega has had its minions weave a tangled web of legislation to ensnare any attempt at regulation. Three members of the House of Delegates did introduce bills to implement the ASMFC cap, but these all met sudden death at the hands of the appropriate subcommittee. As the *Virginian-Pilot* pointed out in an editorial neatly titled "If Only Menhaden Wrote Campaign Checks," five members of the subcommittee, including its chair, were all beneficiaries of Omega's campaign largesse.[51] As Omega spokesman Toby Gascon promptly gloated, "We think our business was taken care of in the Virginia House."[52]

If Virginia failed to implement the cap, the ASMFC's charter gave it congressional authorization to ask the Secretary of Commerce to completely shut down Virginia's menhaden fishery. Yet an entire year went by while the ASMFC took no action despite the open defiance of its authority. The state's attorney general, Robert McDonnell—another recipient of Omega campaign financing—wrote a bizarre brief arguing that the ASMFC had no legal authority to mandate the cap.[53] Omega brazenly announced that it was moving an additional ship from the Gulf to Reedville, effectively expanding its Chesapeake fleet by 10 percent, and then conducted its 2006 fishing season as though the ASMFC didn't exist.[54]

While the ASMFC dithered about what to do in the face of nose-thumbing defiance from both Omega and the state of Virginia, the whole concept of coastal management, especially of migratory species, was plunged into jeopardy. If one company and one state could refuse to implement a token limit on the only species without any limit, why should any state or any other entity comply with any other ASMFC regulation they found onerous? What would this mean for those millions of saltwater anglers who dutifully obeyed the ASMFC limit for every species and who also meticulously measured and released every fish a sixteenth of an inch below ASMFC-mandated minimums?

The whole charade ended in late 2006, when the ASMFC rubber-stamped a "compromise" negotiated between Virginia governor Tim Kaine and Omega. Instead of the previously mandated cap of 105,783 metric tons, the company will be permitted to remove 109,020 metric tons from the Chesapeake annually for the next five years. If the catch falls short in any one year, Omega can add the shortfall to its next year's quota, up to a limit of 122,740 metric tons. As Toby Gascon gleefully acknowledged, "It's not going to reduce the amount of fish we're going to catch."[55]

Toby Gascon also had something else to say: "This allows us to still remain in business."[56] Was the company's survival actually in danger? And if so, why?

The Fish of the Future?

D

OES OMEGA MEAN THE LAST?

Why has Omega been acting as though the corporation—in other words the entire menhaden reduction industry—is fighting for its very life? Because it's true.

But why is it fighting for its life? Because it embodies, in a blatantly naked form, problems fundamental to the industry throughout the history explored in this book.

One might think that Omega, having attained a virtual monopoly over the whole industry, would be an extremely profitable enterprise, but most years it can barely eke out a profit. This may seem surprising, because a monopoly, that pot of gold at the end of the capitalist rainbow, is supposed to grant corporations what economists call "monopoly pricing power" (unless their prices are regulated by the government), which means that if they are providing something that people need or want, they should be able to name their price and make it stick.

The want doesn't have to be a fundamental need such as food, clothing, or shelter. It can be an induced need like tobacco, alcohol, or some other drug. It can be a need or want determined by the nature of society, an occupation, a hobby, or just fashions, fads, and desires (healthy or unhealthy) such as electricity, telephone service, cars, chess sets, plows, computers, prostitutes, casinos, shovels, taxi service, golf clubs, razors, paint, or lipstick. Although Omega has a virtual monopoly on catching the menhaden, none of the products made from menhaden fulfills any need or want that is not satisfied at least as well by some other product. Take paint and lipstick. If a company could maintain a monopoly on either paint or lipstick, it would be enormously profitable. Lots of people need or want paint or lipstick, but nobody particularly wants either paint or lipstick containing menhaden oil from Omega Protein. Chickens, pigs, and cattle need food, but they don't need food made partly from menhaden. Neither you nor your cat needs to eat menhaden, not even to get your omega-3 fatty acids, a topic we will get back to. And so on with each and every one of the products advertised on Omega's Web site, including rust inhibitors, water repellents, alkyd resins, ceramic deflocculants, plant fertilizer, margarine, and insecticide. Most of these are not even the company's actual products.

Omega's actual products are just fish meal, fish oil, and fish solubles — all made from menhaden. That simple fact has to be stated, because of legal requirements, in the mandatory financial reports (Form 10Q and Form 10K) that the company must regularly file with the Securities and Exchange Commission. Omega's reports also reveal that each of these products is in continual competition with a host of other, similar products that have the same functions:

> The principal competition for the Company's fish meal and fish solubles is from other global production of marine proteins as well as other protein sources such as soybean meal and other vegetable or ani-

mal protein products. . . . Other globally produced fish oils provide the primary market competition for the Company's fish oil, as well as soybean and palm oil. . . . Fish meal prices have historically borne a relationship to prevailing soybean meal prices, while prices for fish oil are generally influenced by prices for vegetable fats and oils, such as soybean and palm oils.[1]

Omega doesn't mention that most of the competing fish oils are byproducts of fish caught and prepared for food, and hence don't involve destroying the ecology to produce nonfood industrial commodities. As for the main competing vegetable substance, the fishing industry trade journal *National Fisherman* put the matter quite bluntly: "On the industrial side of the fishery, where menhaden is processed into feed for poultry and pigs, the demand for fish is depressed by a surplus of soy, which serves the same purpose."[2]

Thus Omega as a monopoly has merely inherited the fundamental contradictions of the whole reduction industry throughout its entire lengthy history. For not one of the industrial commodities made out of dead menhaden has ever fulfilled a real need or even a desire that was not met by some other substance that could be obtained without devastating the environment.

There is one reason, and one reason only, why menhaden have been the source material for an industry that has played such important roles in the economic and natural history of the United States during most of the nation's existence. It is the reason the reduction fishery has been, overall, the biggest American fishery for almost a century and a half. It is the reason it has also consistently been the most industrialized and efficient of all fisheries in America and possibly the world. It is because there are—or rather were—so many menhaden, swimming in such huge, densely packed schools, that they were so easy—and therefore so cheap—to catch and convert into industrial products. The key term is "cheap."

For this industry's products to be relatively cheap and therefore profitable, they also had to be mass-produced in vast quantities. But that requires factories and well-equipped fishing vessels, both of which demand significant capital to produce and maintain. Because the cheapness of the industry's products has always depended on both the tremendous quantity of available menhaden and the resultant great volume of production, this capital-intensive industry has throughout its history experienced sudden waves of bankruptcy and consolidation whenever the population of the fish crashed. Why did the menhaden population crash successively in each region of the Atlantic coast, beginning with the 1879 disaster in Maine? Because of overfishing. Why did the industry compulsively overfish, always killing the goose that laid its golden eggs, that favorite metaphor in all those nineteenth-century newspaper articles? Because the industry *had* to overfish to generate its profits. Why did it have to overfish? Because the cheapness of its output, and thus its sole competitive advantage, depended on its vast scale of production. And so on, around and around, the industry has run its vicious cycles.

The history of these industrial commodities demonstrates how entirely *un*necessary the reduction industry's rape of the environment has been. At each stage, the industry has simply reinvented itself to come up with cheap substitutes for competing products. Let's take them in historical order: fertilizer, industrial oils, farm animal and pet feed, farmed fish feed, and finally health food.

Fertilizer in the nineteenth century. Using menhaden to fertilize corn in "old ground," as the Indians taught the Pilgrims—that was a need. Because farmers on Long Island and Connecticut later exhausted their land, by employing monoculture without either rotating their crops or adequately fertilizing with animal or vegetable waste, maybe they needed to catch menhaden and spread them on their fields. Ironically, their ignorance of the land's need for natural forage helped pave the way for what came next, a major industry that would strip the sea of its natural forage.

Of course industrial society needs industrial-scale fertilizer to grow the food for its large nonfarming population, but there was never any need for this fertilizer to be manufactured from huge quantities of dead menhaden. After all, menhaden have never been needed for successful agriculture in any other country. They were just so abundant and so easy to catch on America's Atlantic coast that it was, for a while, cheaper to use them than all the other widely available animal, vegetable, and mineral fertilizers. As soon as the chemical processes of the early twentieth century were able to synthesize cheaper fertilizer, the processing of menhaden into fertilizer was wiped out as an industry.

Industrial oils. Menhaden supplanted whale oil after the Civil War simply because overfishing had made whales scarce, whereas menhaden were superabundant and convenient. Menhaden oil—as lubricant, illuminant, and industrial additive—was for a while nothing more than a cheaper substitute for various readily available vegetable oils, mineral oils, lard, kerosene and other coal oils, and, very briefly, petroleum and natural gas. In fact, much of the menhaden oil that was sold by the industry was used merely to adulterate other oils; a barrel labeled "whale oil" or "linseed oil" often contained mainly menhaden oil.[3] Menhaden oil is no longer used as either a lubricant or illuminant, and today every usage as an industrial additive is merely a cheap substitute for some other kind of oil.

Animal feed. Whatever combination of evolution and human intelligence produced modern chickens, pigs, and cows, there is no evidence that eating fish was part of their design. In fact, because menhaden products offer no real benefit to chickens or chicken producers, they have already lost much of their small share of the poultry feed market to soybeans. (Many people, myself included, are even willing to pay a higher price in the supermarket for eggs labeled from "vegetarian-fed hens.") As for pet dogs and cats, there's always been plenty of animal tissue left over from slaughterhouses and the industrial processing of food fish to satisfy their carnivorous needs and desires.

As Omega Protein tries to reinvent the industry once again, it has been turning to two new usages as clever formulas for converting the cooked and crushed bodies of menhaden into corporate profits: feed for salmon farms and omega-3 health food supplements. Both represent attempts to move beyond the archaic uses of the nineteenth and twentieth centuries into the ethos of the early twenty-first century. But each has major difficulties.

The giant salmon farms that have sprung up in recent years have so many problems of their own that it's not at all clear they will offer a profitable market for huge quantities of menhaden. These problems are so serious that Alaska has actually banned all salmon farming and has thus preserved the nation's healthiest stock of wild salmon. Crowded by the hundreds of thousands into pens extending over hundreds of acres and located near the habitats of wild salmon, farmed salmon have been the source of wildly contagious diseases, some of them new, such as infectious salmon anemia virus (ISAV). Their feces and other wastes have polluted nearby waters, which have also shown oxygen depletion from the packed masses of penned fish. Massive escapes from storm-damaged pens have led to breeding with wild salmon that threatens the long-term survivability of the oceanic species by compromising its genetic stock. And some studies have shown that farmed salmon have high levels of contaminants, especially PCBs and mercury.[4]

Then there is the fundamental irrationality of farming salmon or other predatory fish: these fish need to be fed fish. To produce one pound of farmed salmon, that fish had to be fed three pounds of some other fish. Since only about one-third of the salmon ends up in the fillets lying on the ice in the supermarket (the rest is head, guts, bones, and so on), each pound that you see there took about nine pounds of wild fish to produce. Those nine pounds of wild forage fish—such as menhaden—had to be removed from the ocean, where they would have fed wild fish, and run through an industrial process that converts them into pellets and oil to be fed to a salmon in a pen that is menacing wild salmon and other fish with pollution, genetic threats, hypoxia, and disease. This form of aquaculture is evidently bad, not good, for the marine environment.[5]

These problems with salmon farming by no means apply to all forms of aquaculture. Farming of shellfish, such as oysters, clams, and mussels, is actually quite beneficial to the environment because these are all filter feeders that help clean the waters in which they are raised. For many centuries, herbivorous fish such as carp have been farmed in China, Japan, and Vietnam with great benefit to the ecology, especially in rice paddies. The extensive farming of tilapia, an herbivorous fish originally from the Nile, is producing bountiful quantities of inexpensive food. Farmed catfish are so plentiful that Congress, partly to protect the prices charged by Mississippi catfish farmers and partly in a spiteful act of vengeance against Vietnam, in 2003 passed legislation, signed by President George W. Bush, that makes it illegal for vendors to call Vietnamese catfish "catfish."[6]

The problems inherent in salmon farming, plus the competition from other forms of aquaculture, raise big questions about whether this industry will turn out to be a reliable life preserver for the menhaden reduction industry, even if farmed salmon had to be fed mainly menhaden. But they don't. Most of the fish meal and fish oil being fed to the penned salmon currently consists of anchovies, mackerel, herring, and sardines. Furthermore, in global fish farming, soybean meal is beginning to take market share from fish meal, even for feeding fish in offshore pens, especially in China's huge aquaculture industry. One reason is that food made from soybean meal is more friendly to the environment, since it floats on the surface until eaten by the fish instead of sinking and rotting.[7] So here too, Omega's monopoly on menhaden gives it no monopoly pricing power.

But don't we need "omega"? When Zapata Corporation turned its menhaden subsidiary into a separate corporation in 1998 and gave it the name Omega Protein, it was trying to cash in on growing excitement about the health properties of omega-3 fatty acids. Omega Protein sure sounds like the name of a health-food company, and the corporation plays it for all it's worth. "Healthy Products for a Healthy World" is the slogan at the top of its Web site, where the company describes itself in these words: "Omega Protein is the world's largest manufacturer of heart-healthy fish oils containing Omega-3 fatty acids for human consumption, as well as specialty fish meals and fish oil used as value-added ingredients in aquaculture, swine, and livestock feeds."[8] The company's earnings announcements and other press releases routinely begin: "Omega Protein Corporation, the world's largest manufacturer of heart-healthy fish oils containing long-chain Omega-3 fatty acids, today reported. . . ."[9]

You might think that manufacturing omega-3 fatty acids is the company's main business—unless you read its SEC-mandated financial reports, where it is legally required to tell the truth. There you discover that despite its name and all its efforts, at least since 1998, to capitalize on our desires for magic elixirs to make us healthy and live forever, Omega Protein has yet to make any profit on any of its omega-3 products for human consumption:

> The company has made sales, which to date have not been material, of its refined fish oil, trademarked OmegaPure, to food manufacturers in the United States and Canada. . . . **The Company's strategy to expand into the food grade oils market may be unsuccessful.** The Company's attempts to expand its fish oil sales into the market for refined, food grade fish oils for human consumption may not be successful. The Company's expectations regarding future demand for Omega-3 fatty acids may prove to be incorrect or, if future demand does meet the Company's expectations, it is possible that purchasers could utilize Omega-3 sources other than the Company's products.[10]

Nevertheless, Omega is betting big on this strategy. In 2004, the company completed construction of what Omega calls the Health and Science Center, actually a specialized oil refinery directly attached, by a sort of umbilical-cord pipeline, to the Reedville factory. Financed with a government-guaranteed $17 million loan, this highly automated facility (employing fewer than twenty workers) triples Omega's capacity to produce refined food-grade fish oil. Unwittingly belying the company's claims that it is already the world's greatest manufacturer of this product, Omega president and CEO Joseph von Rosenberg enthused just before the refinery opened, "It's obvious to us the Omega-3 story is something about to happen."[11] The company's omega-3 story was still about to happen in 2006, as Omega was completing construction of a new technical center in Houston, designed specifically to create marketable products from the food-grade fish oil being refined in Reedville.

There seems little doubt that omega-3 fatty acids, especially the form found mainly in oily fish, are exceptionally beneficial to human health. They evidently help prevent heart attacks, strokes, and other cardiovascular disorders, and there is considerable evidence that they may also help prevent or ameliorate various mental disorders and inflammatory diseases such as arthritis. Human bodies cannot produce them, which is why they are classified as an "essential" fatty acid—that is, a necessary component of a healthy diet. The American Heart Association now officially recommends that everybody should consume oily fish or an omega-3 supplement at least twice a week, and that people with coronary disease should do so every day.[12]

However, contrary to the impression Omega Protein creates on its Web site and in press releases, the company is neither the major manufacturer of omega-3 products for human consumption nor the safest. The nonprofit Environmental Defense surveyed seventy-five companies that market more than ninety-five omega-3 supplements in order to evaluate whether they were free from dangerous contaminants, especially mercury, PCBs, and dioxins. More than 80 percent of these companies (sixty-one out of seventy-five) are members of the Council for Responsible Nutrition, a trade association that has established voluntary standards of purity equal to or more stringent than those set by the EPA and California's Proposition 65, which protects the state's citizens from chemicals known to cause cancer, birth defects, or other reproductive harm. Omega Protein is not one of them. In response to the Environmental Defense survey, Omega said it complies with the least stringent standards, those of the Food and Drug Administration (FDA), but did not respond to follow-up inquiries about whether it adheres to the far stricter standards of the EPA, Proposition 65, or the Council for Responsible Nutrition. The differences between these standards are enormous. For example, the FDA's tolerance level for PCBs is an absurdly high 2,000 parts per billion, whereas the State of California's limit is 90 parts per billion.[13]

Almost all of the ninety-five omega-3 supplements marketed by these seventy-five companies are made from various fish oils: some from the flesh of oily fish that store most of their lipids in their muscle tissue, others from the livers of fish that store most of their lipids in that organ—such as cod. ("Omega-3 fatty acids" don't sound quite so jazzy and twenty-first-century when one realizes that oodles of them are still sold in the form of old-fashioned cod liver oil.) Many of these omega-3 supplements are not only safer than Omega Protein's Omega-Pure but also cheaper, making them formidable competitors. And north of Reedville in Columbia, Maryland, sits the company's potentially most formidable competitor, Martek Biosciences, which doesn't use any fish at all to produce extremely pure and potent omega-3. Martek, in fact, is something like a gigantic artificial high-tech menhaden, getting its omega-3 straight from algae.

Human beings aren't the only animals that cannot synthesize their own omega-3. No other mammal can either. Nor, for that matter, can any fish.[14] So how do those oily fish that the American Heart Association tells us to eat, such as bluefish, mackerel, herring, and sardines, get all their omega-3? By eating other animals that are loaded with it. Herring and sardines eat zooplankton that are rich in omega-3. Where did the zooplankton get theirs? By eating phytoplankton, that is, algae. Where do the bluefish and mackerel get theirs? By eating omega-3-rich fish such as herring, sardines, and, most of all, menhaden.

Remember that the one fact central to menhaden's two great environmental roles, as well as their roles in American history, is that they are utterly unmatched as colossal eaters of algae. It was the almost limitless supply of algae that allowed menhaden to become the most abundant of all American fish. Living primarily on algae, they are so oily that just about no human would choose to eat them, whereas just about every finned, feathered, or flippered marine predator eats as many of them as possible. That smelly, oily fish is indeed the greatest source of those vital omega-3 fatty acids available to all of us mammals, fish, and also birds incapable of digesting algae.

So if you want to get your essential omega-3, the most pleasurable way for many of us is to eat the fish that have eaten the menhaden that have eaten the algae that contain this vital substance. Or you can eat pills made from predator fish, or drink yucky-tasting oil made from their livers. Or now, thanks to modern technology, you can go directly to the bottom of the food chain and get your omega-3 directly from the algae, conveniently fermented and packaged by Martek Biosciences today, and probably before long by many competitors with similar processes.[15] Or you can skip the marine food chain altogether and get your omega-3 from flax and flaxseed, soybeans, nuts such as walnuts, and certain grasses and weeds (such as purslane).

Meanwhile, Omega Protein remains vitally dependent on unrestricted catches of billions of menhaden every year in order to eke out its rather skimpy profits. Surrounded by competitors just as eager to cash in on the omega-3 health craze, Omega could be seriously threatened by those hundreds of thousands of environmentalists and recreational anglers, and even some commercial fishermen, demanding some limitation to its catch, at least in the Chesapeake Bay. Since many of these people seem to believe that the fate of the Chesapeake is more important than the fate of Omega Protein, it's no wonder that the company believes it's fighting for its very life.

The company was plunged into even more jeopardy by the actions of Malcolm Glazer, the billionaire formerly in control of Omega who has profited the most from its "harvest" of billions of menhaden. In May 2005, Glazer succeeded in making himself one of the most hated men in the United Kingdom by buying an English national icon, the Manchester United soccer team, and turning it into what one sportswriter called just "another corporate toy."[16] To finance this purchase, Glazer borrowed almost $1.5 billion, more than half from three New York hedge funds, which soon began holding his feet to the fire. To raise cash, in early December 2005 Glazer had Zapata sell off airbag manufacturer Safety Components International, its last remaining holding other than Omega, for $51.2 million. A few days later, Zapata announced that Omega Protein was also up for sale. The *London Observer* greeted this news gleefully with a story headlined "Glazer Starts Selling Off the Family Silver."[17]

Is this British perspective an accurate vision of what the menhaden reduction industry has been reduced to—just part of one man's family silver? The industry is still the third-biggest American fishery and the one having the most impact on the environment. Reedville remains America's second-largest fishery port, as measured by weight of fish landed, and Reedville's catch is dwarfed by Omega's four Gulf ports, with their dozens of ships and fleets of spotter planes. Although the Glazer family didn't own all of Omega, they did own a majority of the company and controlled its decisions and destiny. Thus Malcolm Glazer's need to get rid of Omega Protein may turn out to be the most important event in the long history of the industry.

What does this mean for the future of menhaden?

While waiting for a buyer to materialize, Omega did everything in its power to make itself look alluring, that is, both profitable and destined for an even more lucrative future. This helps explain the corporation's ferocious resistance to any limits or restrictions on its activities as well as its well-publicized, though highly competitive and still not profitable, plunge into the omega-3 health industry.

The most ominous possibility is that Omega could be bought by a major well-capitalized corporation, such as Cargill, Bunge, or Archer Daniels Midland, already in the business of vegetable meals and vegetable oils. That might actually lead to an expansion of the reduction industry. Other possible buyers include private equity groups, which do not have to make public financial reports. There has been some talk of a buyout of the Atlantic coast business by recreational anglers and others, who would shut down Reedville and turn its potentially valuable Cockrell's Creek real estate into upscale residential property. This unlikely outcome would certainly be the best for the Chesapeake, the entire Atlantic menhaden population, and even the economy of Reedville, which would gain more jobs than Omega now provides. But it might also increase the menace to Gulf menhaden, which would then be hit with the industry's full force, including Reedville's ships and planes.

But unsurprisingly, Malcolm Glazer could not find a buyer for this company with a dubious future in time to bail him out of his financial troubles. So in September 2006 he arranged a sale of Omega Protein to itself—at a bargain-basement price. His son Avram and his other representative on Omega's board of directors resigned, leaving the corporation, significantly strengthened by Glazer's desperate fire-sale deal as well as the ASMFC's sweetheart arrangement, prepared to catch as many menhaden as it can—for the next few years anyhow.[18]

Assuming that the industry does continue, either as Omega Protein or as some other corporate entity, its future will depend upon the answers to three questions. Will the population of menhaden be able to withstand continual unlimited catches, or will it crash beyond recovery? Will the industry be able to convert menhaden into new, profitable large-scale industrial commodities, as it once did in the form of fertilizer, then as industrial oil, and most recently as animal feed? The answer to these first two questions may depend on the answer to the third: Will enough people come to realize that the most vital mission of our most important fish is not creating corporate profits but restoring and sustaining our marine environment?

RESURRECTION?

Rhode Island's Narragansett Bay is where menhaden got their name from the Narragansett Indians, who called them *munnawhatteaûg*, "he enriches the land." In the 1870s, Narragansett Bay became the site of a major menhaden fishery, as dozens of steamers and sail ships hunted its waters, pouring millions of fish into the thirteen factories operated by the Narragansett Oil and Guano Company.

A century later, the bay was still visited each summer by some large migrating schools. John Torgan, now the menhaden specialist with Narragansett BayKeepers, remembers "the big menhaden schools," with fish up to twelve inches, when "I was a kid fishing with my dad in the 1970s." But "then it died." Later, he recalls, "we had a major assemblage shift," with very few adults but "large schools of peanut bunkers."[19] Ed Cook, who chairs the menhaden committee of the Rhode Island Saltwater Anglers Association and works as a mate on a charter boat, also remembers the schools of big adults that used to fill the bay in May and June.[20] John Torgan notes that the bay is now increasingly filled with algae. Chris Powell, who monitors the juveniles for the Division of Fish and Wildlife of the Rhode Island Department of Environmental Management, reports massive kills of these babies because of concentrations of algae and the resulting depletion of dissolved oxygen.[21]

Both Torgan and Powell are disturbed by the crash of "river herring" (alewives), whose population plummeted 95 percent from 2000 to 2005, partly because of the deteriorating water conditions and perhaps also because of increased predation from menhaden-starved bluefish and striped bass. EPA environmental scientist Bryan Taplin, whose work on rockfish scales has been so revealing, is based in the Narragansett, where he personally witnessed the destruction of the bay by purse seiners. When I spoke with him in 2000, he reported no longer seeing significant schools of bunker in the bay, and he noted the effects of the absence of their filter feeding. "You have to scratch your head and wonder, since we set quotas for bluefish and tuna, why we don't set quotas for this crucial part of the food chain," he said. "Not to regulate a fishery that's so important is to ask for trouble. I wonder whether we are about to see something go wrong unlike anything we have ever seen."[22]

Over and over in my research for this book, I kept hearing the same alarms: Joe Boone telling me, "You can't overemphasize the importance of this fish to the ecology of the entire East Coast"; Paul Spitzer calling menhaden "the absolute keystone species for the health of the entire Atlantic ecosystem"; Jim Uphoff telling me in 2001 that menhaden are "an incredibly important link for the entire Atlantic coast, and you have a crashing menhaden population with the potential to cause a major ecosystem problem."[23] Even Joe Smith, who monitors menhaden for the National Marine Fisheries Service at the Beaufort Laboratory in North Carolina and who generally supports the industry, acknowledged that "we have not had good recruitment" since 1988. Pointing out that a contracting range is an almost certain sign of a declining population, Smith said, "We have not seen adult menhaden north of Cape Cod since 1993."[24]

The spring and summer of 2005 brought the first hope in more than two decades for menhaden in New England. The Ark Bait Company of Fall River, Massachusetts, had not fished for menhaden in New England since 1993, and for six or seven years had been sending its boat from its own bunker-starved waters all the way to Belford, New Jersey, to fish in Raritan Bay. (As noted earlier, the states that have banned the reduction fishery still permit catching menhaden for bait.) But when large schools of menhaden suddenly appeared in the Narragansett in May, Ark Bait immediately dispatched its boat and spotter plane to begin purse seining in the bay. Ed Cook reports that the Ark boat, which has a capacity of 130,000 pounds, fished for forty straight days in the Narragansett. John Torgan was so excited when he saw the schools that he dug out a snagger treble hook from the bottom of his dad's old tackle box, managed to snag some bunkers, and used them to catch some "giant stripers."

That fall, Joe Smith told me that this was "the first year since 1993 we've had schools reported north of Long Island Sound," and there were "anecdotal reports of adult menhaden all along the beaches and harbors all the way up to Casco Bay in Maine." Bud Brown of the Coastal Conservation Association of Maine remembers the excitement when, during the summer 2005 hearings on menhaden being conducted by the Atlantic States Marine Fisheries Commission, there were reports of schools of adult bunker in Boothbay Harbor. A local bait boat rushed out and, for the first time in years, was able to catch a few bushels of menhaden and sell them for lobster bait.[25]

Was this 2005 reappearance just a one-year quirk? Or did it signal an impending resurrection of the historic abundance of menhaden in New England? I awaited the spring of 2006 and news from New England with a mixture of anxiety and hope. Whether New England would be blessed once again with menhaden would probably depend on New Jersey, which is second only to the Chesapeake as the Atlantic's most important bunker nursery. If 2006 were to be anything like 2005, it would thus also bring another wave of positive results from a major experiment.

Marine science has always had a perplexing fundamental problem. To test a scientific hypothesis, some kind of experiment is usually necessary. To confirm a scientific hypothesis, the experiment should be repeatable. But how in the world is it possible to conduct a verifiable experiment in the vast, dynamic, and changing laboratory of the ocean? Well, about as close as we can get to a hypothesis and an experiment might be something like this:

Hypothesis: Stopping the reduction industry from continuing to fish in a major menhaden nursery will increase the menhaden population and ultimately lead to greater abundance of the predators that feed on menhaden, both in that nursery and in the areas dependent on it for a supply of menhaden.

Experiment: Stop the reduction fishery in a major menhaden nursery and determine what happens next.

Well, we conducted the experiment: New Jersey's 2001 law banning Omega's fleets from the state's waters took effect in the spring of 2002. Almost everybody deeply involved in saltwater recreational fishing in New Jersey—individual anglers, captains of charter boats and party boats, tackle store owners, writers of outdoors columns—believes that ever since then there has been a stunning resurgence of bunkers and, with them, a wonderful abundance of their predators, especially blue-fish and striped bass. In the fall of 2005, an armada of healthy stripers on their southern migration from New England swept into the bays and along the shore, while hordes of bluefish stayed around until almost the end of November, several weeks later than usual. Many of us had never seen anything quite like it. Maybe it wasn't proof, but that fall certainly seemed convincing evidence that the experiment was succeeding—so far.

At 6:30 a.m. on a chilly November 21, three of us accompanied Captain Brian Faust on his *Layla* as we headed out from Cheesequake Creek into the western end of Raritan Bay. The peanut bunkers spawned by the big schools of adults in the spring had already left the creek weeks before, so we intended to race eleven miles east, past Sandy Hook, and then turn south from New York Harbor to pick up the remnants of the migrating stripers wherever we could find them, several miles down the Jersey shore.

But three miles before Sandy Hook, clouds of birds were obscuring the rising sun. Below them, the water was thick with juvenile men-haden. As he cut the engine so we could drift into the school without scaring them away, Brian pointed to the fishfinder and shouted, "I've never in my life seen a screen look like this!" From the bottom up about twenty-five feet, the screen was lit red, solid with the marks of large fish. This could not be the peanut bunkers.

We soon found out what they were. As fast as we could drop our three-ounce metal jigs to the bottom, we caught fat, healthy striped bass, evidently well stuffed with the bunkers they had been chasing around in New England waters all summer. Within a few minutes we each got our two-fish limit, and then we did catch-and-release for almost an hour, until the birds suddenly disappeared as the peanut bunkers raced out to the ocean with the stripers in hot pursuit. As we returned to the dock later that day, we wondered what the following spring would bring.

On May 6, 2006, I went out on Brian's *Layla* along with two other examples of the wealthy sportsmen who persecute Omega Protein: a retired electrician and a young man who makes his living by refinishing furniture in his garage. We found schools of adult bunker in the west end of Raritan Bay, snagged some as large as twelve inches for bait, and then sped east to Old Orchard Shoal, near the mouth of the bay as it opens into lower New York Harbor. There we anchored and spent the next few hours catching striped bass, none smaller than twenty-eight inches, and large bluefish that had shown up in late April, weeks before their normal arrival.

We hadn't been there long before we noticed that perhaps an acre of the water's surface was all rippled and purplish, about a quarter of a mile west of the boat and heading toward us. Soon we heard and saw the characteristic splashes of flipping bunkers. On they came until the boat was enveloped by the school as it continued to swim east into New York Harbor. This was the first of many schools, or perhaps some of the same schools, sweeping back and forth east and west, filtering the water and bringing stripers and bluefish along with them. As the four of us marveled at this encouraging profusion of what we call "bunkers," I thought of those seventeenth-century Dutch travelers who had marveled at the swarms of "marsbankers" and other fish in these very same waters.

When I got home, I found an e-mail from John Torgan: "Big schools of large adult menhaden >12 inches appeared in the Providence River last week." This was as exciting as the day's fishing. Not only were the menhaden back in Rhode Island, but they were big and they were there early. On May 12 I spoke with John, who reported "massive schools of adult menhaden in the Providence River." He had spent most of the day in BayKeeper meetings, watching the menhaden splashing and wishing he were out fishing for the stripers that were no doubt underneath them. John was also encouraged by a sudden and coincident revival of river herring. "We have already counted more river herring this year than we counted in the years 2002 to 2005 all put together," he said. He believes that Rhode Island's ban on fishing for them, which took effect in March of 2006 and thus prevented the usual tremendous fishing pressure on the spring spawning run, was one major factor. To him, this is evidence that fish populations are quite dependent on what we humans do. The river herring are now also spared from the ravages of stripers and bluefish, because once again these predators have lots of menhaden to eat on their way north and when they get to Narragansett Bay.

What does this seemingly miraculous resurrection of menhaden in northern waters mean? For Omega Protein, it means straining at the leash that keeps them from sending their fleet back to New Jersey to grab this bonanza of large adult bunkers, filled with far more oil than the juveniles they are netting in the Chesapeake. For some, it might seem evidence that menhaden populations are inherently cyclical, but that belief depends upon ignoring the true historical cycle: abundance, Gold Rush fever, overfishing, crash, halt to fishing, resurgence. For others, it means that if you give these little fish a chance, they can come back and carry out their two great environmental missions, helping to give us back clear and healthy coastal waters teeming with life. For those concerned about the ecology of the Atlantic and Gulf coasts, it means hope — and inspiration to put a stop to the industrial slaughter, in the rest of the Atlantic and the Gulf, of our most important fish.

Acknowledgments

Earlier versions of parts of the book have appeared in *Discover*, "The Most Important Fish in the Sea" (September 2001), and *Mother Jones*, "Net Losses" (March/April 2006). I am grateful to the dozens of scientists, anglers, and environmentalists who generously gave their time and shared their knowledge of menhaden and the marine environment; their acknowledgement in the text and endnotes cannot adequately describe their contributions. Special thanks go to Dr. Benjamin Cuker, who most helpfully vetted a major part of chapter 3; Dr. Robert Franklin, who provided some key biological insights; and Dick Russell, who read the entire manuscript and made many valuable suggestions. Everyone concerned about the fate of menhaden must recognize the ground-breaking leadership and inspiration of Jim Price, whose boundless knowledge, passion, and dedication have helped make this book possible. Emily Davis of Island Press provided many helpful suggestions about the manuscript and then did a terrific job of coordination. Jonathan Cobb has been a wonderful editor, combining splendid insights, an extraordinary sense of narrative, unerringly practical guidance, and inspirational enthusiasm. As usual, my greatest debts are to the love of my life, Jane Morgan Franklin, who spent countless days of her life helping to create this book, days that she took away from her own writing and other tremendous efforts to make this a better world.

Notes

Chapter 1. Now You See Them, Now You Don't

1. Take, for example, some of the statistical compilations provided by the U.S. National Oceanic and Atmospheric Administration (NOAA) in its annual *Fisheries of the United States*. According to the average provided by NOAA for 1982–87, the annual combined haul of all other finned species was 2.1 billion pounds, while the menhaden haul was 2.75 billion pounds. For previous years, NOAA compiled tables of the total catch for each of the "principal species." In 1955, the combined catch of all the other principal species was 975 million pounds, while the menhaden catch was 1.7 billion pounds; in 1965, the catch of the other principal species was 1.4 billion pounds, while the menhaden catch was 1.8 billion pounds; in 1975, the other principal species catch was 1.1 billion pounds, menhaden 1.8 billion pounds. Since menhaden are small and the other principal species included such large fish as tuna, salmon, and cod, the *number* of menhaden caught is many times the combined totals of the other fish.

2. G. Brown Goode, *A History of the Menhaden* (New York: Orange Judd, 1880), 109–10.

3. Sara J. Gottlieb, "Ecological Role of Atlantic Menhaden *(Brevoortia tyrannus)* in Chesapeake Bay and Implications for Management of the Fishery" (master's thesis, University of Maryland, College Park, 1998), 3. Four gallons is a conservative estimate; others estimate more than six gallons a minute.

4. In 1955, the estimated population of adult Atlantic menhaden (that is, age three and over) was 1.591 billion; by 1999, it was 204.7 million. The annual catch had plummeted from a peak of 712 thousand metric tons in 1956 to 171.2 thousand metric tons in 1999. These figures come from the *Atlantic Menhaden Management Review, 2000* (tables 1 and 2), a report to the Atlantic States Marine Fisheries Commission prepared by the Atlantic Menhaden Advisory Committee, a group dominated by representatives of the menhaden reduction industry.

5. Joseph W. Smith (who monitors menhaden for the National Marine

Fisheries Service at the Beaufort Laboratory in North Carolina), interview with the author, October 26, 2000.

6. Sara Gottlieb, interview with the author, August 28, 2000.

Chapter 2. THE NEW WORLD OF FISH

1. Raimondo de Raimondi de Soncino, Milanese ambassador to England, to Ludvico Maria Sforza, Duke of Milan, December 18, 1497, in *Calendar of State Papers, Milan*, vol. I, ed. A. B. Hinds (HMSO, 1912), no. 552, 336–38. Stockfish are those fish, especially cod and other whitefish such as ling, haddock, and cusk, that can be cured without salt, either by open-air freezing or by otherwise drying.

2. Ida Sedgwick Proper, *Monhegan: The Cradle of New England* (Portland, ME: Southworth Press, 1930), 46.

3. For a detailed and authoritative account, see Harold Innis, *The Cod Fisheries: The History of an International Economy*, rev. ed. (Toronto: University of Toronto Press, 1954). Mark Kurlansky's *Cod: A Biography of the Fish that Changed the World* (New York: Penguin, 1998) brings the history of cod up to date and turns it into a dramatic story with profound ecological significance.

4. John Smith, *A description of New England; or The Observations, and discoveries of Captain John Smith (admiral of that Country) in the north of America, in the year of our Lord 1614 . . .* (London, 1616), 9.

5. Smith, *Description of New England*, 30, 38.

6. Smith, *Description of New England*, 38–39.

7. William Bradford, *Of Plymouth Plantation*, ed. Samuel Eliot Morison (New York: Alfred A. Knopf, 1953), 39.

8. Edward Winslow, *Hypocrisie Unmasked* (London, 1646), 90.

9. *Relation or Journall of the beginning and proceedings of the English Plantation settled at Plimoth in New England* (London, 1622), 26. This document, penned mainly by Edward Winslow, William Bradford, and others, is commonly known as *Mourt's Relation*.

10. *Relation or Journall*, 39. For a powerful narrative of Tisquantum's life and his role in Indian-British relations, told largely from the perspective of the Indians, see Charles C. Mann, *1491: New Revelations of the Americas before Columbus* (New York: Alfred A. Knopf, 2005), 55–66.

11. Bradford, *Of Plymouth Plantation*, 90.

12. *Relation or Journall*, 60.

13. Bradford, *Of Plymouth Plantation*, 85.

14. *Relation or Journall*, 60.

15. Thomas Morton, *New English Canaan* (Amsterdam, 1637), with intro-
ductory matter and notes by Charles Francis Adams, Jr. (Boston: The
Prince Society, 1883), 225.

16. Edward Johnson, *Wonder Working Providence of Sion's Saviour in New-
England* (London, 1654), 83.

17. A decades-long controversy about whether the Indians used fish as fertilizer was kicked off by Lynn Ceci's attempted debunking in her "Fish
Fertilizer: A Native American Practice?" *Science* (New Series) 188,
no. 4183 (April 4, 1975): 26–30. Responses by Howard S. Russell, G. B.
Warden, Sanford A. Moss, and Ceci appeared in *Science* (New Series)
189, no. 4207 (September 19, 1975): 944–50. William Cronon sided with
Ceci in *Changes in the Land: Indians, Colonists, and the Ecology of New
England* (New York: Hill & Wang, 1983), 45; this invaluable book is
marred by a number of errors about fish, including the statement that
Indians caught eels "as they returned from their spawning in the sea"
(American eels all spawn in the Sargasso Sea, where they then die). A
strong attack on the debunkers was made by Nanepashemet in "It Smells
Fishy to Me: An Argument Supporting the Use of Fish Fertilizer by the
Native People of Southern New England," in *Algonkians of New England:
Past and Present*, ed. Peter Benes (Boston: Boston University Press, 1993),
42–50, but even he never mentions menhaden or the origin of their
name. Stephen Mrozowski discusses the dig and its potential significance
in his "The Discovery of a Native American Cornfield on Cape Cod,"
Archaeology of Eastern North America 22 (1994): 47–62. In a telephone interview on February 8, 2006, Mrozowski told me that a graduate student
of his is currently writing a thesis on the bones retrieved from the corn
hills, and they appear to be consistent with either shad or menhaden.

18. Roger Williams, *A Key to the Language of America* (London, 1643), 114;
Goode, *History of the Menhaden*, 10–11; "Menhaden," *The American
Heritage Dictionary of the English Language: Fourth Edition* (Boston:
Houghton Mifflin, 2000).

19. Goode, *History of the Menhaden*, 11–12.

20. Francis Higginson, *Nevv-Englands Plantation. Or, A short and true description of the commodities and discommodities of that countrey* (London, 1630),
n.p. [9].

21. Farley Mowat, *Sea of Slaughter* (Toronto: Seal Books, 1989), 182–83.

22. William Wood, *Nevv Englands prospect: A true, lively, and experimentall*

description of that part of America, commonly called Nevv England (London, 1634), 35. According to Mowat, 193, "Six-footers weighing 140 pounds were not uncommon."

23. John Josselyn, *New-Englands Rarities Discovered in Birds, Beasts, Fishes, Serpents, and Plants of That Country* (London, 1672), 32; Mowat, 191.

24. Higginson, *Nevv-Englands plantation*, n.p. [9–10].

25. Edwin G. Burrows and Mike Wallace, *Gotham: A History of New York to 1898* (New York: Oxford University Press, 1999), 4.

26. William Penn, *A further account of the province of Pennsylvania* (London, 1685), 8.

27. Jaspar Dankers and Peter Sluyter, *Journal of a Voyage to New York and a Tour in Several of the American Colonies in 1679–1680*, trans. from the original manuscript in Dutch and ed. Henry C. Murphy (Brooklyn: Long Island Historical Society, 1867), Plate II.

28. Josselyn, *New-Englands Rarities*, 23.

29. Goode, *History of the Menhaden*, 15.

30. Penn, *Further account*, 8. Penn was probably repeating a popular usage of "herring"; even today the alewife and blueback shad are lumped together as "river herring," an official category of the Atlantic States Marine Fisheries Commission.

31. Goode, *History of the Menhaden*, 15.

32. John Smith, *The Generall History of Virginia, the Somer Iles, and New England* (London, 1624), 59.

33. Dr. Kent Mountford discusses the accuracy of this illustration in "Menhaden: Out of Smith's Frying Pan into Modern Fishery's Crossfire," *Bay Journal* (newsletter of the Alliance for the Chesapeake Bay), October 2005.

34. Dankers and Sluyter, *Journal of a Voyage*, 100. Plate II in this fascinating volume is a picture of this scene, with spouting whales and a bird that looks more like an osprey than an eagle flying off with a fish that resembles a menhaden. One dubious detail is that the bird's talons are holding the fish tail first, whereas both eagles and ospreys almost always carry menhaden and other fish headfirst for better aerodynamics. The passage from Steendam's poem is quoted in Dutch and English in Goode, *History of the Menhaden*, 12.

35. Washington Irving, *A History of New York . . . By Diedrich Knickerbocker*, ed. Michael L. Black and Nancy B. Black (Boston: Twayne, 1984), 279. Goode, *History of the Menhaden*, includes in a footnote this whole sad

story of the death by "moss-bunker" of the legendary trumpeter Antony Van Corlear, who was attempting to rouse the Dutch to resist the English attack on New Amsterdam. The creek at the juncture of the Hudson River and Harlem River is still known as Spuyten Duyvil ("in spite of the devil"), supposedly in memory of this fatal encounter with the giant diabolical moss-bunker.

Chapter 3. MEETING MENHADEN: IN OUR WORLD AND THEIRS

1. "Blue Fishing for Market: A Cruise on a Fulton Market Smack," *New York Times*, September 2, 1877.
2. Karen Wall, "A Fish Story That's Really a Whopper," *Asbury Park (NJ) Press*, June 29, 2004; "Teen Angler's Tale—Hook, Line, and Kayak," Associated Press, June 30, 2004.
3. Goode, *History of the Menhaden*, 156, 158, 159.
4. Gilbert Klingel, *The Bay* (Baltimore: Johns Hopkins University Press, 1984; reprint of original 1951 edition), 45, 127.
5. David Helvarg, *Blue Frontier: Saving America's Living Seas* (New York: Owl Books, Henry Holt, 2002), 3–4.
6. There are also two minor species of American menhaden, the yellowfin menhaden *(Brevoortia smithi)* and the finescale menhaden *(Brevoortia gunteri)*. Two other menhaden in the western hemisphere are *Brevoortia aurea* and *Brevoortia pectinata*, which both range from Brazil to Argentina. There is also a menhaden species found along the western coast of Africa. Samuel F. Hildebrand, *A Review of the American Menhaden, Genus Brevoortia, with a Description of a New Species* (Washington, DC: Smithsonian Institution, 1948); Eduardo M. Acha and Gustavo J. Macchi, "Spawning of Brazilian Menhaden, *Brevoortia aurea*, in the Rio de la Plata Estuary off Argentina and Uruguay," *Fishery Bulletin* 98 (2000): 227–35; Dean W. Ahrenholz, "Population Biology and Life History of the North American Menhadens, *Brevoortia* spp.," *Marine Fisheries Review* 53, no. 4 (1991): 3–19.
7. Quoted in Goode, *History of the Menhaden*, 79.
8. Quoted in Goode, *History of the Menhaden*, 50.
9. Ahrenholz, "Population Biology," 3–19; Allyn B. Powell, "Life History Traits of Two Allopatric Clupeids, Atlantic Menhaden and Gulf Menhaden, and the Effects of Harvesting on These Traits," *North American Journal of Fisheries Management* 14 (1994): 53–64; Sal Cursi (charter boat captain), interview with the author, February 27, 2006.

10. F. C. June and F. T. Carlson, "Food of Young Atlantic Menhaden, *Brevoortia tyrannus*, in Relation to Metamorphosis," *U.S. National Marine Fisheries Service Fishery Bulletin* 68 (1971): 493–512.

11. Linda Deegan, interview with the author, April 19, 2006.

12. John Josselyn, *An Account of Two Voyages to New-England* (London, 1674), ed. Paul J. Lindholdt (Hanover, NH: University Press of New England, 1988), 77.

13. Mark Catesby, *The Natural History of Carolina, Florida, and the Bahama Islands*, vol. 1 (London, 1771), xxxiii.

Chapter 4. WHALES, MENHADEN, AND INDUSTRIALIZED FISHING

1. Catesby, *Natural History of Carolina*, xxxiii.

2. Much of this analysis is drawn from Cronon, *Changes in the Land*, 149–51. The only error in Cronon's fine discussion comes from ignoring the role of fish fertilizer in Indian agriculture, as I discuss in chapter 2, note 17.

3. Bradford, *Of Plymouth Plantation*, 85.

4. Cronon, *Changes in the Land*, 150–51.

5. Ezra L'Hommedieu, "Communications Made to the Society, Relative to Manures, *Transactions of the Society for the Promotion of Agriculture, Arts, and Manufactures, Instituted in the State of New York*, vol. I, 1801, 65, as quoted and cited in Goode, *History of the Menhaden*, 485. Goode reproduces major sections of L'Hommedieu's paper as an appendix, citing the 1801 reprint of the 1792 first volume.

6. Goode, *History of the Menhaden*, 484–85. The year after publishing this article, L'Hommedieu purchased Robins Island, which had been confiscated from a British loyalist during the Revolution; the island sits in Peconic Bay, where it was in that period surrounded by menhaden all summer.

7. Timothy Dwight, *Travels in New England and New York*, 4 vols., ed. Barbara Miller Solomon (Cambridge, MA: Harvard University Press, 1969): Vol. III (1822), "Journey to Long Island," Letter II, 213; Vol. II (1821), "Journey to Provincetown," Letter I, 357.

8. George Brown Goode, *The Fisheries and Fishery Industries of the United States*, sec. V, vol. I (Washington, DC, 1887), 367, 371–72; in this report prepared for the U.S. Commission of Fish and Fisheries, Goode includes almost forty folio pages in fine print from a fascinating three-hundred-page manuscript diary of a farmer-fisherman who traces the evolution of these companies. Ralph H. Gabriel, "Geographic Influences

in the Development of the Menhaden Fishery on the Eastern Coast of the United States," *Geographical Review* 10, no. 2 (August 1920): 91–100; Ralph Henry Gabriel, *The Evolution of Long Island* (New Haven, CT: Yale University Press, 1921; reprint ed., Port Washington, NY: Ira J. Friedman, 1968), 79.

9. Gabriel, "Geographic Influences," 94.

10. Dwight, *Travels*, vol. II, 359, 362, in reference to his 1800 trip in Connecticut; Dwight repeats this complaint about the "fetor" on his 1804 trip on Long Island, vol. III, 213.

11. G. Browne Goode, "The Use of Agricultural Fertilizers by the American Indians and the Early English Colonists," *American Naturalist* 14 (July 1880): 473–79, 477.

12. Goode, "The Use of Agricultural Fertilizers," 474.

13. Lance E. Davis, Robert E. Gallman, and Karin Gleiter, *In Pursuit of Leviathan: Technology, Institutions, Productivity, and Profits in American Whaling, 1816–1906* (Chicago: University of Chicago Press, 1997), 19, 28, 30. Baleen was widely known as "whalebone." Although this book correctly distinguishes between the oil derived from sperm whales ("sperm oil") and that from all other whales ("whale oil"), for simplicity I lump the two together under the latter term.

14. Goode, *Fisheries*, 361; also Goode, *History of the Menhaden*, 190.

15. Goode, *Fisheries*, 360; Barbara J. Garrity-Blake, *The Fish Factory: Work and Meaning for Black and White Fishermen of the Menhaden Industry* (Knoxville: University of Tennessee Press, 1994), 18.

16. Goode, *Fisheries*, 334; Davis et al., *In Pursuit of Leviathan*, 19.

17. Herman Melville, *Moby-Dick; Or, The Whale* (Evanston and Chicago: Northwestern University Press and the Newberry Library, 1988), chapter 6.

18. "A New Enterprise," *New Bedford (MA) Standard*, reprinted in *Scientific American*, August 8, 1863, 96.

19. "Chasing the Bony-Fish," *New York Times*, May 26, 1884, 5.

20. John Frye, *The Men All Singing: The Story of Menhaden Fishing*, 2nd ed. (n.p.: The Donning Company, 1999), 50, 52, 54, 76. Frye has some marvelous details about the spectacular growth of Reedville as well as pages of pictures of these mansions.

21. John Frye's *Men All Singing* (1978, 1999) and Barbara Garrity-Blake's *Fish Factory* (1994) are the only two full-length books on menhaden and their history published since the 1880s.

22. Goode, *History of the Menhaden*, 162–63; "The Menhaden Oil Mania," *Scientific American*, March 9, 1867, 154.

23. Davis et al., *In Pursuit of Leviathan*, 41.

24. "The Way Menhaden Oil Is Made," *Scientific American*, September 27, 1862, 198; "The Newport Fisheries," *Scientific American*, March 19, 1864, 178. These two articles were first discussed by Nathan Adams in two unpublished 2005 papers: "'Not Without Value': Menhaden, Fertilizer, Oil & a Migratory Fishery in the 19th and Early 20th Century" and "Closing Destiny: The Menhaden Fishery of the 19th and Early 20th Century."

25. "Menhaden Oil Mania," 154.

26. "Eastern Long Island—Menhaden Oil and the Fisheries," *Scientific American*, January 7, 1871, 21.

27. Gilbert Burling, "Long Island Oil-Fisheries," *Appleton's Journal of Literature, Science and Art* 6, no. 127 (September 2, 1871): 268–73.

28. "Menhaden Oil Mania," 154.

29. Davis et al., *In Pursuit of Leviathan*, 15.

30. Sperm whales sometimes contained the precious but rare ambergris used in some pricey perfumes, and the sailors themselves often did use whale teeth as canvases for their etched art, known as scrimshaw. Also, what was left of the blubber after the oil was tried out was used to feed the flames of the try-works.

31. "Manure from the Sea (from *The Maine Farmer*)," *Southern Planter*, June 1855, 169.

32. "Artificial Guano from Fish," *Cultivator*, June 1856, 17. See also "Manufacture of Fish Guano," *New England Farmer*, July 1856, 335, and "Menhaden Oil," *Plough, the Loom and the Anvil*, October 1857, 213.

33. Adams, "Closing Destiny," 13, makes the suggestion about the Union soldiers.

34. Goode, *History of the Menhaden*, 90–91.

35. Rob Leon Greer, *The Menhaden Industry of the Atlantic Coast: Appendix III to the Report of the U.S. Commissioner of Fisheries for 1914* (Washington, DC: GPO, 1915), 5. Greer incorrectly states that the *Ranger* was the first floating menhaden factory; at least two and possibly four were already operating in Long Island Sound. Frye, *Men All Singing*, 50, gives a few more details about the *Ranger*.

36. Frye, *Men All Singing*, 49. Frye, who did important research in the Reed

family papers, has three chapters with fascinating details on the establishment and development of the menhaden fishery in the Chesapeake.

37. Garrity-Blake, *Fish Factory*, 15.

38. Garrity-Blake, *Fish Factory*, 16. This book is primarily a fine study of the relations of blacks and whites, especially workers, in the southern menhaden industry.

39. Edward J. Boyd, report in *Rural New-Yorker* reprinted in *Scientific American*, November 29, 1879, 344.

40. Charles Burr Todd, "The Menhaden Fishery and Factories," *Lippincott's Magazine of Popular Literature and Science*, December 1883, 545–56, 546.

41. Todd, "Menhaden Fishery," 546, 555.

42. Goode, *Fisheries*, 335.

43. "Food Fishes of America: How They Are Caught on Our Coasts, Lakes, and Rivers," *New York Times*, May 30, 1874, 10.

44. Edward Richard Shaw, "The Millions of Menhaden," *Potter's American Monthly*, July 1882, 1-7, 1.

Chapter 5. THE DEATH OF FISH AND THE BIRTH OF ECOLOGY

1. Thomas Henry Huxley, "Inaugural Address," The Fisheries Exhibition, London, 1883.

2. George Perkins Marsh, *Report Made under Authority of the Legislature of Vermont on the Artificial Propagation of Fish* (Burlington: Free Press Print, 1857), 51.

3. George Perkins Marsh, *Man and Nature*, ed. David Lowenthal (1864; repr., Cambridge, MA: Harvard University Press, 1965), 106; *The Earth as Modified by Human Action* (New York: Scribner, Armstrong, 1874), 107. Marsh's citation of menhaden is in a footnote referring to the writing of Timothy Dwight, which I cited in the previous chapter, about farmers netting the fish for fertilizer; this was written in 1864, before the advent of the major reduction industry, and not revised for the 1874 edition.

4. "Food Fishes of America: How They Are Caught on Our Coasts, Lakes, and Rivers," *New York Times*, May 30, 1874, 10.

5. Dean C. Allard, *Spencer Fullerton Baird and the U.S. Fish Commission: A Study in the History of American Science* (New York: Arno, 1978), 70–71, 76. Allard describes the successful 1868 fight in Connecticut to restrict the nets and the increasingly volatile struggles in the next few years in Massachusetts and Rhode Island.

6. Anthony Netboy, *The Atlantic Salmon: A Vanishing Species?* (Boston: Houghton Mifflin, 1968), 314, 323.

7. Netboy, *Atlantic Salmon*, 323.

8. Henry David Thoreau, *A Week on the Concord and Merrimack Rivers*, rev. ed. (1849; repr., Boston: James R. Osgood and Company, 1873), 40–41.

9. Allard, *Spencer Fullerton Baird*, 89.

10. For a full account, see Allard, *Spencer Fullerton Baird*, 60–110.

11. "The Decrease of Our Fish Supply," *Scientific American*, August 3, 1872, 72; Dean C. Allard, "Spencer Fullerton Baird and the Foundation of American Marine Science," *Marine Fisheries Review*, vol. 50, no. 4 (September 22, 1988): 124–29.

12. Allard, *Spencer Fullerton Baird*, 92–98. Allard shows how Baird's proposal was defeated first by rivalry between Rhode Island and Massachusetts, then by his inability to win congressional support.

13. Jim Lichatowich, *Salmon without Rivers* (Washington, DC: Island Press, 1999), 123.

14. Lichatowich, *Salmon without Rivers*, 123–28; "The Fish Car Era of the National Fish Hatchery System" (Washington, DC: GPO, 1970), http://www.railroadextra.com/fishcar.html.

15. Allard, *Spencer Fullerton Baird*, 297, 308–9.

16. This was a somewhat revised version of Goode's monograph titled *The Natural and Economical History of the Menhaden*, which was included in the *Report of the United States Commission of Fish and Fisheries* for the year 1877, actually published as a government document in 1879.

17. A fine exploration of this work is Brian Payne's "George Brown Goode and the Technological Development of the Fisheries," a paper originally presented at the Middle-Atlantic New England Council for Canadian Studies, October 2002, and available in *khronikos*, an online journal published by the University of Maine at http://www.library.umaine.edu/khronikos/html/good/goode.htm.

18. Two volumes of text and the accompanying atlas of illustrations were published in 1887 under the collective title *Section V: History and Methods of the Fisheries*. The first contains Goode's new article on menhaden, which reprints portions of his 1880 *A History of the Menhaden* but also includes some significant additional information and source material.

19. Goode, *History of the Menhaden*, 109. In discussing this and the following passages, I quote the entire section titled "The place of menhaden in nature," not omitting or rearranging a single word.

20. Goode, *History of the Menhaden*, x. Dean Allard has a differing interpretation of Spencer Baird's similar welcoming of the challenge to the Maine law by the menhaden manufacturers, arguing that "his ultimate hope was for a U.S. Supreme Court decision that would clarify this issue not only for the coastal area but also for navigable inland lakes and rivers" (Allard, *Spencer Fullerton Baird*, 286).

21. In the *Report of the Commissioners Appointed to Inquire into the Sea Fisheries of the United Kingdom*, 1866. Huxley had been the main scientist appointed by the Crown to prepare this investigation, which in many ways was the precedent for Spencer Baird's original commission from Congress. Like both Baird and Goode, Huxley saw his role as scientist primarily as someone who could help the commercial fisheries become more efficient. In his 1883 inaugural address at the Fisheries Exhibition, he equated this efficiency in capturing more fish with "progress."

22. G. Brown Goode, "The Enemies of the Menhaden," *New York Times*, November 9, 1879, 4. This article includes a slightly differently worded statement of the menhaden's place in nature.

23. Goode, *History of the Menhaden*, 108–9.

24. The classic account of the tragedy of the passenger pigeon is Edward Howe Forbush, "Passenger Pigeon: *Ectopistes migratorius (linnaeus)*," in *Game Birds, Wild-Fowl and Shore Birds*, Massachusetts Board of Agriculture; reprinted in *Birds of America*, ed. T. Gilbert Pearson, 1917 (Garden City, NJ: Garden City Publishing, 1936), 36–46.

25. For an insightful discussion of this, see Lawrence Buell, *Writing for an Endangered World: Literature, Culture, and Environment in the U.S. and Beyond* (Cambridge, MA: Belknap Press, 2001), 200.

26. "Chasing the Bony-Fish," *New York Times*, May 26, 1884, 5.

27. *United Service: A Quarterly Review of Military and Naval Affairs* 11, no. 3 (March 1894): 277.

28. "Menhaden Fishers Taking Food Fish," *New York Times*, May 30, 1882, 8.

29. "Fish in the Long Island Waters," *New York Times*, June 30, 1873, 2.

30. "To Preserve Weakfishing," *New York Times*, July 13, 1884, 3; "Wanton Food Fish Destruction," *Forest and Stream*, July 17, 1884, 486; "Will Fight for Their Fish," *New York Times*, June 10, 1887, 8.

31. "Menhaden in Raritan Bay," *Forest and Stream*, June 14, 1888, 416.

32. "Extraordinary Haul of Fish," *New York Times*, August 26, 1853, 2.

33. "Bluefish and Menhaden," *Forest and Stream*, August 19, 1886, 67; the

story was taken from the *Southside (NY) Signal*, a paper that frequently reported on fishing in Long Island's Great South Bay.

34. "Protecting the Food Fish; Complaints against the Large Catches of Menhaden . . . The Enormous Menhaden Industry Injuring the Supply of Food Fish," *New York Times*, September 7, 1882, 2. The *Times* story is reprinted, with additional information, in "The Vexed Menhaden Question," *Forest and Stream*, September 14, 1882, 131.

35. "The Menhaden Fisheries; Evils Following the Use of the Present Methods . . . Valuable Edible Fish Caught and Turned into Fertilizers," *New York Times*, September 24, 1882, 3.

36. "Destruction of Food Fishes," *Forest and Stream*, July 13, 1882, 463. See also "Taking Mackerel for Oil," *Forest and Stream*, August 17, 1882, 50.

37. "The Menhaden Fisheries," 3.

38. "The Destruction of Mackerel; Menhaden Steamers Engaged in the Business," *New York Times*, October 22, 1882, 13.

39. John Z. Rogers, "Mackerel and Mackerel Seines," *Outing*, October 1891, 64. See also John Z. Rogers, "Decline of Our Fisheries," *New York Times* (Sunday Magazine), August 11, 1901, p. 11, in which Rogers describes in detail the wanton destruction of mackerel by the menhaden steamers.

40. Goode, *History of the Menhaden*, 114, 164–65, 185.

41. Goode, *History of the Menhaden*, 156.

42. "The Menhaden Question," *Forest and Stream*, April 5, 1888, 209. Goode, *History of the Menhaden*, 156, is more equivocal about the riot and factory burning.

43. Goode, *History of the Menhaden*, 156.

44. "The Menhaden Industry; Why the Fish Did Not Visit Maine This Season," *New York Times*, January 15, 1880, 8.

45. "Menhaden Movements—A New Theory," *Forest and Stream*, September 30, 1880, 176.

46. "Chasing the Bony-Fish," *New York Times*, May 26, 1884, 5.

47. "The Menhaden Fisheries. Conditions of the Business—Wanting No Concessions to Its Opponents," *New York Times*, January 10, 1884, 3.

48. Goode, *Fisheries*, 329, 331.

49. "Catching Moss-Bunkers," *Harper's Weekly*, August 2, 1879, 609.

50. "Menhaden Season Closed," *New York Times*, December 16, 1888, 14.

51. Helvarg, *Blue Frontier*, 39.

52. "The Menhaden Question," reprinted from the *New Jersey Coast Pilot* (Camden) in *Forest and Stream*, October 5, 1882, 19.

53. "New Jersey's Menhaden Fisheries," *Forest and Stream*, February 16, 1882, 54.

54. "Disorderly Legislators," *New York Times*, January 11, 1882, 5.

55. "New-Jersey Acts Disapproved," *New York Times*, April 30, 1882, 7.

56. "The Menhaden Question," *Forest and Stream*, March 3, 1887, 111.

57. "Threaten to Fire upon Jersey Fishing Pirates," *New York Times*, September 29, 1922.

58. The Treaty of Washington compensated the United States for the destruction of hundreds of American ships by Confederate raiders built in England. It also settled rival American and Canadian fishing claims, which had posed a continual threat of war, by devising complex formulas guaranteeing reciprocity of fishing rights and privileges.

59. "For Fighting Fishermen," *New York Times*, July 7, 1895, 17.

60. See Cronon, *Changes in the Land*, 132–34, on this ongoing effort to wipe out wolves to protect livestock.

61. Among freshwater fish or saltwater shellfish, we have long relished scavengers such as catfish and crabs, and filter feeders such as oysters, mussels, and clams. Then there is the recent introduction of that farm-raised herbivore originally from the Nile delta, the tilapia, for anyone who doesn't mind eating completely tasteless flesh.

62. "Murder Most Foul," *Forest and Stream*, September 3, 1885, 107.

63. "Questions of Food Fish," *New York Times*, September 10, 1882, 8.

64. "The Menhaden Question," *Forest and Stream*, September 10, 1885, 121.

65. Letter signed by Louis G. d'Homergue as secretary of the United States Menhaden Oil and Guano Association in the *New York Herald*, September 10, 1882, reprinted in *Forest and Stream*, September 28, 1882, 168.

66. "The Menhaden Question" (Fall River, MA: J. H. Franklin & Co., 1882), reprinted in its entirety in *Forest and Stream*, March 8, 1883, 110.

67. Barney White, interview with the author, June 12, 2001.

68. "Menhaden Fishing. The Fishermen Replying to the Charges of Their Accusers," *New York Times*, January 20, 1888, 3.

69. "The Menhaden Question," *Forest and Stream*, January 26, 1888, 1; February 23, 1888, 81. The following year, A. Foster Higgins concluded his widely read article "Striped Bass Fishing" with these words: "Nearly, if not quite all bass fishermen agree in the opinion that the steam menhaden fishermen have greatly injured the bass fishing—both by depriving them of the food they most eagerly seek, and also by driving them off

their feeding grounds, by their huge nets" (*Scribner's Magazine*, June 1889, 681).

70. "Bluefish and Menhaden," *Forest and Stream*, August 26, 1886, 81.

71. "Food for Predatory Fish, *New York Times*, December 24, 1893. There were quite a few other articles in the 1890s that expounded on the ecological functions of menhaden and the dangers of continuing human slaughter of them. Two especially interesting examples are Mrs. N. Pike, "The Destruction of Animal Life and Its Consequences," *Scientific American* 44, January 17, 1891, 37, and Merritt W. Pharo, "The Menhaden Fishery on the N.J. Coast," *Friend: A Religious and Literary Journal*, April 4, 1896, 293.

Chapter 6. At War with Menhaden

1. "A Menhaden Trust," *New York Times*, December 22, 1897, 1; "American Fisheries Company," *New York Times*, January 9, 1898, 1; "To Lay Off Menhaden Steamers," *New York Times*, July 29, 1899, 7. Nathan Adams first called my attention to these news stories.

2. Roger W. Harrison, *The Menhaden Industry*, U.S. Department of Commerce, Bureau of Fisheries, Investigational Report No. 1 (Washington, DC: GPO, 1931), 1–4. See also Garrity-Blake, *Fish Factory*, 15–18.

3. Gabriel, *Evolution of Long Island*, 76–77. A slightly different version appeared in Gabriel, "Geographic Influences," 91.

4. When I use the word "men," I mean males of our species. I try to use "fishermen" to refer to males, "anglers" or "fishers" to refer to those of more than one gender.

5. Greer, *Menhaden Industry of the Atlantic Coast*, 6, 8.

6. Rogers, "Decline of Our Fisheries," 11–12; Robert A. Widenmann, "Extermination Threatens American Sea Fishes," *New York Times* (Sunday Magazine), July 26, 1914, 4–6; "New York's Polluted Waters," *New York Times*, July 27, 1919, 38; "Oil on Troubled Waters," *Outlook*, April 16, 1924, 638; David M. Neuberger, "The Disastrous Results of Pollution of Our Waters," *Outlook*, May 30, 1924, 88–90.

7. Greer, *Menhaden Industry of the Atlantic Coast*, 25.

8. "Wants More Fish Meal: Federal Bureau Plans Greater Use of It as Food for Hogs," *New York Times*, July 21, 1918.

9. "Fish Meal for Pigs: A Valuable Food Product Added to Animals' Diet," *New York Times*, June 6, 1920. Reprinted as "Give the Hogs a Fish Course," *Independent*, August 7, 1920.

10. Orville M. Kile, "Down to the Sea for Fatbacks," *McClure's Magazine*, March 1924, 11–13, 125–26.

11. Harrison, *Menhaden Industry*, 111–12.

12. Greer, *Menhaden Industry of the Atlantic Coast*, 25.

13. "Earl N. Finprey," "The Seaplane Turns from War to Fish-Scouting," *New York Times* (Sunday Magazine), November 7, 1920, 53. This article appears in a slightly rewritten form as "Seaplanes Turn from War to Fish Scouting," *Current Opinion* 30, no. 1 (January 1921): 111.

14. For a full story and its significance, see the chapter "Billy Mitchell and the Romance of the Bomber" in my *War Stars: The Superweapon and the American Imagination* (New York: Oxford University Press, 1988).

15. "Finprey," "Seaplane," 53.

16. Greer, *Menhaden Industry of the Atlantic Coast*, 11.

17. Harrison, *Menhaden Industry*, 6.

18. Harrison, *Menhaden Industry*, 1–2.

19. *Statistical Abstract of the United States*, "Fisheries—Catch of Principal Species: 1931–1959."

20. Frye, *Men All Singing*, 84, 132.

21. All statements by Hall Watters are from an interview with the author on July 16, 2000.

22. William R. Nicholson, "Changes in Catch and Effort in the Atlantic Menhaden Purse-Seine Fishery 1940–1968," *Fishery Bulletin* 69, no. 4 (1971): 765–81.

23. Leonard C. Roy, "Menhaden—Uncle Sam's Top Commercial Fish," *National Geographic*, June 1949, 813–23.

24. "Biggest Ocean Harvest: The lowly menhaden, top U.S. commercial fish, is hunted by scientifically equipped task force," *LIFE*, November 19, 1951, 140–42.

25. *Statistical Abstract of the United States*, "Fisheries—Catch of Principal Species: 1931–1959."

26. *Statistical Abstract of the United States*, "Domestic Fish and Shellfish Catch and Value, by Species: 1982–1987."

27. All figures specifically on the areas of the Atlantic catch are from Nicholson, "Changes in Catch and Effort," "Table 4—Atlantic menhaden purse-seine catch by year and area," 769. This table also shows total Atlantic catch from 1940 through 1968. For estimated landings of Atlantic menhaden by weight, and numbers from 1955 through 1999, see *Atlantic Menhaden Management Review, 2000, by Atlantic Menhaden*

Advisory Committee: Report to the Atlantic Menhaden Management Board of the Atlantic States Fisheries Commission (Washington, DC: June 2000), table 1, 12. These two documents are the sources for the graph.

28. Jim Uphoff, interview with the author, August 10, 2001.

29. Frye, *Men All Singing*, 132.

30. Daybrook Fisheries in Louisiana and Beaufort Fisheries in North Carolina. Under Department of Commerce regulations, for example, Omega would have to make public disclosure of its annual catch in each region if there were no competitor.

31. "The Old Man and the Lisa," *The Simpsons*, April 20, 1997.

Chapter 7. ECOLOGICAL CATASTROPHES

1. Frye, *Men All Singing*, 52.

2. Omega Protein Corporation, 1999 Annual Report, 1999 Form 10-K, Form 10-Qs from 2000 through 2005. In 2006, Omega moved one of its Gulf of Mexico ships to Reedville, ostensibly because of problems associated with Hurricane Katrina, which devastated the Gulf in 2005.

3. "Public Comment Draft, Addendum II to Amendment 1 to the Interstate Fishery Management Plan for Atlantic Menhaden," Atlantic States Marine Fisheries Commission, May 2005, 5. Since, as noted in footnotes on pages 10 and 17, this federal agency chooses to keep Omega's landing reports confidential, I have had to extrapolate from the figures given for total coast wide landings, which included two vessels from a small, independent North Carolina company that was not fishing in the Chesapeake.

4. "Public Comment Draft, Addendum II," 13.

5. Omega's annual catch from the Chesapeake has averaged more than 105,000 metric tons for the five years up to 2005. This is more than 233 million pounds. If the average fish weighs 6 ounces, this equals more than 617 million fish.

6. Nicholson, "Changes in Catch and Effort," 781.

7. Bill Matuszeski, interview with the author, June 15, 2001.

8. Robert H. Boyle, "Bringing Back the Chesapeake," *Audubon*, May–June 1999, 78–84.

9. Daniel Pauly and Jay Maclean, *In a Perfect Ocean: The State of Fisheries and Ecosystems in the North Atlantic Ocean* (Washington, DC: Island Press, 2003) 9.

10. R. Malcolm Keir, "Fisheries: An Example of the Attitude toward Resources," *Bulletin of the American Geographical Society of New York* 44, no. 1 (1912): 582–89, 587. This extremely interesting article traces the periods of abundance, waste, and conservation for the lobster, shad, and oyster.

11. Jeremy B. C. Jackson, Michael X. Kirby, Wolfgang H. Berger, Karen A. Bjorndal, Louis W. Botsford, Bruce J. Bourque, Roger H. Bradbury, Richard Cooke, Jon Erlandson, James A. Estes, Terence P. Hughes, Susan Kidwell, Carina B. Lange, Hunter S. Lenihan, John M. Pandolfi, Charles H. Peterson, Robert S. Steneck, Mia J. Tegner, and Robert R. Warner, "Historical Overfishing and the Recent Collapse of Coastal Ecosystems," *Science* 293 (July 27, 2001): 629–38, 634. Nineteen scientists from a variety of fields collaborated to produce this exceptionally important article, which, unlike much ecological research, goes beyond local field studies to explore a vast range of historical records and other material.

12. On one hand, there are unknown risks to an environment whenever an alien species is introduced. On the other hand, the environment may not be hospitable to the aliens, and here early results are not promising. In 2006, cownose rays—which had shown up weeks ahead of schedule because of early warming of the bay—practically annihilated an entire reef of the Asian oysters a few days after they were planted. "Hungry Rays Thwart River Oyster Restoration Effort," Associated Press, May 28, 2006.

13. For current and historical information on the degradation of the bay and the progress of restoration, see the Web site of the Chesapeake Bay Program (http://www.chesapeakebay.net), the regional partnership of Maryland, Virginia, Pennsylvania, the District of Columbia, and the EPA and other federal agencies.

14. Scott Harper, "State Cites Cyanide Violations at Menhaden-Processing Facility," *Virginian-Pilot* (Hampton Roads), September 9, 2006.

15. Howard R. Ernst, *Chesapeake Bay Blues: Science, Politics, and the Struggle to Save the Bay* (Lanham, MD: Rowman & Littlefield, 2003), 10, 71–74.

16. James D. Hagy, Walter R. Boynton, Carolyn W. Keefe, and Kathryn V. Wood, "Hypoxia in Chesapeake Bay, 1950–2001: Long-term Change in Relation to Nutrient Loading and River Flow," *Estuaries* 27 (August 2004): 634–58.

17. Benjamin Cuker, interview with the author, November 28, 2005.
18. Pamela Wood, "Chesapeake Bay Gets a D on Annual Health Report Card," *Capital* (Annapolis), November 14, 2005.
19. James Dixon Hagy III, "Eutrophication, Hypoxia and Trophic Transfer Efficiency in Chesapeake Bay" (dissertation, University of Maryland Center for Environmental Science, 2002), 249.
20. Hagy, "Eutrophication," 239, 248.
21. Bill Matuszeski, interview with the author, November 26, 2005.
22. Gretchen Parker, "Fishermen Call for Catch Limits on Menhaden to Help Bay," Associated Press, March 31, 2005.
23. Jim Uphoff, interview with the author, August 10, 2001.
24. Bill Goldsborough, interview with the author, November 30, 2005.
25. J. L. McHugh, "Estuarine Nekton," *Estuaries*, ed. G.H. Lauff (Washington, DC: American Association for the Advancement of Science, 1967), 581–620, as cited in A. G. Durbin and E. G. Durbin, "Grazing Rates of the Atlantic Menhaden *Brevoortia tyrannus* as a Function of Particle Size and Concentration," *Marine Biology* 33 (1975): 265–77, 265–66, and also in Ann G. Durbin and Edward G. Durbin, "Effects of Menhaden Predation on Plankton Populations in Narragansett Bay, Rhode Island," *Estuaries* 21 (September 1998): 449–65, 450. I have converted liters to gallons.
26. Gottlieb, "Ecological Role of Atlantic Menhaden," 45.
27. This inspiring story is told in Dick Russell's fine *Striper Wars: An American Fish Story* (Washington, DC: Island Press, 2005).
28. Jim Price, interview with the author, August 17, 2000.
29. Anthony Overton, interview with the author, August 16, 2000.
30. Gretchen Parker, "Fishermen Call for Catch Limits on Menhaden to Help Bay," Associated Press, March 31, 2005. A report issued by the Chesapeake Bay Program in 2006 gives an official estimate of 60 to 70 percent of the bay's rockfish infected with mycobacterial diseases ("Chesapeake Bay 2005: Health and Restoration Assessment; Part One: Ecosystem Health," draft, 3).
31. Elizabeth Williamson, "Chesapeake's Rockfish Overrun by Disease," *Washington Post*, March 11, 2006. For an analysis of the relationship between the debilitated condition of the rockfish and these infections, see A. S. Overton, F. J. Margraf, C. A. Weedon, L. H. Pieper, and E. B. May, "The Prevalence of Mycobacterial Infections in Striped Bass in

Chesapeake Bay," *Fisheries Management and Ecology* 10, no. 5 (October 2003): 301–8.

32. Merrill Leffler, "Uncommon Blooms: The Nitrogen Factor," *Maryland Marine Notes*, May–June 1998, 1–4, 1.

33. J. H. Uphoff, Jr., "Predator-Prey Analysis of Striped Bass and Atlantic Menhaden in Upper Chesapeake Bay," *Fisheries Management and Ecology* 10, no. 5 (October 2003): 313–22; Jim Uphoff, "Biomass Dynamic Modeling of Atlantic Menhaden in Chesapeake Bay: 1965–2000," Maryland Department of Natural Resources Fisheries Service, August 4, 2003.

34. Francis X. Clines, "Warnings Don't Sway Watermen's Faith in the Blue Crab," *New York Times*, May 13, 2001; Craig Timberg, "For Resurgent Rockfish, the Special Is Bay Crab," *Washington Post*, March 16, 2001.

35. J. C. Griffin and F. J. Margraf, "The Diet of Chesapeake Bay Striped Bass in the Late 1950s," *Fisheries Management and Ecology* 10, no. 5 (October 2003): 323–28, 325.

36. R. J. Pruell, B. K. Taplin, and K. Cicchelli, "Stable Isotope Ratios in Archived Striped Bass Scales Suggest Changes in Trophic Structure," *Fisheries Management and Ecology* 10, no. 5 (October 2003): 329–36; Bryan Taplin (one of the authors of this study), interviews with the author, August 20, 2000, and October 13, 2005. The relationships among menhaden, rockfish, and crabs get more complex whenever the menhaden population declines enough to reduce the number of rockfish, which leads to a reduced consumption of crabs and thus a misleadingly high crab harvest. Ron Lester has convincingly plotted these interrelations from 1950 to 2004; his graphs and conclusions are at http://www.intercom.net/~slester/menhaden.html.

37. Gene Mueller, "With Rockfish, Will History Repeat?" *Washington Times*, June 4, 2006.

38. Russell, *Striper Wars*, 5.

39. Vince Guida, NOAA Fisheries, Sandy Hook, New Jersey, interview with the author, May 9, 2006.

40. John McPhee's *The Founding Fish* (New York: Farrar, Straus and Giroux, 2002) is a hymn to shad from a devoted pursuer and devourer.

41. See the official Atlantic States Marine Fisheries Commission Web site's page on shad and river herring at http://www.asmfc.org.

42. Bob Sampson, Jr., "Shad Runs Decrease Despite Work of Fishery Management," *Norwich Bulletin*, April 29, 2006.

43. John Torgan and Christopher Powell, interviews with the author, April 11, 2006.

44. Sampson, "Shad Runs Decrease."

45. Elizabeth Williamson, "R.I. Shellfish Offer Clue to Health of Chesapeake," *Washington Post*, May 8, 2006; "'Dead Zone' Summer Killed Billions of Ocean State Mussels," *Science Daily*, April 12, 2006, http://www.sciencedaily.com/releases/2006/04/0604.

46. Goode, *History of the Menhaden*, 189.

47. Alexander Wilson, *American Ornithology*, vol. 5 (Philadelphia, 1812), 13–26; Paul Spitzer, "A Proposal to Use the Declining Osprey Colony on Gardiner's Island, New York, as a Bioindicator," December 1999 draft, 1–2.

48. Paul Spitzer, interview with the author, August 19, 2000; see also Spitzer, "Osprey Reproductive Failure and Population Decline at Gardiner's Bay, NY: A Diagnostic Report," 2002 draft.

49. Paul Spitzer, "An Investigation of Source-Sink Population Dynamics in Ospreys," March 2005 draft, 1.

50. Paul Spitzer, "A Brief Review of Bird-Menhaden Connections," Report to the Atlantic States Marine Fisheries Commission, October 2004; Spitzer, interview with the author, July 22, 2005.

51. The two significant sources on the early history of the Gulf industry are W. R. Nicholson, *Gulf Menhaden*, Brevoortia patronus, *Purse Seine Fishery*, U.S. Department of Commerce, NOAA, NMFS, Technical Report SSRF-722, and Frye, *Men All Singing*, 92–97.

52. Steven J. VanderKooy and Joseph W. Smith, eds., *The Menhaden Fishery of the Gulf of Mexico, United States: A Regional Management Plan, 2002 Revision*, Gulf States Marine Fisheries Commission, March 2002, 6-2.

53. VanderKooy and Smith, *Menhaden Fishery of the Gulf of Mexico*, 6-1.

54. Joseph W. Smith, "The Atlantic and Gulf Menhaden Purse Seine Fisheries: Origins, Harvesting Technologies, Biostatistical Monitoring, Recent Trends in Fisheries Statistics, and Forecasting," *Marine Fisheries Review* 53, no. 4 (1991): 28–41, 38, 39.

55. Douglas S. Vaughan, Joseph Smith, and Michael Prager, "Population Characteristics of Gulf Menhaden, *Brevoortia patronus*," NOAA Technical Report NMFS 149 (Seattle: U.S. Department of Commerce, April 2000), 2–3; VanderKooy and Smith, *Menhaden Fishery of the Gulf of Mexico*, 6-1 to 6-9.

56. Smith, "Atlantic and Gulf Menhaden," 39.

57. Vaughan, Smith, and Prager, "Population Characteristics," 2; Vander-Kooy and Smith, *Menhaden Fishery of the Gulf of Mexico*, 6-3 to 6-9.

58. Steve VanderKooy, interview with the author, April 17, 2006.

59. Gulf States Marine Fisheries Commission, "Gulf Menhaden," http://www.gsmfc.org/menhaden (accessed August 17, 2006).

60. Ross E. Molloy, "Texas Oyster Industry Hurt as Red Tide Sweeps Coast; Deadly Algae Has Killed Millions of Fish," *New York Times*, October 2, 2000.

61. Mark Schleifstein, "The Dead Sea," *Times-Picayune* (New Orleans), March 25, 1996.

62. James Hagy, interview with the author, December 2, 2005.

63. Nancy Rabalais and Donald Scavia, "Origin, Impact, and Implications of the 'Dead Zone' in the Gulf of Mexico," USGCRP seminar, July 13, 1999, http://www.usgcrp.gov.

64. Shannon Tompkins, "Gulf Boils with Angling Opportunity during the Summer," *Houston Chronicle*, June 8, 2006.

65. Stanley Clisby Arthur, "The Emblematic Bird of Louisiana," *Louisiana Historical Quarterly* 2, no. 3 (1919): 255–56.

66. Durbin and Durbin, "Effects of Menhaden Predation," 449–65, 462.

67. Monty Graham, interview with the author, October 3, 2000.

68. VanderKooy and Smith, *Menhaden Fishery of the Gulf of Mexico*, 9-4.

69. VanderKooy and Smith, *Menhaden Fishery of the Gulf of Mexico*, 4-9 to 4-10.

70. VanderKooy and Smith, *Menhaden Fishery of the Gulf of Mexico*, 9-2.

71. Vaughan, Smith, and Prager, "Population Characteristics," 18.

72. VanderKooy and Smith, *Menhaden Fishery of the Gulf of Mexico*, 4-8 to 4-10, 9-3.

73. Gulf States Marine Fisheries Commission, "Gulf Menhaden."

74. Vaughan, Smith, and Prager, "Population Characteristics," 4.

75. Vaughan, Smith, and Prager, "Population Characteristics," 4–6.

76. VanderKooy and Smith, *Menhaden Fishery of the Gulf of Mexico*, 8-1.

77. VanderKooy and Smith, *Menhaden Fishery of the Gulf of Mexico*, 9-5.

78. VanderKooy and Smith, *Menhaden Fishery of the Gulf of Mexico*, 9-5. For some details on government-aided financing of the industry, see Omega Protein Corporation, Form 10-Q for the quarterly period ending September 30, 2005, 31 and 33.

79. Omega Protein Corporation, Form 10-Q for the quarterly period ending September 30, 2005, 34.

80. Kenneth R. Weiss and Usha Lee McFarling, "Altered Oceans: Part One, A Primeval Tide of Toxins," *Los Angeles Times*, July 30, 2006. The entire excellent series (July 30–31 and August 1–3, 2006) is available as a multimedia presentation at http://www.latimes.com/news/local/oceans/la-oceans-series,0,7842752.special.

Chapter 8. Collision Courses

1. Smith, *Description of New England*, 38–39.
2. Cronon, *Changes in the Land*, 55–57. Of course, as Cronon points out elsewhere, the Indian males' fishing and hunting was an essential component of their economy.
3. "The Menhaden Question," *Forest and Stream*, March 3, 1887, 111.
4. "For Fighting Fishermen," *New York Times*, July 7, 1895, 17.
5. Captain Fitz J. Babson, "Outlaws and Criminals," originally published in the *Cape Ann (MA) Advertiser* and reprinted in *Forest and Stream* with the journal's reply, February 23, 1888, 81 and 91.
6. For detailed accounts of the leading roles of recreational anglers, their organizations, and their publications in the development of conservationism, see John F. Reiger, *American Sportsmen and the Origins of Conservation*, rev. 3rd ed. (Corvallis: Oregon State University Press, 2001). Reiger notes that such iconic figures in modern environmentalism as Thoreau and George Perkins Marsh were avid lifelong anglers.
7. The congressional act establishing Yellowstone was quite explicit in legislating "against the wanton destruction of the fish and game found within said park, and against their capture or destruction for the purposes of merchandise or profit." Yellowstone National Park Act, 42nd Cong., 2nd sess. (March 1, 1872), chap. 24.17 Stat. 32.
8. Contradictions between the "preservationist" and "wise use" wings of conservationism are nothing new. See Roderick Frazier Nash's classic history, *Wilderness and the American Mind*, 4th ed. (New Haven, CT: Yale University Press, 2001).
9. My analysis of the discord between anglers and environmentalists, especially over MPAs, is greatly indebted to Ted Williams, a prominent presence in both groups. See his "Marketing MPAs: Enviros Alienate Anglers over Marine Protected Areas," *Fly Rod & Reel*, November 2002; "Feuding While the Fish Flicker Out," *Blue Ridge Press*, January 13, 2003; and "Guns & Greens: If Sportsmen and Environmentalists Worked Together, They Would Be Invincible," *Audubon Magazine*, January 2005.

10. Most recreational anglers actually support various forms of MPAs, according to a survey reported in Ronald J. Salz and David K. Loomis, "Saltwater Anglers' Attitudes towards Marine Protected Areas," *Fisheries* 29, no. 6 (June 2004): 10–17.

11. Although many conservation-minded anglers now routinely practice catch-and-release and use circle hooks or even barbless hooks, there is some mortality for all species; for deep bottom-dwelling fish, whose air bladders pop through their bodies when brought to the surface, mortality is about 100 percent. Well-informed anglers argue for regulations appropriate to these facts of piscine life, such as banning all fishing for deep-dwelling groundfish where their populations are endangered. Many recreational anglers also argue that regulations should distinguish between fish resident in these areas and migratory fish that are just passing through much closer to the surface.

12. For most of the early colonists, "wilderness" was something that ought to be replaced by civilization. "Wilderness" as a desirable state has been a concept defined and then redefined from the early nineteenth century through the present. One ongoing tussle has long been over whether wilderness is something to be used and enjoyed or something to be kept as sequestered as possible from use. In addition to Nash's penetrating history (cited above), see the volume of essays edited by J. Baird Callicot and Michael Nelson, *The Great New Wilderness Debate* (Athens: University of Georgia Press, 1998).

13. Mark Hertsgaard argues in "Green Goes Grassroots: The Environmental Movement Today," *Nation*, July 31/August 7, 2006, 11–18, that the major environmental organizations, with the exception of Greenpeace, have until very recently tended not to mobilize or activate their members, relying instead primarily on litigation and lobbying.

14. Ransom A. Meyers and Boris Worm, "Rapid Worldwide Depletion of Predatory Fish Communities," *Nature* 423 (May 15, 2003): 280–83.

15. "Big-Fish Stocks Fall 90 Percent since 1950, Study Says," *National Geographic News*, May 15, 2003.

16. See Richard Ellis, *The Empty Ocean: Plundering the World's Marine Life* (Washington, DC: Island Press, 2003), 14–21, for some particulars on the devastation wrought by this industrialized fishing.

17. Niels Moore, "Scientific Report Shows New Jersey Menhaden Stocks Are Healthy and Properly Managed, Contrary to Claims by N.J. Recreational Fishermen" (press release of National Fisheries Institute), May

16, 1997. Moore was one of the Gulf State Marine Fisheries commissioners who prepared the current Menhaden Fisheries Management Plan. He now serves as one of Virginia's three representatives on the Atlantic States Marine Fisheries Commission.

18. Frye, *Men All Singing*, 12.

19. Barney White, interview with the author, June 12, 2001.

20. According to the 2006 Proxy Statement (Form 14A) filed by Omega Protein Corporation, "Malcolm I. Glazer beneficially owns 51.9% of outstanding common stock of Zapata that are held by the Malcolm I. Glazer Family Limited Partnership, . . . a partnership in which Malcolm I. Glazer controls the general partner. By virtue of such ownership, Mr. Glazer may be deemed to beneficially own the 14,501,000 shares of common stock owned by Zapata." See chapter 9, note 18.

21. Frank Delano, "Raising a Flap over a Fishery, Greenpeace Protests Omega," Fredericksburg.com, July 24, 2005, http://fredericksburg.com/News/FLS/2005/072005/07242005/117173.

22. Jay Hancock, "Proposed Limit Angers Big Bay Fish Processor," *Baltimore Sun*, March 1, 2006.

23. Scott Harper, "Report Says Menhaden Is a Little Fish with a Big Effect," *Virginian-Pilot* (Hampton Roads), April 29, 2006; "The Oily Politics of an Oily Fish," *Virginian-Pilot*, May 8, 2006.

24. "The Menhaden Question," reprinted from *New Jersey Coast Pilot* in *Forest and Stream*, 19.

25. Clyde L. MacKenzie, Jr., *The Fisheries of Raritan Bay* (New Brunswick, NJ: Rutgers University Press), 63.

26. "Arguing about Menhaden," *New York Times*, June 9, 1888.

27. The U.S. Fish Commission was an independent agency of the government until 1903, when it was renamed the Bureau of Fisheries (BOF) and placed in the Department of Commerce and Labor. In 1939, the BOF was transferred to the Department of the Interior, where it became the Bureau of Commercial Fisheries, a division of the U.S. Fish and Wildlife Service, parallel to its Bureau of Sport Fisheries. But then in 1970, both the Commercial and Sport bureaus were taken away from the resource-oriented Department of the Interior and placed in the business-oriented Department of Commerce under its newly created National Oceanic and Atmospheric Administration (NOAA). NOAA unified the two bureaus under the name National Marine Fisheries Service (NMFS, later officially renamed NOAA Fisheries but still mainly known as NMFS), essentially dismantled the old Sports Bureau,

and got down to business by having NMFS focus on aiding commercial fisheries. The official history is at http://www.nefsc.noaa.gov/history. Some of the interpretation comes from "Fixing a Broken System: Fisheries Management," *Makin' Waves* (newsletter of the Recreational Fishing Alliance), Spring 2002, 5.

28. "State Fishery Rights; The Menhaden and Mackerel Industries in Congress. A Bill to Vest Their Control in the Government Declared Unconstitutional—Contest between Shore and Off-Shore Fishermen," *New York Times*, March 24, 1892.

29. *Atlantic States Marine Fisheries Compact*, Public Law 539, 77th Cong., Chap 283, 2nd Sess., 56 Stat. 267; as Amended by Public Law 721, 81st Cong., Articles I, II, and III.

30. Al Ristori, "Fluke Reduction Eased but Still Silly," *Star-Ledger* (Newark), July 3, 2005. Ristori is the regular saltwater fishing columnist for the *Star-Ledger*.

31. Tom Fote, interview with the author, April 15, 2006.

32. "A Tiresome Game We're Tired of Playing: Ring around the Pogy," *Florida Sportsman*, November 1997.

33. However, even today one of Virginia's representatives is Niels Moore.

34. "2005 Seafood Harvest Figures Released," North Carolina Division of Marine Fisheries, April 28, 2006, http://www.ncfisheries.net; Patricia Smith, "Fish Landings in 2005 Continue Recent Downward Trend," *New Bern (NC) Sun Journal*, April 30, 2006; Frye, *Men All Singing*, 82, 88; Lawrence Latané III, interview with the author, May 12, 2006.

35. Karen E. Wall, "The Stink about Bunker," *Asbury Park (NJ) Press*, July 1, 2005.

36. Karl Blankenship, "Commission Proposes Cap for Bay's Menhaden Catch," *Bay Journal* (newsletter of the Alliance for the Chesapeake Bay), March 2005.

37. See pp. 121–22.

38. "Commission Limits Menhaden Fishing," *Wall Street Journal*, August 18, 2005; Karl Blankenship, "ASMFC Votes to Impose Cap on Bay's Menhaden Industry," *Bay Journal* (newsletter of the Alliance for the Chesapeake Bay), September 2005.

39. Ryan Grim, "Menhaden Madness," *Baltimore City Paper*, August 10, 2005.

40. Candus Thomson, "Menhaden Defense Fund: Lots of Hot Air, Some Roiled Water," *Baltimore Sun*, August 14, 2005.

41. Joseph Gordon, Greenpeace organizer, personal communication with the author, July 15, 2005.

42. Charles Hutchinson, interview with the author, May 1, 2006.

43. Keith Walters, interview with the author, May 1, 2006.

44. Matthew Barakat, "Greenpeace Boaters Thwart Commercial Fisher's Menhaden Catch," Associated Press, August 9, 2005; John Hocevar, personal communication with the author, May 23, 2006.

45. "Public Comment Draft, Addendum II," 4, 5, 6.

46. "Public Comment Draft, Addendum II," 4, 5, 13.

47. "Public Comment Draft, Addendum II," 6.

48. "Compact & Rules and Regulations," Atlantic States Marine Fisheries Commission, December 2003, Article IX.

49. "A Fish Called Menhaden" (editorial), *Washington Post*, February 5, 2006.

50. "Good News: The Chesapeake Bay Got a Gift—But Not from Virginia" (editorial), *Daily Press* (Newport News), September 6, 2005.

51. "If Only Menhaden Wrote Campaign Checks" (editorial), *Virginian-Pilot* (Hampton Roads), April 10, 2006.

52. Scott Harper, "Bills to Cap Harvest of Menhaden Are Sunk in House Subcommittee," *Virginian-Pilot* (Hampton Roads), February 1, 2006; "Menhaden Cap Sent to Sleep with the Fishes" (editorial), *Virginian-Pilot*, February 6, 2006.

53. "If Only Menhaden Wrote Campaign Checks." McDonnell's brief is at http://www.oag.state.va.us/media. Governor Timothy Kaine evidently retained the authority to implement the cap and indicated that he was planning to act. But then it turned out that a law passed under Omega's guidance the year before had stripped the governor of this authority whenever the Assembly was in session, and the Assembly stayed in session until Omega began its fishing season on May 1, 2006 (Lawrence Latané III, "Governor Thwarted on Limiting Menhaden Catch: His Spokesman Says Kaine Can't Set a Cap while Assembly Meets," *Richmond (VA) Times-Dispatch*, April 2, 2006). The Newport News *Daily Press* editorialized that "this slick trick of a bill," pushed by an "aggressive, hard-lobbying company," was "better suited to be chum than law," and "resources critical to the common good should be managed by someone other than a profit-driven, out-of-state corporation" ("Little Fish, Big Mess" (editorial), *Daily Press*, April 13, 2006).

54. Lawrence Latané III, "Menhaden Fleet Grows by 1; Omega Protein Will Have 11 Ships This Season, Raising Anxiety of Conservationists," *Richmond (VA) Times-Dispatch*, April 24, 2006.

55. Fred Carroll, "Kaine: Limit Set for Menhaden Catch," *Daily Press* (Newport News), July 31, 2006; Pam Wood, "New Menhaden Cap Moves

Forward," *Capital* (Annapolis), August 17, 2006. The agreement, titled "Addendum III to Amendment 1 to the Fishery Management Plan for Atlantic Menhaden," is on the ASMFC Web site, http://www.asmfc.org.

56. Tom Pelton, "Virginia Agrees to Fishing Limit," *Baltimore Sun*, August 1, 2006.

Chapter 9. THE FISH OF THE FUTURE?

1. Omega Protein Corporation, Form 10-Q for the quarterly period ending September 30, 2005, 31.

2. "June 2000 Market Update," *National Fisherman*, October 21, 2000.

3. Goode, *History of the Menhaden*, 192.

4. An especially alarming study was conducted in 2003 by the Environmental Working Group; this and subsequent work is on the organization's Web site, http://www.ewg.org.

5. Ellis, *Empty Ocean*, 82–92; Helvarg, *Blue Frontier*, 173–74; Rod Fujita, *Heal the Ocean* (Gabriola Island, BC: New Society, 2003), 50–51; Bruce Barcott, "Aquaculture's Troubled Harvest," *Mother Jones*, November/December 2001, 39–45. There are numerous other sources on the problems of salmon farms.

6. "The Great Catfish War," *New York Times*, July 22, 2003.

7. "China Looks beyond U.S. Farmers to Satiate Its Growing Soybean Appetite," *Wall Street Journal*, August 21, 2006.

8. Omega Protein Corporation, "Who We Are," http://www.buy-omegaprotein.com/about.html.

9. "Omega Protein Reports $2.5 Million Profit for 2006 First Quarter" (press release), May 8, 2006.

10. Omega Protein Corporation, Form 10-Q for the quarterly period ending September 30, 2005, 29, 42. Bold print in original.

11. Lawrence Latané III, "Menhaden Plan Could Boost Virginia Fisheries," *Richmond Times Dispatch*, April 25, 2004. See also Frank Delano, "A Fish-Oil Bonanza; Northern Neck Menhaden Firm Is Building a Big Refinery and Planning to Cash In on Omega-3 Health Craze," *Fredericksburg (VA) Free Lance-Star*, July 12, 2004.

12. American Heart Association, "Fish and Omega-3 Fatty Acids," http://www.americanheart.org/presenter.jhtml?identifier=4632.

13. Environmental Defense, "Fish Oil Supplements: Is the Brand You're Taking Safe?," Oceans Alive, http://www.oceansalive.org. Full details, with a list of all the companies and products, are on this Web site.

14. Vince Guida, interview, May 9, 2006. Guida is a specialist on lipids in fish.

15. Martek is continually lowering the cost of producing its omega-3; in 2006, it signed a contract with Kellogg, which will use this algae-derived omega-3 to enrich cereals.

16. Kevin Kozel, "Coming to Terms with the Future," Goal.com, December 1, 2005, http://www.goal.com.

17. Zapata Corporation, Form 8-k, December 8, 2005; "Zapata Corporation Authorizes Exploration of Sale of Its Omega Protein Corporation Holdings" (press release), December 8, 2005; John Duncan, "Glazer Starts Selling Off the Family Silver," *London Observer*, December 11, 2005; "Glazer in the Mire," *Red Issue: The Definitive Manchester United Website*, December 28, 2005, http://www.redissue.co.uk; "Man Utd in Hock to Glazer's Lender," January 1, 2006, http://www.telegraph.co.uk/money.

18. Following the terms of a deal announced in Omega's press release of September 8, 2006, Omega purchased from Glazer's Zapata Corporation 9,268,292 shares of its own stock at $5.125 per share, far below its market value of $6.58 per share the day the deal was announced and just half its $10.25 per share price in 2004. The immediate cost to Omega was $47.5 million, financed by a $35 million term loan and a $30 million revolving credit facility from hedge fund Cerberus Capital Managment. Then on December 4, 2006, Zapata sold its remaining 5.23 million shares of Omega to a group of institutional investors for $29 million in cash, or $5.54 per share.

19. John Torgan, interview with the author, April 11, 2006.

20. Ed Cook, interview with the author, April 11, 2006.

21. Christopher Powell, interview with the author, April 12, 2006.

22. Bryan Taplin, interview with the author, August 20, 2000.

23. Jim Uphoff, interview with the author, August 10, 2001.

24. Joseph W. Smith, interview with the author, October 26, 2000.

25. Joseph W. Smith, interview with the author, November 23, 2005; Bud Brown, interview with the author, December 12, 2005.

Index

About the Author

One of America's leading cultural historians, H. Bruce Franklin has written and edited eighteen books and hundreds of articles on American culture and history. He has taught at Stanford, Yale, Wesleyan, and Johns Hopkins and is currently the John Cotton Professor of English and American Studies at Rutgers University in Newark. Before becoming an academic, he flew for three years as a navigator and intelligence officer in the Strategic Air Command. His years of pondering the sea have included working as a deckhand and mate on tugboats in New York Harbor, serving as president of the Melville Society, and doing as much saltwater fishing as he can.

About Island Press

Island Press is the only nonprofit organization in the United
States whose principal purpose is the publication of books
on environmental issues and natural resource management.
We provide solutions-oriented information to professionals,
public officials, business and community leaders, and concerned citizens who are shaping responses to environmental
problems.

Since 1984, Island Press has been the leading provider
of timely and practical books that take a multidisciplinary
approach to critical environmental concerns. Our growing
list of titles reflects our commitment to bringing the best
of an expanding body of literature to the environmental
community throughout North America and the world.

Support for Island Press is provided by the Agua Fund,
The Geraldine R. Dodge Foundation, Doris Duke Charitable
Foundation, The Ford Foundation, The William and Flora
Hewlett Foundation, The Joyce Foundation, Kendeda
Sustainability Fund of the Tides Foundation, The Forrest &
Frances Lattner Foundation, The Henry Luce Foundation,
The John D. and Catherine T. MacArthur Foundation, The
Marisla Foundation, The Andrew W. Mellon Foundation,
Gordon and Betty Moore Foundation, The Curtis and Edith
Munson Foundation, Oak Foundation, The Overbrook
Foundation, The David and Lucile Packard Foundation,
Wallace Global Fund, The Winslow Foundation, and other
generous donors.

The opinions expressed in this book are those of the author
and do not necessarily reflect the views of these foundations.